TAX COMPLIANCE IN TANZANIA

ANALYSIS OF LAW AND POLICY AFFECTING VOLUNTARY TAXPAYER COMPLIANCE

TAX COMPLIANCE IN TANZANIA

ANALYSIS OF LAW AND POLICY AFFECTING VOLUNTARY
TAXPAYER COMPLIANCE

KIBUTA ONGWAMUHANA

MKUKI NA NYOTA
DAR – ES – SALAAM

Published by

Mkuki na Nyota Publishers Ltd.
Nyerere Road, Quality Plaza Building
P. O. Box 4246
Dar es Salaam, Tanzania
Website: www.mkukinanyota.com

© Kibuta Ongwamuhana, 2011

ISBN 978-9987-08-073-1

Contents

Acknowledgments

There are many people who have made invaluable contributions to this work. Professor Richard Jooste and Professor Jennifer Roeleveld of the University of Cape Town, the late Professor Jwani Mwaikusa of the University of Dar es Salaam, Dr. Khoti Kamanga and Mr. Beatus Malima. Their encouragement and assistance is deeply appreciated.

I also thank officers of the Tanzania Revenue Authority and the Bank of Tanzania, staff of the Ministry of Finance and those of the Ministry of Planning, Economy and empowerment, for providing me with the data which enriched the book.

I thank my wife Minnie, my son Sami, and my two step daughters Rafikiel and Lulu, for their love and sacrifice in putting up with my working hours and my absences, as I worked on this project. Their collective loving support has enabled me to finish the book.

There are others who may have put in a valuable word, or an idea, that found expression in the book. To all of them, I say thank you.

Abbreviations and Acronyms

BA	American Bar Association
ADB	African Development Bank
ASYCUDA	Automated System for Customs Data
BOT	Bank of Tanzania
CIAT	Centro Interamericano de Administraciones Tributarias
COMESA	Common Market for Eastern and Southern Africa
DANIDA	Danish International Development Assistance
DI	Destination Inspection
DFID	Department for International Development (UK)
EAC	East African Community
ESAURP	Eastern and Southern African Universities Research Programme
ESRF	Economic and Social Research Foundation
FAST	Flexible Anti-Smuggling Teams
FCL	Full Container Load
GATT	General Agreement on Tariffs and Trade

GDP	Gross Domestic Product
GGM	Geita Gold Mining Company Ltd
GTZ	German International Cooperation Agency
HS (Code)	Harmonised Commodity Description and Coding System
IMF	International Monetary Fund
ISO	International Organization for Standardization
ITA	Income Tax Act
ITAX	Integrated Tax Administration
KRA	Kenya Revenue Authority
LSD	Legal Services Department
NGO	Non-Governmental Organisation
NIPPA	National Investment Promotion and Protection Act
OECD	Organisation of Economic Cooperation and Development
PAYE	Pay As You Earn
PI	Pre-shipment Inspection
PIN	Personal Identification Number
PWC	PricewaterhouseCoopers
QMS	Quality Management System
QMSA	Quality Management System Auditor
RRA	Rwanda Revenue Authority
SADC	Southern Africa Development Cooperation
SBE	Single Bill of Entry
SIDA	Swedish International Development Assistance
TBL	Tanzania Breweries Limited
TBS	Tanzania Bureau of Standards

TCC	Tanzania Cigarette Company Limited
TFDA	Tanzania Food and Drugs Authority
TIC	Tanzania Investment Centre
TID	Tax Investigations Department
TIN	Tax Identification Number
TISCAN	Tanzania Inspection Service Company
TPA	Tanzania Ports Authority
TPRI	Tanzania Pesticides Research Institute
TRA	Tanzania Revenue Authority
UN	United Nations
UNCTAD	United Nations Conference on Trade and Development
UNDP	United Nations Development Program
URA	Uganda Revenue Authority
WB	World Bank
WTO	World Trade Organisation
ZRA	Zambia Revenue Authority
ZRB	Zanzibar Revenue Board

1

Tax Compliance

Introduction and Background

In defining tax, Professor Tiley quotes from the *Oxford English Dictionary* describing tax as "a compulsory contribution to the support of government levied on persons, property, income, commodities, transactions etc, now at a fixed rate mostly proportionate to the amount on which the contribution is levied"[1]. However, Professor Tiley says that this definition of tax, when stripped of its limited view as to the purpose of taxation, its irrelevant description of the tax base and its undue stress on proportionate as opposed to progressive taxation, tells very little beyond the fact that taxes are compulsory.

The compulsory nature of taxation is underscored by many who attempt to define taxation. Cooley's definition[2] describes taxes as "the enforced contributions from persons and property levied by the state by virtue of its sovereign power for the support of government and for all

---

1 J. Tiley 2008: p. 3.
2 Quoted in *Blacks Law Dictionary*, 9th ed, 2009: p. 1594 [from T. M. Cooley, *The Law of Taxation*, 4th ed, 1924: p. 61-63].

public needs". Whitehouse and Vaines[3] strip the tax definition to three elements: "a compulsory levy, imposed by government, to raise money for public purposes." The 2009 edition of the *Oxford Dictionary of Law*[4] also underlines the compulsory nature of taxation, saying that "tax is a compulsory contribution to the state's funds." Unlike the *Oxford English Dictionary*, the *Oxford Dictionary of Law* does not refer to the purpose or manner of imposition, as these are indeed irrelevant to the essential character of taxation.

Given the compulsory character of taxes, it may seem odd that this study sets out to make a case for voluntary tax payment and to speak against the predominant use of coercion in securing taxpayer compliance with taxes.

Even though taxes are compulsory, they are readily justified by many. There are those who justify taxation on account of the role government plays in sustaining the protection of life, liberty and the pursuit of happiness.[5] There are others who justify taxation on account of the public services provided by government such as education, health and security.[6] All of these functions are funded largely by revenues from taxation. Therefore, there is inherent good in the existence of government and taxation is seen as a necessary consequence.

The imperative of government and the resulting need for taxation gives rise to a duty for the public to comply with tax payment. The obligation to pay tax is not only self evident, but should also be readily acceptable. Professor Bird says that:

> In an ideal law abiding society, people would pay taxes they owe. Tax administration in such a setting would amount to little more than the provision of facilities for citizens to discharge this responsibility. No such country exists, or is likely to exist. Compliance with tax laws must be created, cultivated, monitored, and enforced in all countries.[7]

However, voluntary payment of tax remains largely illusory. Broomberg and Kruger say that "most people, at the best of times, dislike paying tax."[8] This is a widely held view. With regard to Tanzania, Maliyamkono, writing with colonial history in mind, notes that "the history of taxation in the country (Tanzania) has led to a situation where many people and companies see no shame in avoiding paying tax

---

3   C. Whitehouse and P. Vaines, 2002: p. 5.
4   *Oxford Dictionary of Law*, 7th ed, 2009: p. 541.
5   T. Maliyamkono et al 2009: p. 2.
6   C. Whitehouse and P. Vaines 2002: p. 6.
7   R. M. Bird, 1999: p. 71.
8   E. B. Broomberg and Des Kruger 1998: p. 1.

and where small enterprises will find it beneficial to remain outside the formal taxed economy."[9] Attributing the dislike for taxes on the colonial history of Tanzania is not sound, because even in countries which have not known colonialism, taxation is not readily accepted.

Nonetheless, tax compliance remains an important component in designing tax systems and in administering tax legislation. The need to secure compliance is an unavoidable imperative. Bird sums it up:

> Given the universality of the free rider instinct, an element of coercion seems inherent in the financing of public goods. Tax compliance to a considerable extent thus depends ultimately upon the perceived ability of the tax administration to detect and bring tax offenders to book.[10]

All taxation is based on law. Most constitutions prohibit taxation except in accordance with laws duly enacted by the legislative authority. In Tanzania, Article 138 (1) of the Constitution provides that "No tax of any kind shall be imposed save in accordance with a law enacted by Parliament or pursuant to a procedure lawfully prescribed and having the force of law or by virtue of a law enacted by Parliament".[11]

Tax laws are enacted in the belief that taxpayers will comply with them. Looking at the laws, the policy statements, and the conduct of tax administrators, the underlying assumptions behind tax laws appear to be that:

    i. there is a sufficiently high legal literacy amongst the population to understand the taxation laws and the obligations which tax laws impose;

    ii. there is a high enough sense of civic duty among taxpayers to easily and rapidly appreciate the need for tax laws;

    iii. the high sense of civic duty will drive taxpayers to accept tax laws and willingly bear tax obligations; and

    iv. the few errant taxpayers will find the enforcement measures in the tax laws a sufficient deterrent to guide them back into the fold.

It would appear from prevailing tax practice that tax policy framers and tax administrators believe that, in the absence of the above assumptions, it would be pointless to enact laws which are unlikely to be respected.

Statement of the Problem

The problem to be examined in this study is why tax compliance level

---

9   T. Maliyamkono et al 2009: 7.

10 R. M. Bird 1999: p.72.

11 The Constitution of the United Republic of Tanzania of 1977: p.123.

in Tanzania is poor. The proposition put forward is that complimentary relationship which must exist between enforcement and voluntary tax payment is not adequately recognised. The near singular emphasis placed on tax enforcement undermines voluntary tax payment and alienates taxpayers from the tax system.

The factors which show that Tanzania has not succeeded in the important task of securing high level taxpayer compliance are the narrow tax base, the prevalence of dissatisfaction with taxation, and a perception that the tax administration is high-handed and severely tainted with corruption.

The Tanzania Revenue Authority (TRA), established by law as a semi-autonomous government agency is responsible for the administration and collection of central government taxes in Tanzania. The TRA is acutely aware of the problem of tax non-compliance and has been addressing aspects of non-compliance in implementing the First, Second and Third Corporate Plans.[12] In the meantime, however, faced with a general dissatisfaction with taxation, and low levels of voluntary taxpayer compliance, the TRA has tended to rely heavily on detection and punishment of non-compliant taxpayers. With detection and punishment underpinning tax administration strategies in Tanzania, audits and inspections have become a regular, rather than random, feature of tax law administration. There is a culture of criminal prosecutions and fiscal penalties which characterises the response of tax administrators to non-compliance.

However, it is argued in this study that enforcement measures are costly in both monetary and psychological terms. A tax system which is heavily reliant on tax enforcement needs a large team of tax auditors and tax investigators who all must be well equipped to do their job. It also needs to involve court bailiffs and property auctioneers. It also needs to involve as well the police for protection, or to give police powers to tax administrators. All this effort increases the cost of tax collection and eats into tax revenues. Tax enforcement is also limited by the capacity of the country to allocate tax enforcement resources. As a result, enforcement can have only limited success in boosting compliance with taxes.

It is also noted in the study that undue reliance on tax enforcement can be counter-productive and may reduce taxpayer compliance. Enforcement procedures are by their very nature intrusive. Fear and punishment can work only up to a point, beyond which they generate

---

12   See Chapter Two, section 2.6 discussing the 'Public Perception of the Tax System in Tanzania'.

resentment and resistance from taxpayers. The greater the extent of tax enforcement powers, and the more often they are used, the more taxpayer-hostility they tend to generate.

The study puts forward the proposition that if the factors which account for the low level of voluntary taxpayer compliance are addressed and remedied, a much higher tax compliance level can be achieved. Stated differently, the level of tax compliance will significantly improve if there is a high level of voluntary tax payment.

The study attempts to dispel the suggestion that voluntary taxpayer compliance is merely an ideal, possibly a myth. It demonstrates how voluntary tax payment can be made a reality. It also discusses wider governance issues which have been shown to impact significantly on taxpayer compliance patterns. The study attempts to formulate compliance principles which may be used to realize voluntary taxpayer compliance and improve the administration of taxes.

The Relevance of the Book
The relevance of this study is to make a case that it is not only the threat of prosecution, fines and jail terms which make taxpayers comply with their tax obligations. In fact, there are many taxpayers who will evade taxes notwithstanding that there are severe penalties for tax evasion.

There are several factors which make people comply with tax laws. Some taxpayers pay their taxes voluntarily because deep in their hearts they believe that paying taxes is their civic responsibility in respect of which they need no one to push them or threaten them. Others believe that it is in their best interests to comply with tax obligations because they receive benefits from the government worthy of their tax contributions. There are also those who believe in paying their taxes because of the culture they have inherited and they are proud of such culture. They were born in that culture and will do everything to continue it because it is their obligation to do so. Others comply with tax because of a religious belief which equates non-payment of tax with theft, which is a sin. Yet others do so because of their desire to belong and interact socially. The stigma associated with tax evasion is so powerful in the psychology of this group that people feel ostracised if they become associated with tax cheats.

At the other end of the spectrum, there are those groups who resent taxation and believe that there is no justification for it. They perceive taxation and the whole matter of government as an intrusion into one's privacy. Some use the government's failure to deliver public services to an acceptable level as justification for not paying their taxes. Even when government delivers public services efficiently, they are quick to say that the government has that duty, and there should be no *quid pro quo* to justify taxation. They will use the failings of government (corruption, authoritarianism, wastefulness and unfairness in the tax system) to claim legitimacy for non-payment of tax and for their resistance. This study makes a case that even this class of people can be made to comply voluntarily with their tax obligations through a mix of tax compliance strategies which have persuasion (rather than threat and sanctions) at the centre of the mix.

The study proposes that a tax administration can win the hearts and minds of taxpayers by treating them with respect. Through responsible administration the government can influence positive taxpayer attitudes by ensuring that the benefits flowing from taxes are visible to the public and the taxation system is balanced and fair.

Much of the funding which is now overbearingly in favour of tax enforcement could be redirected towards promoting voluntary tax compliance so that savings thereof and enhanced tax revenues can be realized and be channelled to improve services in education and health, and in government investment in the productive sectors.

The conclusions from this study are relevant because they proceed from an understanding (rarely appreciated by tax administrators) that governments are generally limited in their ability to fund tax enforcement. The governments of developing countries such as Tanzania are more severely limited in this regard because of the shortage of money and the skills necessary to make tax enforcement work. Given these circumstances, a mix of enforcement and persuasive strategies is an imperative, and resource allocation is best maximized by investing as well in voluntary tax payment schemes.

Objectives of the Research

The primary objective of this study is to examine why the level of tax compliance in Tanzania is poor. Four secondary objectives that follow are based on the fact that there is not enough recognition in Tanzania of the complimentary relationship which needs to exist between enforcement and voluntary tax payment, and that the undue emphasis placed on tax enforcement undermines voluntary tax payment and alienates taxpayers from the tax system. They are:

　　i. To show the complimentary relationship that needs to exist between enforcement and persuasion, and show that inordinate reliance on enforcement is counter-productive and may undermine tax compliance;

ii. To explore and reveal the factors which influence taxpayer behaviour and which account for taxpayer compliance;

iii. To underscore the interface between good governance and voluntary taxpayer compliance, and show how governance impacts on compliance; and

iv. To show how immensely complex and multifaceted taxpayer compliance is, and therefore, the need for multidimensional strategies for achieving it.

Research Methodology

The research conducted used a variety of methods. The first is documentary research. This method entailed the collection and review of policy documents, legislation, research reports and recorded information from public debates which are relevant to the subject. Documentary research also involved the identification and critical examination of literature which is available on the subject so as to establish the state of knowledge on voluntary taxpayer compliance. The sources of literature and documents included institutional libraries, the internet for electronic information, government offices, especially the Tanzania Revenue Authority (TRA), the Ministry of Finance, the Ministry of Planning, Economy and Empowerment, the Bank of Tanzania, the office of the Attorney General, the National Bureau of Statistics, the Eastern and Southern African Universities Research Programme (ESAURP), the Economic and Social Research Foundation (ESRF), the Research on Poverty Alleviation (REPOA), the Institute of Resource Assessment, and university libraries. Other sources included country offices of organisations such as the World Bank (WB), the International Monetary Fund (IMF), and the African Development Bank (ADB).

Selective interviews was the second method. Although it was initially intended to conduct wider surveys to gauge perceptions and attitudes towards the tax system, the review of the literature at the outset showed that sufficient data already existed from very recent surveys carried out by the National Bureau of Statistics and PricewaterhouseCoopers (PWC). These two surveys were done in 2003 and 2007 and contain adequate data to satisfy the purposes of this book.[13] There was not much point in undertaking a largely similar survey which would very likely only replicate results already documented.

A third research method relied on was the examination and analysis of the existing laws in Tanzania, and where possible, the other countries in Eastern Africa. This method also included examination and analysis of the current Practice Notes and Rulings issued by the Tanzania Revenue Authority; an examination and analysis of decided cases (both tax and non-tax), and the examination and analysis of the existing tax policy documents.

Hypotheses
The following hypotheses have guided the preparation of this book:

  i. There is not enough transparency and public involvement in the making of tax laws in Tanzania, which impacts on taxpayer compliance with tax laws.

  ii. The content of existing tax laws to a large measure does not encourage taxpayers to comply voluntarily with taxes;

  iii. The manner of tax administration alienates taxpayers and fails to inspire them to take ownership of the tax system;

  iv. Serious governance issues exist in Tanzania which impact negatively on taxpayer compliance attitudes;

  v. Public perception of the government in Tanzania and of the tax system affects taxpayer compliance attitudes;

  vi. Taxpayers can voluntarily pay their taxes if they perceive the tax laws to be just, the tax administration to be fair, and the government to be responsible, and

  vii. The manner in which tax money is spent/used has an impact on tax compliance.

Conceptual Framework
This book also proceeds from the conceptual framework that taxpayer compliance is central to the success of any tax system. Unless taxpayer compliance is secured at sufficient levels, the performance of the tax system will be significantly impaired.

---

13 The two surveys were carried out meticulously and covered a sufficiently wide field of respondents, generating reliable results. The data from the two surveys is examined and used in this book.

Tax laws are enacted on the assumption that people will comply with them and pay their taxes to the levels expected by government. Every time the government introduces new taxes, or reviews existing ones, the underlying assumption is that the taxes associated with those laws will be paid to the projected levels so that projected revenues are realized to fund government activities. With this assumption as the guiding premise, compliance with taxes has become the most important aspect of tax administration. It is no surprise, therefore, that a large part of the literature on tax administration is dedicated to tax compliance issues.

Much effort has gone into researching how best to secure taxpayer compliance, change taxpayer attitudes, and get taxpayers to accept taxes and the tax system.[14] A host of variables said to affect compliance have been investigated: these include legal sanctions,[15] social stigma,[16] likelihood of being audited,[17] morality,[18] self interest,[19] opportunity,[20] perception of fairness,[21] and demographic features.[22] However, Taylor[23] argues that while each of these factors appears to have a causal effect or a correlated connection with compliance, there is difficulty in determining the links between individual elements. What seems to be agreed according to Taylor is that strategies for improving tax compliance which are based solely on audits and sanctions are inadequate[24] or counterproductive[25] and do not explain voluntary compliance that occurs in the absence of audits.

Nonetheless, the need for high level compliance is underscored in much of the tax literature examined in this study, as time and again, it is emphasized that unless people pay their taxes, budget targets critical to funding government spending cannot be achieved.

For Tanzania, the importance of taxation as a revenue source for the government cannot be over-emphasised. Tax revenue accounts for around 60% of government spending, supplemented only by non-deficit

---

14 J. A. Roth et al 1989.
15 H. Grasmick and W. Scott 1982: p.213.
16 T. Pocarno and C. Price 1993: 197.
17 P. Webly 1987: p.267.
18 R. Schwartz and S. Orleans 1967: p.274.
19 K. M. McGraw and J. T. Scholz 1991: p.471.
20 S. Klepper and D. Nagin 1989: p.1.
21 M. L. Roberts and P. A. Hite 1994: p.27.
22 J. C. Baldry 1987: p.357.
23 N. Taylor 2003: p.71.
24 E. Kirchler 1998: p.117; S. James and C. Nobes 1998; T. R. Tyler 1998: p.269.
25 R. Schwartz and S. Orleans 1967: p.274; M. Blumenthal, C. Christian and J. Slemrod 2001.

foreign financing. Non-tax revenue is negligible. This composition of revenue makes it imperative to increase tax revenues through higher compliance with taxes.

Globally, the importance of taxation is recognized in much of the literature. Gretz, Reinganum, and Wilde[26] provide the reasons which make tax compliance a priority, namely that:

i. The revenue losses which arise from non-compliance are significant;

ii. Non-compliance with tax law could extend to disrespect for other laws, creating a nation where there is no respect for the law; and

iii. The fairness of the tax system requires that equals should pay equal tax.

Taylor adds that as tax systems begin to rely more heavily on voluntary self reporting and self assessment, the need to understand the processes underlying tax compliance is increasingly urgent.[27]

Defining 'voluntary taxpayer compliance'

'Voluntary taxpayer compliance' is now a common-place phrase which has come to dominate tax compliance literature. Eliminating the middle word "taxpayer" which largely refers to the person paying the various levies collected by government, the two key words which remain in this phrase are "voluntary" and "compliance". In explaining these concepts, it is best to start with the word "compliance", a noun derived from the verb "to comply", meaning "to act in accordance with a wish or command, to meet specified standards."[28] In relation to law(s), "to comply" means to obey and act in terms of the law. "Compliance" in relation to law is the act of submitting oneself to law.

The word "voluntary" means "done, given, or acting of one's own free will",[29] the underlying factor being the lack of compulsion, or coercion, behind the act done.

Braithwaite,[30] who has written extensively on tax compliance, suggests that a definition of tax compliance should be one that captures issues of theoretical importance, as well as giving practical direction for measuring compliance. He believes that James and Alley have offered

26 M. Graetz, J. Reinganum and L. Wilde 1986, "The tax compliance game: Toward and interactive theory of law enforcement," (1986) 2 (1) *Journal of Law, Economics and Organization.*
27 N. Taylor 2003: p.72.
28 J. Pearsall 2002: p.292.
29 *Ibid.,* at p.1606.
30 V. Braithwaite "Dancing with Tax Authorities" in V Brathwaite(ed) *Taxing Democracy* (Chapter 2) Ashgate Publishing Company (2003) Aldershot 24.

a definition which meets this criterion. They define compliance as "the willingness of individuals and other entities to act within the spirit as well as the letter of tax law and administration without application of enforcement activity."[31] In these terms though, this definition is more of 'voluntary tax compliance' rather than general tax compliance.

Braithwaite has also questioned the accuracy of speaking about a willingness to comply without enforcement when the compliance itself is required by law as is always the case with taxation. By law, non-compliance invites sanctions.

Putting aside this polemical issue, in this study, the phrase 'voluntary tax compliance' is used in the sense proposed by James and Alley above. In that sense, 'voluntary taxpayer compliance' can be described as a civic state of mind which accepts that the payment of tax is a necessary and important public duty, and from this acceptance arises a desire to comply with the taxes levied without the need for a sanction or other form of state coercion. Voluntary taxpayer compliance may also refer to a taxpayer's desistance from subterfuge or unfair attempts to reduce the tax burden on him/her. Commonplace tax burden reduction methods include: deliberate understatement of taxable income, overstating allowable deductions, falsifying tax information, committing tax fraud, and resisting or delaying tax payment.

Scope of Study

The geographical focal point of the inquiry is Tanzania. An attempt is made to use data from, and include some discussion of other countries in the Eastern African region (Kenya, Uganda, Rwanda, Burundi and Zambia). However, such discussion is limited. South Africa is also excluded from the discussion. This exclusion is done for two reasons. Although this study is being submitted for examination at a South African University, the researcher's access to field data in South Africa would have been too limited because he is not a South African and has not worked or lived in South Africa to enable him to forge the sort of contacts and access to officers he has in Tanzania, and to a limited extent in the rest of Eastern Africa. In any case, the researcher believes that South Africa is in a more developed position, and has a level of resources and know-how that is not available to Tanzania or to other countries of Eastern Africa that are examined. These factors put South Africa at too different a level of play in relation to the issues examined in this book, to make it an example for Tanzania and the other East African countries to follow.

---

31   S. James and C. Alley 1999: 3.

The study undertaken demonstrates that the taxpayer compliance level in Tanzania is poor. Existing tax laws do not facilitate, or encourage, voluntary taxpayer compliance. They are more tilted towards enforcement, with audits and sanctions standing out as pre-eminent elements. This situation, coupled with negative perceptions of government and the tax system, create the tax resistance which feeds tax evasion and tax avoidance.

The assumptions, noted above at 1.1 regarding tax laws and compliance with those laws, are not borne out in Tanzania. Investigation shows that, as is the case in many countries, tax legislation in Tanzania is generally not understood by taxpayers because it is too complex.

In this regard, Tanzania is no different from other jurisdictions where complexity of tax legislation is a problem. In their attempt to develop tax compliance principles, Kidder and McEwen[32] have identified two key issues affecting tax compliance: the first is lack of clear language, and the second is complexity. They argue that tax laws must be made less complex and must be drafted using clear language if they are to be understood, and complied with, by those who pay taxes. The comments of Kidder and McEwen on complexity and lack of clear language in taxation laws echo concerns which have long been expressed by the courts in the United Kingdom. Referring to some tax provisions in England, Lord Simonds in *St Aubyn v Attorney General*[33] said that they "are, I think of unrivalled complexity and difficulty and couched in language so tortuous and obscure that I am tempted to reject them as meaningless." In *Associated Newspapers Group v Fleming*[34] Lord Reid came very close to dismissing a tax provision for being "obscure to the point of unintelligibility".

The failure to understand tax legislation is one of the many factors which lead to poor taxpayer compliance. Complexity of tax legislation leads those with means to engage tax advisers and leave it to them to make sense of the tax laws, and to either find ways for the taxpayers to live with the tax obligations, or to avoid them. To a large extent too, the complexity and the perception of unfairness in tax burden distribution and/or procedural inequity in administering tax, accounts for the tolerance society has for tax avoidance in stark distinction to the intolerance there is for tax evasion.

---

32 R. Kidder and C. McEwen '1989: p.47 at 64.

33 *St Aubyn v Attorney General*, 1952, AC 15 at 30.

34 *Associated Newspapers Group v Fleming*, 1973, AC 628 at 639.

Although tax avoidance has the same cost to the nation as does tax evasion, tax avoidance is generally tolerated, even encouraged at times. Judicial vindication of the legality of tax avoidance has ensured that there is no stigma for indulging in the tax avoidance vice as there is for tax evasion. In *CIR v Newman*[35], a judge felt it quite appropriate to say that "...there is nothing sinister in so arranging one's affairs as to keep taxes as low as possible, for no one owes any public duty to pay more than the law demands...." This restatement in the United States of America of the virtue of tax avoidance echoes what has been the position for many years in the United Kingdom. Lord Tomlin's statement in *IRC v Duke of Westminster*[36] is still good law to this day. He said,

> Every man is entitled if he can to order his affairs so that the tax attaching under the appropriate Acts is less than it otherwise would be. If he succeeds in ordering them so as to secure this result, then however unappreciative the commissioners of Inland Revenue or his fellow taxpayers may be of his ingenuity he cannot be called to pay increased tax.

Tax avoidance, however, is an equally complex and expensive exercise. Those without means to engage tax planners either suffer in silence, or complain against tax burdens they cannot appreciate, or resort to crude ways of beating the tax system, including, as is the case in Tanzania, bribing tax officers.

Widespread ignorance of tax laws in Tanzania also results from the legislative process not being inclusive enough. It is quite uncommon to have broad purposeful consultation with stakeholders on proposed legislation. It is also rare to have a well thought out strategy for disseminating enacted laws to the public. The passing of a tax law is bureaucratic and secretive. Invariably it is triggered by a need for the Ministry of Finance to collect additional tax revenue, or a need by the tax authority to improve the administration of a particular tax or an aspect of taxation. Whatever the cause for law, the write-up leading to legislation proceeds with much secrecy.

The TRA is the architect of all draft tax laws and amendments to existing laws. TRA legislative proposals are sent to the Ministry of Finance to be sanctioned. The Ministry of Finance in turn prepares a cabinet paper and seeks the approval of the Cabinet. However, discussions and views of ministers are never made public. When Cabinet approval is obtained,

---

35 *CIR v Newman*, 1947, 159 F 2d 848.
36 *IRC v Duke of Westminster,* 1936, AC 1.

instructions are sent to the Attorney General's office to prepare a bill.

There is much secrecy surrounding tax bills. No one must know the content of proposed tax measures, as it is feared that such knowledge will compromise their effectiveness. When new tax proposals are tabled in Parliament, discussion is limited and is managed by government to ensure quick passage. There is rarely an attempt by government to encourage a real understanding by parliamentarians of the tax measures they are asked to legislate, nor is there an attempt to educate the public on what is proposed before it becomes law. As a result, widespread ignorance persists, and optimum compliance with tax law remains difficult and elusive.

For Tanzania, there is also a real risk that this reliance on the tax administration to drive the tax legislation process will promote legislation which suits tax administrators and alienates the tax-paying public. Overtime, this can only lead to significant tax resistance.

It is fair though to say that all tax systems experience some form of resistance to taxation, not only because taxation is intrusive, but also because of the financial and other incentives arising from non-compliance with tax laws. It has been said that it is impossible to reduce the tax gap to zero, whether taxpayers are persuaded to pay taxes voluntarily or are compelled to do so forcibly. Rosenberg[37] argues that neither persuasion nor force offers a guarantee for compliance with taxes by every person. He concludes that the most that can be done is to use a mix of strategies to try to achieve optimum tax compliance and bridge the tax gap.

Various factors account for taxpayer compliance as well as taxpayer resistance. Ignorance of law and complexity of taxation as alluded above, are just two of the many factors that affect tax compliance. For most people as well, taxes are a considerable burden in terms of money, time and aggravation.[38] In a study undertaken in his country, Carroll[39] reveals that 57% of the taxpayers studied over a period of three years evaded taxes by either understating their income or overstating their allowable deductions on income.

Research undertaken in Tanzania by the Eastern and Southern African Universities Research Programme (ESAURP), whose results were published in 2009,[40] shows that the untaxed informal sector in

---

37   J. D. Rosenberg 1996: p.181-182.
38   J. S. Carroll 1992: p.43.
39   *Ibid.*
40   T. Maliyamkono et al 2009: p.25.

Tanzania accounted for 28.1% of Tanzania's GDP in 1986; 36.1% in 1996; and 48.1% in 2006. The ESAURP research also revealed that the estimated tax gap for Tanzania in 2005/2006 was around 20% of potential revenue. When broken down in tax type, it shows the tax gap for income tax was 6.6%; for excise duty 18.4%; for VAT 15.2%, and for import duty 37.7%.[41] Statistical projections by the TRA of the tax gap behaviour also show an upward increase. Data from the TRA Third Corporate Plan[42] shows the tax gap rising from 17.8% in 2010/11 to 20.1% in 2011/12 and to 22.7% in 2012/13. This steady increase in the size of the untaxed public is quite worrisome. This data also supports the view that tax payment is a burden that many wish to escape.

Attempts to justify taxes on account of services provided by the government fail to win the hearts and minds of taxpayers. Some argue that services provided by the government are generally so removed from the payment of taxes that it is difficult for the taxpayers to see the direct benefits they have received from the taxes they have paid.[43] Moreover, as most taxes have a redistributive effect, many taxpayers will receive less in benefits than they pay in taxes.[44] Even those who receive net benefits from the payment of taxes might prefer reduced or less costly benefits in exchange for lower taxes.[45] Others reasonably perceive that their benefits would not decrease if they were not to meet their tax obligation.[46]

Whatever, the motive for non-compliance, the end result impacts negatively on the nation's economy. Non-compliance of some is also unfair and unjust on the compliant taxpayers because it narrows the tax base, and results in compliant taxpayers being heavily taxed as there are fewer taxpayers supporting the tax base. Non-compliance is also damaging to the nation's economy because it prevents the government from meeting its revenue collection targets, and impairs the ability of the government to deliver essential public services.

A narrow tax base leads to higher rates of tax. As the tax rates rise, the compliant taxpayers become disgruntled with the increasingly unbearable burden of supporting the free riders. In turn, this unfair tax burden encourages more people to cheat the tax system. Therefore it is critical that each and every taxpayer be made to meet their tax obligations as fully as possible.

One program used by many countries to monitor and expand the tax base is registration of taxpayers. Each taxpayer is assigned a Tax Identification Number (TIN); in some jurisdictions this is called a Personal Identification Number (PIN). The TIN or PIN is a unique computer generated number which is non-repeating and is used to identify a taxpayer in connection with various tax related activities for

41 *Ibid* at p.26.
42 TRA "Third Corporate Plan 2008/09 – 2012/13", March 2010.
43 R. W. McGee, 1994: p.432-33.
44 J. D. Rosenberg, *supra* Note 6, p.183.
45 *Ibid.*
46 *Ibid.* (The typical case of a free rider is one who would like to enjoy the benefits without wanting to share the cost which brings the joy).

which possession of a TIN is required. For many countries the TIN program enables the tax administration to identify and keep track of taxpayers and the taxable activities in which they engage. The more people assigned TIN numbers, the wider the scope for enforcement of taxes on those registered.

Bird has cautioned that in emerging economies the effectiveness of a TIN program depends upon how widely the requirement for TIN is enforced on various transactions.[47] If the requirement for a TIN on various documents is not wide ranging, the TIN program will not force new taxpayers to come into the tax net. In relation to Tanzania, Maliyamkono argues that:

> If taxes are to be collected from the small and medium enterprises sector, tax regimes need to be developed which recognize the distinctive characteristics of small and medium enterprises. Most self employed people do not keep adequate records which would allow them to be accurately taxed. This is partly a result of illiteracy and inadequate skills, but also due to the family nature of the business which leads to a confusion between family and business finances. Moreover, since many businesses are conducted in the home, they can be invisible for tax purposes. Most transactions are conducted in cash and most traders do not operate bank accounts, and, in a situation where there is no culture of tax compliance, the scale of the operations cannot directly be estimated. Furthermore the turnover is high and, since the barriers to entry are low, traders may frequently change their operations.[48]

The easy entry into the informal sector and easy mobility within the informal sector enabling traders to frequently change income activities without any reporting or compliance requirement partly explains why the informal sector in Tanzania has grown at 10% every 10 years to stand at 48.1% of the official GDP by 2006.[49]

Tanzania had a population of 33.6 million by 2002 (the last census figures issued by the government), at least 54% of whom are above the age of 15 years.[50] The TIN registration program was launched in 1996. However, as of June 2010, there were only 686,980 TIN registrations (up from 334,724 in June 2008). This number includes both individuals and corporate entities engaged in trades. Those deriving income solely

---

47 R. M. Bird '1999: p.69.

48 T. Maliyamkono et al 2009: p.9-10.

49 T. Maliyamkono et al 2009: p.25.

50 http://www.tanzania.go.tz/census; See also *The Economic Survey 2006*, issued by the Ministry of Planning, Economy and Empowerment, Dar es Salaam, June 2007, which estimates the current population in 2007 to be 37.5 million (Table A at xv).

from employment covered by the PAYE scheme are excluded from TIN. The number of taxpayers registered for VAT stood at 14,292 in December 2010. The number of VAT registrations had risen to 15,320 by June 2004 but dropped significantly to 8,010 in July 2005 because the VAT registration threshold was increased from Tanzania shillings 20 million to Tanzania shillings 40 million. Those who were no longer eligible were weeded out. These numbers show that there are still far too many potential taxpayers remaining outside the electronic tracking system afforded by the TIN program.

For Tanzania, the low level of taxpayer compliance is additionally attributed to the high tax rates, which are levied because of the narrow tax base. The tax base is narrow because the size of the untaxed public is big. The tax base is also drained by widespread non-payment of tax. Non-payment of tax is compounded by wide-ranging tax exemptions granted under existing tax laws. The Income Tax Act 2004[51] gives the Minister for Finance wide powers to exempt persons, entities, and institutions from payment of income tax. The Minister can also exempt any class of income from taxation. Section 10 of the Income Tax Act 2004 reads as follows:

10   (1)   The Minister may by Order in the Gazette, provide

      a.   that any income or classes of incomes accrued in or derived from the United Republic shall be exempt from tax to the extent specified in such Orders; or

      b.   that any exemption under the Second Schedule shall cease to have effect either generally or to such extent as may be specified in such Order.

   (2)   The Minister may by Order in the Gazette, amend, vary or replace the Second Schedule.

   (3)   Notwithstanding any law to the contrary, no exemption shall be provided from tax imposed by this Act and no agreement shall be concluded that affects or purports to affect the application of this Act, except as provided for by this Act or by way of amendment to this Act. (This proviso is meaningless because the Minister has the powers to vary or amend the whole schedule which provides for exemptions.)

---

51   Act No. 11 of 2004, which came into operation on 1st July 2004, replacing the Income Tax Act of 1973 (Act No. 33 operative from 1st January 1974).

Similar provisions exist in the VAT Act of 1997,[52] and also in the Customs Management Act of 2005.[53] Not one of the three statutes provides clear guidelines or principles for the Minister to use when granting tax exemptions. The unwritten assumption appears to be that tax exemptions will be given in line with government policy and that such discretion will be exercised prudently. However, as documented practice has shown, this is not always the case. This ministerial discretion and the tax exemptions account for a large part of taxpayer-dissatisfaction with the tax system and in turn, the resistance to taxation.

It is a principle of the rule of law that every power must have limits, whether implied or explicit.[54] A power granted without limits can be abused. This is the reason why in many countries the power to tax derives from the constitution. The role of the constitution is to specify who should wield what amount of powers, how those powers are to be applied, and what limits are placed on the exercise of such powers.[55] The act of the legislature to grant unbridled powers to the Finance Minister, and to the Council[56] in the case of the customs exemptions, is inconsistent with responsible governance. The imprudent use of tax exemption powers has demoralized those who would otherwise be compliant taxpayers and has generated widespread distrust for the tax system.

It is also a fact that the tax administration itself (the TRA) has been given, and is allowed to wield, immense powers. It may, without a court order, attach a person's bank account and direct the bank to pay to the TRA money out of the attached bank account. This extra-judicial power can be exercised whether or not the TRA tax claim is lawfully disputed. The TRA has also the power to attach and sell property to recover disputed taxes even where there are on-going proceedings in respect of

---

52   Act No. 24 of 1997, Sections 9, 10, 11 and 12. Section 9 provides that certain supplies may be zero-rated, while Section 10 deals with exempt supplies, and Section 11 provides for exempt persons and exempt organizations. These substantive provisions cross refer to the First, Second, and Third Schedules to the VAT Act.

53   Act No. 1 of 2005 (East African Community Laws). Section 114 of the East African Customs Management Act 2005 read together with the Fifth Schedule Parts A and B (this customs law applies to Tanzania, Kenya and Uganda).

54   A. Michael and B. Thompson 2002: p.24.

55   Ibid.

56   The Council is the policy organ of the East African Community and is made up of Ministers responsible for Regional Cooperation drawn from Kenya, Tanzania, and Uganda. The Council is established under Article 13 of the Treaty for the Establishment of the East African Community signed on 30th November 1999, which was ratified and brought into force on 7th July 2000. The functions of the Council are set out in Article 14.

the dispute. The TRA also has power to collect taxes from third parties, or transfer a tax claim to a third party as if the third party owed the taxes directly.

Although a Bill of Rights[57] exists in Tanzania which proclaims lofty inalienable rights for all persons living in Tanzania, these constitutional protections have not been used to curb the powers of the TRA, and/or protect taxpayers from the wielding of taxation powers.

From a perception perspective, rather than facilitating compliance with tax laws, the laws in place undermine taxpayer compliance. The taxpayer seems to hold an underlying mistrust of the content of the tax laws, which project the taxpayer as a cheat who must be reigned in, in order to secure compliance.

Literature Review

In reviewing the existing literature, this study attempts to explore the extent of existing knowledge on taxpayer compliance. The first point noted is that, while there is ample written material on tax compliance generally, there is not much literature specific to voluntary tax compliance. The second point is that the written material on voluntary taxpayer compliance does not sufficiently project the complimentary relationship between tax enforcement and voluntary tax compliance, nor the existing link between voluntary taxpayer compliance and good governance. This gap is addressed by this study. It is argued here that to achieve high level tax compliance, a combination of enforcement and voluntary tax compliance strategies is necessary. In addition, since legitimacy of government and good governance impact on compliance attitudes, the source of legitimacy and the elements of good governance are examined.

In the study, it is argued that generally people will not comply with what they do not respect. For a tax system to command the respect of the people, it needs to be just and beneficial to them. Government must deliver on its duty to its people in order for the tax claims it makes to be accepted with ease. In addition, the tax system must be just. A just tax system is reflected through its sound administrative principles, the fairness of its rules and the safeguards it puts in place for the protection of taxpayers.

---

57 Part Three of the Constitution of the United Republic of Tanzania 1977, Articles 21 and 24 provide for the right to participate in the governance of the country, the right to own property, and the right to protection of personal property (references used here are taken from the current 2005 edition of the Constitution).

To demonstrate these links, this study explores the strategies for tax compliance currently in use in Tanzania. It notes that there is a predominance of enforcement strategies as against persuasive strategies, concluding that not enough is being done to promote voluntary taxpayer compliance. The study also explores issues of governance starting with the governance concept itself, its underlying principles, the influence good governance has on compliance generally, and how good governance impacts voluntary taxpayer compliance.

The study notes as well that there is little taxpayer compliance material on Africa and none on Tanzania. Professor Maliyamkono,[58] who is the Executive Director of ESAURP, has spearheaded research on the taxation of the informal sector in Tanzania, but much of that research and the literature flowing from it is dedicated to formalization of the informal sector with a view to expanding the tax base. Voluntary compliance of the informal sector traders has not been a focal issue in the ESAURP writings. Another relevant author is Odd-Helge Fjeldstad, who works with the Chr. Michelsen Institute[59] and does a lot of work for the Research Council of Norway and the Danish International Development Agency (DANIDA). Fjeldstad has published several works on taxation in Africa.[60] Though not directly on voluntary taxpayer compliance, his general discourse on African tax administration offers some insights on compliance.

Wallschutzsky[61] has provided additional literature on taxation in developing countries. He has attempted a comparative examination of taxpayer compliance in developing countries and developed countries, showing the disparity that exists. The study by Morgan and Murphy[62] on rural taxpayers in Australia is also instructive of the differences that exist

---

58 Two works have been published: T. L. Maliyamkono and M. S. D. Bagachwa *The Second Economy in Tanzania* 1990; T. L. Maliyamkono, H. Mason, A. Ndunguru, N. E. Osoro and A. Ryder (eds) *Why Pay Tax*2009.

59 The Chr. Michelsen Institute is the largest independent non-profit research institution in Scandinavian countries. It is based in Norway and was founded in 1930 as an international centre for policy oriented and applied development research.

60 O.H. Fjeldstad "Why People Pay Tax: A Study of Tax Compliance in Tanzania"; O. H. Fjeldstad "Taxation, Coercion and Donors: Local Government Tax Enforcement in Tanzania" 2001: p.289-306; O. H. Fjeldstad and J. J. Semboja "Why People Pay Taxes: The Case of the Development Levy in Tanzania"2001: p.2059-2074; O. H. Fjeldstad and J. J. Semboja "Dilemmas of Fiscal Decentralisation: A Study of Local Government Taxation in Tanzania" 2001: p.7-41.

61 Wallschutzsky, "Achieving Compliance in Developing Countries" (May 1989) *Bulletin de la Societe Geologique de France*, 234-244.

62 S. Morgan and K. Murphy "The Other Nation: Understanding Rural Taxpayers"December 2001.

in attitudes between rural and urban taxpayers, more so for developing countries where the rural population is a dominant proportion (true for Africa). These works, however, do not address compliance within a tax administration framework and in the context of governance.

McGee's[63] numerous writings are focused more on tax evasion generally and on tax non-compliance in the transition economies of the former Eastern Block countries. His earlier book on the philosophy of taxation offers good insights into the concept of 'just taxation'.[64] In a more recent book (2008)[65], he has a solitary article on tax evasion in the West African country of Mali. Ayoki's[66] monograph on tax reform in Uganda, addresses more the issue of revenue mobilization, looking at the structure of taxation and the tax administration processes. He does not discuss compliance issues.

There are several other authors who have written on the subject of tax compliance, but many look at the subject from the perspective of taxpayer behaviour (attitude). The causal link which exists between taxpayer behaviour and general governance is not sufficiently projected. These include Bird and Jantscher,[67] Silvani and Baer,[68] Barbone,[69] Tanzi and Pellechio,[70] and Frampton[71].

63 R. W. McGee (ed) *The Ethics of Tax Evasion* 1998; R. W. McGee "Tax Advice for Latvia and Other Similarly Situated Emerging Economies" 1996: p.223; R. W. McGee "Principles of Taxation for Emerging Economies: Some Lessons from the U.S. Experience" 1993: p.29; R. W. McGee (ed) *Taxation and Public Finance in Transition and Developing Economies* 2008.
64 R. W. McGee *The Philosophy of Taxation and Public Finance* 2004.
65 R. W. McGee and G. G. and B. M'Zali "Attitudes Towards Tax Evasion in Mali"2008.
66 M. Ayoki, M. Obwona and M. Ogwapus *Tax Reforms and Domestic Revenue Mobilisation in Uganda* 2008.
67 R. M. Bird and C. D. Jantscher (eds.) *Improving Tax Administration in Developing Countries International Monetary Fund* 1992; and M. Casanegra de Jantscher "Necessary Attributes for a Sound and Effective Tax Administration" 1997: p.3.
68 C. Silvani and K. Baer "Designing a Tax Reform Strategy: Experiences and Guidelines" 1977: 1; and *Striking the Balance: Tax Administration, Enforcement and Compliance in the 1990s* 1993.
69 L. Barbone, A. Das-Gupta, L. De Wulf and A. Hansson (World Bank Tax Policy and Administration Thematic Group) "Reforming the Tax Systems: The World Bank Record in the 1990s" 1999.
70 V. Tanzi and A. Pellechio "IMF Working Paper 95/22" 1995.
71 D. Frampton *Practical Tax Administration* 1993.

In Tanzania, a short study was made by Osoro[72] and a short paper written by Luoga[73] touches on the governance concept. Neither undertakes a sustained discourse on tax compliance. There are a few more studies on voluntary taxpayer compliance, but these have not sought to examine the special problems confronted by developing countries in aligning tax administration with democratic good governance.[74]

At the global level, voluntary taxpayer compliance has assumed much prominence in tax compliance literature over the last decade. Voluntary taxpayer compliance is hailed for two parallel reasons. On the one side is the sound economics of voluntary taxpayer compliance. It reduces the cost of tax administration and is good for the economy. On the other side, is the sociological and psychological aspect of compliance, centred on taxpayer motivation and responsible citizenship. Some of this literature lauds the fear factor arguing that the fear of detection and punishment makes many comply with taxes.

Taxpayer compliance literature at the global level appears unanimous in treating voluntary taxpayer compliance as a priority. The justification for this priority status is premised on the cost of non-compliance. Graetz, Reinganum and Wilde[75] (referred to previously) point to three reasons why non-compliance is costly. The first reason is the significant revenue losses that occur from non-compliance. The second is the real risk that the disrespect for tax laws which breeds non-compliance can quickly extend to widespread disrespect for other laws. The third reason is that tax non-compliance undermines the fairness of the tax system that requires that equals should pay equal taxes.

Given the priority which the promotion of voluntary taxpayer compliance has come to occupy in developing efficient tax systems, Smith has identified a number of incentives which drive voluntary compliance.[76] He points to responsive service and procedural fairness as key incentives for voluntary taxpayer compliance. He also points to the need for an appropriate balance between enforcement and cooperative

---

72 N. E. Osoro et al "Enhancing Transparency in Tax Administration in Tanzania" 1999.

73 F. D. A. M. Luoga "Tax Reform, Constitutionality and the Human Rights Dimension: An Analysis of the Pitfalls in the Tanzanian Tax Reform Approaches" 2002; Luoga "Formulation of Tax Policy in a Developing Country: Some Suggestions for Tanzania" 1995; Luoga "Divergent Tax Administration Practices and the Collapse of Accountability in Taxation: the Emerging Realities in Tanzania" 2004.

74 J. A. Roth et al 1989; P. Sawicki 1983; J. Slemrod "Complexity, Compliance Costs and Tax Evasion" 1989: p.156-174.

75 M. Graetz et al 1986: p.1.

76 K. W. Smith "Reciprocity and fairness: Positive incentives for tax compliance" 1990.

strategies to reinforce voluntary taxpayer compliance. Further, he underlines the need for effective detection and punishment of non-compliance as both a deterrent and an incentive for compliance. Finally, he argues that legitimacy and/or allegiance to authority reinforces voluntary taxpayer compliance. However, his examination of voluntary taxpayer compliance as an issue in governance is peripheral.

In the United States of America, Milliron and Toy are among the authors who have written on the subject, mostly from a behavioural perspective.[77] This is the case too with Boyd[78], Erard[79] and Mansfield[80]. However, in a recent book edited by McGee,[81] a link is established between bureaucracy, corruption and tax compliance. The findings of research by Riahi-Belkaoui[82] in 30 developed and developing countries indicate that tax compliance is highest in countries with less corruption and a smaller bureaucracy. The tax morale is higher when citizens are protected from official corruption and bloated bureaucracy. This finding confirms the link between good governance and tax compliance attitude.

Overall, the literature on taxpayer compliance is heavily weighted towards measures and mechanisms for compelling compliance, but it is shifting. Many of the studies available were produced before the debates on taxpayer rights, the human rights dimension in taxation, democratic taxation and good governance, assumed prominence. These debates are now influencing a new series of writings which acknowledge the multidimensional aspects of taxpayer compliance and have informed this study. They include the works of Braithwaite[83], Bentley[84], Brenan and Buchanan,[85] McGee[86], Howarth and Maas[87], and Croome.[88]

---

77 V. Milliron and D. Toy "Tax compliance: An investigation of key features" 1988: p.84-104.
78 C. W. Boyd "The enforcement of taxpayer compliance: Some theoretical issues" 1986: p.588-599.
79 B. Erard "The influence of tax audits on reporting behaviour" 1992: p.95-114.
80 H. K. Mansfield "The role of sanctions in taxpayer compliance" 1983.
81 R. W. McGee (ed) *Taxation and Public Finance in Transition and Developing Economies* 2008.
82 A. Riahi-Belkaoui 2008: p.8.
83 V. Braithwaite (ed) *Taxing Democracy: Understanding Tax Avoidance and Evasion* 2003.
84 D. Bentley (ed) *Taxpayers' Rights: An International Perspective* 1998; D. Bentley *Taxpayers' Rights Theory, Origin and Implementation* 2007.
85 G. Brennan and J. Buchanan *The Power to Tax: Analytical Foundations of a Fiscal Constitution* 1980.
86 R. W. McGee *The Philosophy of Taxation and Public Finance* 2004.
87 P. Howarth and R. Maas *Taxpayer Rights and Revenue Powers* 2004.
88 B. Croome *Taxpayers' Rights in South Africa* 2010.

The lack of literature on the subject of voluntary taxpayer compliance in Africa and on Tanzania and the predominance of writings examining the subject from a developed country perspective is a challenge for this study. This challenge will need to be surmounted. Notwithstanding, a critical examination of the subject is still possible, and is undertaken here to assist in developing tax administration principles which will foster voluntary taxpayer compliance in Tanzania and hopefully in the other Eastern African countries to which this study is relevant.

Outline

Having observed that the level of tax compliance is low in Tanzania, the general proposition emerging from Chapter One is that there is undue reliance on tax enforcement measures and not enough emphasis on promoting voluntary tax payment. It is suggested that the level of tax compliance will improve if there is a good mix between enforcement and voluntary tax payment strategies. This chapter has also touched on the impact of governance on tax compliance, a subject discussed in detail in Chapter Two.

Chapter Two examines the governance issue. It pursues the proposition that voluntary tax compliance is a function of confidence and trust in the government, resulting from good governance and the perception people have of the government. The chapter seeks to demonstrate the extent to which good governance can inspire voluntary taxpayer compliance. A case is made that optimum taxpayer compliance can be achieved where there is a responsible government and the process of tax legislation is inclusive enough to enable taxpayers to take ownership of the tax system.

Chapter Three uses both literature and available data to demonstrate that tax resistance is largely attributable to the failure to respect the constitution and to observe the rule of law and good governance. The chapter contains a thoroughgoing discussion on the protection of taxpayers and taxpayer rights.

Chapter Four focuses on tax administration in Tanzania. It examines the tax regime through the working of the TRA, and the interplay between the TRA and the Ministry of Finance. The chapter discusses in detail the powers of the Commissioner General, the Commissioners, and the institutional relationship which exists between the taxpayers and the tax authority and how all this impacts on taxpayer compliance.

Chapter Five analyses the tax framework in Tanzania, paying particular attention to the tax laws which govern the taxation of income, the imposition of customs duties and the administration of value added tax. These three are the most important taxes for Tanzania because of their significant revenue yield and the complexity of their design. The aim of the analysis is to ascertain whether the tax laws governing income tax, value added tax and customs in Tanzania facilitate voluntary tax compliance or hinder such compliance.

Chapter Six discusses tax policy with a view to establishing whether the tax policy in Tanzania is driven by the needs of institutions and government, or the needs of the people whom the institutions and government aim to serve. It also discusses the interaction between taxpayers and tax officials in order to determine whether there is recognition of a common endeavour and whether there are policies in place aimed at maximizing taxpayer acceptance of the tax system. The questions posed are: whether taxpayers are treated respectfully; whether they are made to understand the tax system and the tax obligations placed on them; and whether there is recognition of their ownership of the tax system.

Chapter Seven discusses the tax enforcement strategy of the TRA. It examines the effectiveness of the enforcement initiatives (such as investigation and prosecution) undertaken by the Tax Investigations Department (TID), the problems preventing effective punishment of tax delinquency and the overall limitations of tax enforcement.

Chapter Eight draws conclusions from the study. In line with the overall inquiry undertaken in this work, this concluding chapter underlines the complimentary relationship between voluntary taxpayer compliance and tax enforcement essential to the performance of a successful tax system and essential to desired increases in tax revenue yield. The chapter suggests possible steps to be taken to improve the tax system and to improve voluntary taxpayer compliance, which has lagged behind, so that tax administration is improved.

2

Good Governance and Tax Compliance

Trust in Government

It is imperative that there is trust between the public and the government for tax compliance to work. Professor Bird[89] underlines the link which exists between governance and compliance. His general proposition is that tax compliance levels not only reflect the effectiveness of the tax administration, but also taxpayer attitudes towards taxation and towards government in general. He argues that that,

> ...attitudes affect intentions and intentions affect behaviour. Attitudes are formed in a social context by such factors as the perceived level of evasion, the perceived fairness of the tax structure, its complexity and stability, how it is administered, the value attached to government activities and the legitimacy of government.[90]

Chapter One already alluded to the general dislike people have for taxation. Professor Bentley suggests that,

---

89 R. M. Bird 2004: p.134.
90 *Ibid* at p.136.

if you are going to do something that people do not like and you want them to tolerate or even enjoy it, make sure that you do it with as much fairness, transparency, consultation and engagement as possible. If you are going to tax people, make sure they know that they are doing something for the greater good, that the process is as painless as possible and that they don't feel that they are paying more than their fair share.[91]

Later in this chapter the study will refer to a tax perception survey undertaken in Tanzania which demonstrates that perceived legitimacy of government and the state of governance affect public reaction to taxation.[92]

Trust engenders compliance. De Juan, M. A. Lasheras, and R. Mayo[93] have published findings which show that tax compliance decreases significantly where the level of trust in the government is low. Taxpayers are reluctant to give money to a government which does not command their confidence.[94] Likewise, taxpayers' willingness to pay taxes voluntarily decreases when they disagree with how taxpayer money is spent, or where they feel alienated from what the government is doing.[95]

The question, however, is how does a government gain and maintain the trust of its taxpayers? Good governance is a key factor in creating and maintaining trust between taxpayers and government.

Good Governance

Santiso[96] traces the genesis of the concept of 'good governance' to a 1989 World Bank Report[97] on Sub-Saharan Africa which described the crisis in the region as "a crisis of governance". This view of the World Bank was prompted by concern over the continuing lack of effectiveness of the aid provided to Africa. It called into question the ability, capacity and willingness of political authorities to govern effectively.

---

91 D. Bentley 2007: p.2.
92 National Bureau of Statistics "Assessment of the Effectiveness of Taxpayer Awareness Program and Attitude of Taxpayers Towards Tanzania Revenue Authority," September 2003.
93 A. De Juan, M. A. Lasheras and R. Mayo "Voluntary Tax Compliant Behaviour of Spanish Income Tax Payers" 1994: p.90-105; L. Feld and B. S. Frey "Trust Breeds Trust: How Taxpayers Are Treated" 2002: p.87-99; J. T. Scholz and M. Lubell "Trust and Taxpayers: Testing the Heuristic Approach to Collective Action" 1998: p.398-417.
94 L. Lederman "Tax compliance and the Reformed IRS" 2003: p.971-1011; see also M. E. Kornhauser "The Rhetoric of the Anti-progressive Income Tax Movement: A Typical Male Reaction" 1987: p.465.
95 Ibid.
96 C. Santiso "Good Governance and Aid Effectiveness: The World Bank and Conditionality" 2001: p.1.
97 World Bank Sub-Saharan Africa: From Crisis to Sustainable Development 1989.

In its 1991 Report[98], the World Bank defined 'governance' as the manner in which power is exercised in the management of a country's economic and social resources for development. It identified three distinct aspects of governance: the form of political regime; the process by which authority is exercised in the management of a country's economic and social resources; and the capacity of governments to design, formulate and implement policies and discharge functions.

In the succeeding years (1992, 1993, 1994 and 2000),[99] the World Bank refined its definition, progressing from a value neutral definition to a more normative definition which recognized the existence of 'good governance' (as against 'bad governance'). When speaking of good governance, it put additional requirements on the process of decision-making and public policy formulation. In the words of Santiso,[100] good governance extends beyond the capacity of the public sector to the rules that create a legitimate, effective and efficient framework for the conduct of public policy. It implies managing public affairs in a transparent, accountable, participatory and equitable manner. It entails effective participation in public policy-making, the prevalence of rule of law and an independent judiciary.

The Organization for Economic Cooperation and Development (OECD) and the International Monetary Fund (IMF) also emphasize the normative character of governance. They do this by linking governance with participatory development, human rights and democratization. Kofele-Kale,[101] expanding on this context of good governance, writes that it focuses on legitimacy of government (degree of democratization); accountability of political and official elements of government (media freedom, transparency of decision making, accountability mechanisms); competence of governments to formulate policies and deliver services; and respect for human rights and rule of law (individual and group rights, security, framework for economic and social activity, participation).

---

98 World Bank *Managing Development: The Governance Dimension* 1991 (A good analysis of the Bank report is given in J. Faundez, M. E. Footer and J. J. Norton (eds), *Governance, Development and Globalization*, 2000: p.152.

99 World Bank *Governance and Development* 1992; World Bank *Governance* 1993; World Bank *Governance: The World Bank Experience* 1994; World Bank *Reforming Public Institutions and Strengthening Governance* 2000.

100 C. Santiso 2001: p.5.

101 N. Kofele-Kale "Good Governance as a Political Conditionality: An African Perspective" 2000: p.153.

There are other writers such as Pierre[102] who offer a definition of governance which refers to the ability of the government to sustain coordination and coherence among a wide variety of actors with different objectives (institutions, interest groups, civil society, non-governmental and transnational organizations), suggesting that governance is broader than government. However, writing with Peters,[103] Pierre adopts a more state-centric view of governance, perceiving it to refer to processes in which the government plays a leading role, making priorities and defining objectives (that steer society and the economy). Hirst[104] prefers a more general definition that governance is the means by which an activity or ensemble of activities is controlled or directed, such that it delivers an acceptable range of outcomes according to some established standard.

Good Governance is the exercise of power by various levels of the government that is effective, honest, equitable, transparent and accountable.[105] The true test of good governance is the degree to which it delivers on the promise of human rights: civil, cultural, economic, political and social rights.[106] This is done through organizational, administrative and policy reform.

Good governance exists when the authority of the government is based on the will of the people and is responsive to them; when open, democratic institutions allow full participation in political affairs; and when human rights protections guarantee the right to speak, assemble and dissent. Equally, it exists when government and governmental institutions are pro-poor, promoting sustainable human development of all citizens.[107]

The United Nations Development Program (UNDP) understands good governance (i.e. the quality of a government's exercise of power) to mean the degree to which government institutions (such as parliament) and processes (such as elections) are transparent. It also understands the term to mean the extent to which institutions of government are

---

102 J. Pierre (ed) *Debating Governance: Authority, Steering and Democracy* 2000.

103 J. Pierre and B. G. Peters *Governance, Politics and the State* 2000.

104 P. Hirst "Democracy and Governance" 2000 .

105 The Canadian International Development Agency (CIDA) has adopted this definition of good governance and uses it to measure a country's rating with regard to human rights.

106 United Nations High Commission for Human Rights "Development: Good Governance" http://www.unhcr.ch/huridocda.nsf.

107 United Nations Human Development Report Office *Human Development Report 2000*.

accountable to the people, allowing them to participate in decisions that affect their lives and the extent to which these institutions are not susceptible to corruption. It means, as well, the degree to which the private sector and organizations of civil society are free and able to participate in the affairs of government.[108] This study adopts this definition wherever reference to good governance is made.

According to this definition of good governance, a government exercising good governance is one which has the qualities proposed by Hayden and Bratton.[109] It promotes equity, participation, pluralism, transparency, accountability and the rule of law, and it is effective, efficient, responsive and sustainable over the long term. Good governance must be rooted in these principles to move society towards greater human development through poverty eradication, environmental protection and regeneration, gender equality and sustainable livelihoods. In practice, these principles of good governance translate into tangible things such as free, fair and frequent elections; a representative legislature that makes laws and provides oversight; an independent judiciary that interprets laws; guarantees for human rights and the rule of law; and transparent and accountable institutions. This is the view also taken by the UN High Commission for Human Rights which has identified the key attributes of good governance as being: transparency, responsibility, accountability, participation and responsiveness (to the needs of the people).[110] It echoes the UN Secretary General's emphasis that good governance means greater participation coupled with accountability.[111]

An article by the United Nations Economic and Social Commission for Asia and the Pacific,[112] points out that good governance has four major characteristics: It follows the rule of law; and is transparent; consensus oriented; equitable and inclusive; effective and efficient; and accountable.

Good governance ensures that corruption is minimized, the views of minorities are taken into account, and that the voices of the most vulnerable sections of people in the society are heard and included in the process of decision-making. It is also responsive to the present and future needs of society.

---

108 UNDP "Policy paper on governance and how it relates to human development" 1997; UNDP "Governance for sustainable human development" 1997.
109 G. Hayden and M. Bratton (eds) *Governance and Politics in Africa* 1993.
110 UNHRC Resolution 2000/64.
111 K. Annan "Preventing War and Disaster" 1999.
112 UNHRC *Millennium Report 2000*.

In today's interconnected and globalized world, the terms 'governance' and 'good governance' are being increasingly used in the same context in development literature when speaking about a country's credibility and respect on an international basis. Needless to say, bad governance is regarded as one of the root causes of all evil within our societies. International finance institutions, multilateral lending agencies, and donor countries now subject loans and development assistance to a 'good governance' test.

The *existence of rule of law* as an attribute of good governance deserves discussion. The discourse on rule of law pre-dates the discourse on good governance. However, the concept of governance, broad as it is, has now subsumed the rule of law, such that rule of law is presented as a pre-requisite for good governance. The origins of the concept of rule of law are attributed to Dicey.[113] He stated that rule of law means no person shall be punished or be deprived of property except by a law validly enacted. This statement reinforced not only the limits on government power, but emphasized as well a requirement for individuals to comply with law under the notion of 'law and order' necessary for public safety.[114] Tamanaha[115] accepts that in its most basic formulation the rule of law means that the government is limited by law. Beyond this, he says, there is substantial disagreement on the content of rule of law in the modern era.

Raz has argued that rule of law as an idiom imparts a very simple concept "that people should obey the law and be ruled by it."[116] But Raz notes that in a political and legal theory context, rule of law is understood in a narrower sense to mean that government shall be ruled by law and be subject to law such that actions not authorized by law cannot be "actions of government as government".[117]

Trebilock and Daniels argue that, when spoken of in relation to development, the conception of rule of law focuses on two elements of the legal system: procedural justice, referring to transparency in law making and adjudicative functions; and the predictability, stability and enforceability of laws. These last elements impart 'due process' or

---

113 A. V. Dicey *Introduction to the Study of the Law of the Constitution, 10th Edition* 1960: p.183.
114 M. Neumann *The Rule of Law Politicizing Ethics* 2002: p.23-48.
115 B. Z. Tamanaha *On the Rule of Law; History, Politics and Theory* 2004: p.32.
116 J. Raz *The Authority of Law, Essays on Law and Morality* (See the chapter on 'The Rule of Law and its Virtue') 1979: p.212.
117 *Ibid.*

'natural justice'.[118] Rule of law also focuses on institutional values such as 'independence' and 'accountability'.[119]

The rule of law requires fair legal frameworks that are enforced impartially. It also requires full protection of human rights, particularly those of minorities. Impartial enforcement of laws requires an independent judiciary and an impartial and incorruptible police force.

Transparency underpins rule of law and good governance because with it there is a requirement for decisions to be made and enforced following laid down rules and regulations in conformity with the law. Transparency also means that information is freely available and directly accessible to those who are affected by such decisions and their enforcement. In addition, it means that enough information is provided to the people in easily understandable form and media. This accessibility is especially relevant to taxation.

Good governance requires *consensus building*, the mediation of the different interests in society to reach a broad consensus in society on what is in the best interest of the whole community and the methodology through which this can be achieved. It also requires a broad and long-term perspective on what is needed for sustainable human development and how to achieve the goals of such development. This perspective of good governance resonates with the views of Peters and Pierre who see the role of government as that of "steering society and the economy".[120]

A society's well-being also depends on *equity and inclusiveness.* One must ensure that all members feel that they have a stake in the society and do not feel excluded from the mainstream of society. This requires all groups, but particularly the most vulnerable, to have opportunities to improve or maintain their well being. This inclusiveness makes every member of society feel part of the government process.

Good governance means that there is an *effective and efficient government*, whose processes and institutions produce results which meet the needs of society, while making the best use of resources at their disposal. The concept of efficiency in the context of good governance also covers the sustainable use of natural resources and the protection of the environment, for the benefit of all sections of people in the society. The government must be seen to care for its people and the resources of the nation.

---

118 M. J. Trebilcock and R. J. Daniels *Rule of Law Reform and Development* 2008:.
119 *Ibid*: p.31.
120 J. Pierre and B. G. Peters 2000.

Accountability is another key requirement of good governance for good reason. Governmental institutions, as well as the private sector and civil society organizations must be accountable to the public and to their institutional stakeholders. Every institution is accountable to those who will be affected by its decisions or actions. Accountability cannot be enforced without transparency and the rule of law.

The United Nations (UN), basing itself on these principles, is trying to strengthen the capacity of weak states to govern because countries that are well governed are both less likely to be violent and less likely to be poor. When people's interests, needs and human rights, are at the centre of governance institutions and practices, there can be real progress in combating poverty. In short, a more peaceful and more prosperous nation contributes to a more peaceful and more prosperous world.[121]

Overall, good governance reinforces acceptability of government and social perception of its legitimacy. This acceptability and legitimacy, in our view, affects and determines the level of people's readiness to comply with existing rules and regulations imposed by government, including the requirement to pay taxes.

While good governance is driven by rule of law, the existence of rule of law is itself predicated on the existence of constitutionalism in government and for those governed. Constitutionalism, as a concept, is the notion that government can, and should, be legally limited in its exercise of power by a constitution.[122] The authority and legitimacy of government depends on observing the constitutional limitations placed on government. These refer firstly to the existence of rules which create three separate arms of government: the legislature (with power to make laws), the executive (to implement those laws), and the judiciary (to adjudicate disputes under the laws).

Constitutionalism also means the rules which limit the scope of authority of the state[123] and the procedural requirements governing the exercise of power given to each of the three arms of government. However, the limits on government power are reflected as well by the entrenched rights of individuals written into the constitution or in a separate bill of rights or charter document. Constitutionalism in this latter context refers to the extent to which the exercise of power by the government is constitutionally conditioned to the observance of the civil and human rights of its subjects.

---

121 United Nations Economic and Social Council "Report of the Committee of Experts on Public Administration" 2006.
122 Stanford Encyclopedia of Philosophy at http://setis.library.usyd.edu.au/stanford.
123 The terms 'state' and 'government' are, in this context, used interchangeably.

Professor Yash Ghai, in one of his writings, says,

constitutionalism…is premised on the belief that the primary function of a constitution is to limit the scope of governmental power and to prescribe the method for its exercise, thereby preserving the autonomy of civil society. In its modern form, the constitution performs these functions typically through the separation of powers, the incorporation of democratic principles and some form of judicial review. The constitution validates certain fundamental values and, subject to their overriding supremacy, establishes a framework for formation of government and the conduct of administration.[124]

In essence then, constitutionalism refers to the extent to which the constitution entrenches the separation between the three arms of government, the rights of individuals and the procedural mechanisms for the exercise of the power given to government. All this is, in truth, the measure of the constitutionalism of any state, and the more there is of it, the more good governance exists.

Constitutionalism is concerned with ensuring that the exercise of state power, which is essential to the realisation of the values of the society, should be controlled in order that it should not itself be destructive of the values it was intended to promote. Constitutionalism is averse to unlimited power. Thus, in its traditional meaning, constitutionalism means the restraints imposed upon any usage of state power. All state power should have certain limits. There is to be no power without limits.

For the ordinary citizen, the power to tax is the most familiar manifestation of the government's power to coerce. This power to tax involves the power to impose on individuals and private institutions, charges that can be met only by a transfer to government of private property, or financial claims to such property. These tax charges carry with them elaborate powers of enforcement which underpin the tax system.[125]

Historically, governments have always possessed taxation powers, although in recent times the public have come to demand that sweeping powers of taxation must be constrained. Controls over the sovereign have been exercised through constraints on the taxing authority. The ascendancy of regional organizations and their desire to harmonize governance structures and political culture at the regional level have greatly helped in placing the rights issue at the centre of both political and economic debate, but also in enforcing supranational protections.

---

124 Y. Ghai, "Constitutions and Governance in Africa: A Prolegomenon" 1993: p.53-54.
125 G. Brennan and J. M. Buchanan 1980: p.8.

The exercise of power by governments is now constrained by protections afforded by both the regional union(s) (in the case of the European Union under the EU Treaty) and multilateral treaties and institutions such as the European Convention on Human Rights and the European Court of Human Rights.[126] The corresponding institutions for Africa are the African Union (AU), the African Commission on Human and Peoples Rights, and the African Court of Justice and Human Rights.

Even for countries that are not aligned to formal regional structures, the quest for constitutionalism and rule of law has meant that a service standard is now set for tax administrations at the heart of which is protection of taxpayer rights. Canada, Australia and New Zealand are among the non-European countries which have made significant strides in this direction.[127]

Constitutional restraints on tax administrations have an enormous impact on the legitimization of taxes. The restraints and taxpayer protections help to bring understanding and acceptance of the tax system.

Limiting the power to tax, as well as the powers of the tax authority, is not inimical to government interests in collecting taxes. It is often the case that taxing authorities operate outside the constitutional and administrative law because of perceived vital government interests in imposing and collecting taxes. However, when viewed from the perspective of constitutionalism, it emerges that constraining the powers of taxation does not undermine the vital interests of a government in taxing its people. On the contrary, limiting taxing powers constitutionally enhances trust in the constitutionality of taxation and encourages taxpayers to voluntarily pay their taxes. The public assumption is that, when taxing powers are subject to constitutional limitations, legitimacy of taxation is achieved and the justification for tax compliance is entrenched.

The proposition here is that limiting the powers of tax collection is, in the long run, in the best interests of the state, because it encourages voluntary tax compliance. Constitutional limitation of taxing powers also plays another important role in tax administration. It helps provide a better guarantee for taxpayer rights which is another motivation for voluntary tax compliance. Taxpayer rights and the power to tax are not opposite forces; they are complementary features. When the power

---

126 D. Bentley "Chapter 2: Classifying Taxpayers' Rights" in *Taxpayers' Rights* 1998: p.19.
127 D. Bentley traces the origins of taxpayer rights in Chapters 1 and 2 of *Taxpayers' Rights* 2007: p.1-58.

to tax is exercised within constitutional and legal limitations, good governance is achieved and with it the legitimacy of taxation.

It was previously mentioned that good governance requires responsible use of tax revenue. Governments are not usually limited in their use of tax money. They may tax revenues to finance public needs, or they may give part of the revenue to citizens in welfare payments. However, one needs to distinguish sharply between the *need for taxing power* and the *manner of exercise* of the power to tax. The power to tax, per se, does not carry with it any obligation to use the tax revenue raised in any particular way. The power to tax does not logically imply rational spending.

Seen in this way, the power 'to tax' is simply the power 'to 'take'. If the government wishes to obtain a particular piece of property, it is of no relevance whether it does so simply by direct appropriation, or by purchase, or by taxation. Both government and the owner are in an identical position after government action, irrespective of the precise details of the means of appropriation. The government takes and the person loses. Therefore, if any distinction between taking and taxing is to be sustained, the tax alternative must involve certain additional requirements not present with direct appropriation. For example, if the power to tax is constrained by some generally uniform requirements that apply to all persons in similar circumstances (for example as regards persons with the same aggregate net wealth), then it may be accepted. Whereas the direct appropriation or other arbitrary taking may not survive electoral scrutiny, the tax alternative would do so. In this case, the fair distribution of tax burdens ensures (or, more accurately, increases) the likelihood that electoral processes will vindicate and compliment the constraints placed on taxation.

Responsible use of taxation revenues as a feature of good governance helps to create and maintain public confidence in the government. Control of expenditure has two aspects to it. The first is accountability. The need to fully account for all tax revenues collected and expended by government. The second is responsible spending. Braithwaite[128] insists that the priorities of government in public spending must coincide with public opinion as to current priorities. Levi[129] agrees and adds that where government spending priorities sharply conflict with the way taxpayers feel their tax money ought to be spent, the seeds of resentment against

---

128 V. Braithwaite "Communal and Exchange Trust Norms: Their Value Base and Relevance to Institutional Trust" 1998.
129 M. Levi *Of Rule and Revenue* 1988: p.78.

the tax system are sown, and, with that, tax resistance creeps in. The way the government expends public funds has a considerable impact on taxpayers' compliance with taxes.[130] Unwise spending of public funds fuels non-compliance with taxation.[131] The wisdom of this Hindu saying, that "the ruler must act like a bee which collects honey without causing pain to the plant "[132] cannot be ignored.

In Tanzania, opposition against public spending patterns is common-place. A survey by the National Bureau of Statistics in Tanzania revealed that only 2 in every 10 taxpayers who were interviewed have confidence in the tax system. Even the tax administration officers who were interviewed for this survey agreed that the tax system in Tanzania is unfair.[133] The survey showed the dim view taxpayers have of the lavish lifestyle of the TRA as an organization and the opulence of its officers. This lavishness was seen as an example of wasteful government spending which the public does not approve. There are other examples often mentioned, including government ownership and use of expensive four-wheel drive vehicles or luxury cars, which add nothing to the ability of government to deliver services. The vehicles are used mostly in the city where the public officers live and work and are never used to go to remote rural areas which reason is often advanced to justify their purchase. The public also resents that every five years the government gives interest free loans for luxury vehicles to its 285 parliamentarians. Maintenance and repair of the vehicles is borne by the government. Tanzania also has cabinets consisting of 61 ministers,[134] too big for a small country ranked by donor agencies among the three poorest countries in the world. Ministers enjoy an opulent lifestyle,

---

130 *Ibid.*
131 *Ibid.*
132 These words are quoted from *The Mahabharata*, a sacred Hindu writing..
133 The report by the National Bureau of Statistics in September 2003 is an indictment of the TRA and the Government of Tanzania. The report reveals that only two in every ten taxpayers who were interviewed have confidence in the tax system. Even the TRA officers who were interviewed for this survey agree that the tax system is unfair.
134 The size of the cabinet was in February 2008 reduced to 49 following a crisis of public confidence in government in the wake of a serious corruption scandal and abuse of government office by the Prime Minister and two senior ministers. Further reduction of Cabinet size was implemented after the general election in October 2010, but the public remains unconvinced that enough is being done.

often with two official residencies.[135] The expensive lifestyle extends to senior officers and heads of public institutions. In contrast, one notes the lack of funding for hospitals and schools, the failure to maintain roads or build public facilities, and the failure to adequately fund law enforcement agencies such as the police. Opposition to this pattern of government spending becomes the justification for tax resistance.

Official corruption also undermines trust in government. Corruption is an assault on the legitimacy of government. Obedience to government stems from the public approval of the government of the day. Odd-Helge and Bertil[136] argue that public approval is the basis of the legitimacy of government. When institutions are legitimate, citizens have a predisposition to consider obedience to them as reasonable and appropriate.[137] Where a government lacks legitimacy, or loses its legitimacy, the public equally loses the moral justification for obeying the laws of such government.[138]

Odd-Helge and Bertil have cautioned that the disrespect for tax laws can lead to disrespect for other laws and contribute further to undermining the legitimacy of the government.[139] Therefore, there is a danger of a vicious circle emerging whereby distrust breeds more distrust. In contrast, trust in government and wide-spread public approval tends to legitimize everything related to government and reinforces the payment of tax as a social norm.[140]

The proposition made in this study is that when a government is perceived to be trustworthy, citizens are more likely to comply with its demands in general.[141] From this perspective, trust in government is closely linked to public perceptions of the capacity of the government to make credible decisions about the use of taxes, as well as the design and administration of taxes. Trust and responsibility bolster taxpayer inclination to pay taxes voluntarily.[142]

---

135 In 1980, the government decided to move the seat of government to Dodoma, a town in central Tanzania that had to be built and upgraded for this purpose. The project is still ongoing to-date with the result that ministers have residences in Dar es Salaam, where most of the official business is still carried out, but also in Dodoma in anticipation of the move.
136 F. Odd-Helge and T. Bertil "Fiscal Corruption: A Vice or a Virtue?" 2003: p.1463.
137 *Ibid.*
138 *Ibid.*
139 *Ibid.*
140 *Ibid.*
141 M. Levi and L. Stoker "Political Trust and Trustworthiness" 2002: p.475.
142 *Ibid.*

Governance and Tax Compliance

Generally taxpayers have no problem with the justification for taxation. They accept that governments need money to meet their obligations to the public they govern. Taxpayers seem to recognize too that government's main source of revenue is taxation. Governments have three major sources of revenue: borrowing, income from asset ownership, and taxation. Government borrowing is an expensive source of revenue because at the end it must be repaid. Government ownership of income producing assets is now largely discredited. Most governments have moved away from ownership of business entities and have privatized their assets, reverting to the role of regulator and policy maker. This change has further elevated taxation to the most important source for funding governments.

However, opinions seem to vary greatly as to how best the obligation to tax must be carried out. It seems that many taxpayers prefer that the burden of taxation comes with as little pain and with as much respect, as possible. For governments, expediency and efficiency often override the convenience to the taxpayer. The government interest in collecting more revenue at times means it will cast a blind eye to the excesses of the taxation authority. There is some fear that if a tax administration is forced to observe good governance principles, tax collections could suffer. Governments need to recognize, however, that unfair taxation is ultimately self-destructive. Professor Bentley says that "without justice and the rule of law, taxation becomes an arbitrary exaction at whim."[143]

The ideal situation is to have high levels of voluntary taxpayer compliance, with as little cost of tax administration as possible and as minimal enforcement as absolutely necessary. In other words, taxpayers comply with their tax obligations because they are ready and willing to pay without forcible intervention by the tax authority. When non-compliant taxpayers dictate the attitudes of tax authorities in making them act with mistrust and suspicion against the taxpayers as a group, and when, in so acting, tax authorities excessively use enforcement to extract tax, taxpayers will most likely resent the intrusive character taxation assumes in their lives. Therefore, in line with the ideal situation, voluntary tax compliance must be a priority for effective administration and collection of taxes.[144]

---

143 D. Bentley *Taxpayers' Rights* 2007: p.2.
144 M. Blumenthal, C. Christian and J. Slemrod 2001: p.125. Also see C. Silvan and K. Baer1977: paragraph 30.

In putting forward a conceptual framework for this study,[145] Chapter One underscores the complimentary relationship between enforcement and persuasive strategies for effective tax administration. The proposition that taxpayers obey laws only when doing so is in their own self interest was discounted.[146]

There is an economic perception that compliance with tax laws is driven by choice, often dictated by an individual's desire to maximise outcomes.[147] This economic view holds that tax compliance decreases when audits decline, because the fear of being caught is reduced.[148] Writers who uphold this economic perception of tax compliance suggest a tax compliance approach focused on the cost/benefit model.[149] This approach is made up of intensified audits, followed by increases in the severity of penalties for non-compliance (non-disclosure or under reporting of income). Supporters of this view believe that increasing the cost of non-compliance directly reduces non-compliance.[150]

However, this study argues that an economic perception of compliance does not fully explain tax behaviour. It is known that some people obey laws even when the laws are against their self interest.[151] This altruism in tax compliance shows that, apart from self interest, there are other factors which account for compliance. Non-economic factors, such as the trust which the government commands among its people, the social norms dictating behaviour for taxpayers as members of society, the sense of fairness to others, as well as the integrity of oneself and moral constraints which may derive from religion or upbringing, all influence

---

145 Chapter One, Part 1.5 Conceptual Framework.
146 The economic theory of crime deterrence starts from the premise that individuals are willing to breach rules if the expected benefits of such non-compliance exceed the expected benefits of compliance. Neoclassical economists rely on this theory as propounded by Garry Becker to push the view that tax evaders are motivated to bend rules of compliance as long as the benefits of doing so outweigh those of compliance. See G. S. Becker "Crime and Punishment; An Economic Approach" 1968: p.169; M. Block "Optimal Penalties, Criminal Law and the Control of Corporate Behaviour" 1991: p.395-419; M. Wenzel "Tax Compliance and the Psychology of Justice: Mapping the Field" 2003: p.41.
147 *Ibid.*
148 M. E. Kornhauser "Doing the full Monty: Will Publicizing Tax Information Increase Compliance?" 2005: p.2.
149 *Ibid.*
150 *Ibid.*
151 D. M. Kahan "Signaling or Reciprocating? A Response to Eric Posner's Law and Social Norms" 2002: p.367, at 377.

tax behaviour and compliance with tax laws.[152] Bankman and Griffith[153] make a compelling argument against attributing tax compliance entirely to the intensity of audits; they observe that higher rates of compliance have been shown to exist even where there are no stringent audits and the chances of being caught are at the lowest levels.

The question as to what role the standing of the government of the day plays in influencing taxpayer compliance behaviour has been dealt with in earlier sections of this chapter. At this stage the study attempts to provide more correlative evidence by examining the legal framework governing taxation in Tanzania to see if it is structured in a way that cultivates trust between taxpayers and the government and between taxpayers and the tax administration. The question asked is whether existing laws enable government to command the trust and confidence that lead to acceptable levels of voluntary tax compliance.

Firstly, the reciprocity between taxpayers and the tax authority *vis a vis* the tax laws in place is examined. This reciprocity is central to the concept of equity and inclusiveness. Do the existing tax laws ensure that every person pays tax to the fullest level required? Are the tax laws effective? Do they carry an ability to drive compliance?

The need to have tax laws apply equally to everyone is important because taxpayers' sense of fairness stems from the belief that all persons will fulfil their tax obligation so that the costs of running the country are evenly distributed. No person should cause another to bear more tax burden by escaping his/her own tax obligation.

Together with the need for fairness, there is a need for accountability of the government to taxpayers. The main argument is that, when the government is seen as accountable to the taxpayer, the taxpayer's desire to voluntarily pay taxes is enhanced. Good laws are not enough to drive compliance if the government is not acting responsibly. Good governance acts as the bedrock for tax laws to function in a society. The existence of a responsible government increases the taxpayer's inclination to voluntarily comply with the tax obligations imposed by the government, because good governance justifies the right to tax.

Public Perception of the Tax System in Tanzania
The link between perceived legitimacy of government, the state of governance and taxpayer reaction to taxation is aptly demonstrated by

152 *Ibid.*
153 J. Bankman and T. Griffith "Social Welfare and the Rate Structure: A New Look at Progressive Taxation" 1987: p.1905.

two surveys conducted in Tanzania. The first was carried out in 2003[154] and the second in 2006.[155]

In the first taxpayer survey undertaken by the Tanzania National Bureau of Statistics in 2003, it is reported that 56.6% of the 2,399 taxpayers surveyed considered the tax rates in Tanzania to be either high or too high. The respondents in this interview included 270 staff of the TRA. More than half of the TRA officers interviewed believed that the value added tax (VAT),[156] in particular, is a burden to businesses.[157] The survey shows that a significant number of taxpayers and tax administrators perceive the current tax system to be unfair. As a result, they have no confidence in it.[158] The survey further shows that only 2 in 10 taxpayers interviewed have confidence in the current tax system.[159]

In a latter perception survey undertaken by PricewaterhouseCoopers in September 2006 focusing only on large taxpayers, similar concerns were again noted. The survey, commissioned by the TRA, sought to gain understanding of taxpayers' perceptions on a variety of tax matters. It also aimed at soliciting opinions on reforms implemented, so as to inform the development of the responsive taxpayer services and the TRA taxpayer education programs.

The major areas covered by the survey included customs modernization reforms, the TRA service provision and VAT refunds. The survey result shows that, in respect of fundamental functions such as valuation in customs, , only 43% of respondents agreed that goods are valued correctly for taxation purposes and that the TRA is correctly applying the WTO Agreement on customs valuation. As regards clearance of imported goods at points of entry into the country, only 26% said that goods are not cleared in a timely manner.

On the provision of service, only 45% of the respondents agreed that complaints are dealt with promptly. As to assistance taxpayers get from the customs department, 23% of those surveyed reported that they do not receive complete, accurate and easy to understand information.

Results on VAT refund claims show that 33% of the respondents were not aware of new procedures for handling VAT claims introduced in

---

154 National Bureau of Statistics '2003.

155 PricewaterhouseCoopers "Stakeholders Perception Survey Report" 2006.

156 Value Added Tax (VAT) was first introduced in Tanzania in 1997 and replaced the Sales Tax, which was only applicable to the sale of goods. VAT applies as well to payments for services.

157 *Ibid*: p.6.

158 *Ibid*: p.11, 14, and 18.

159 *Ibid*: 14.

October 2004.[160] Only 25% believed that these procedures would be implemented impartially. Nonetheless, 40% believed that the procedures would improve the VAT refund process.

The VAT refund procedures introduced in 2004 sought to speed up the VAT refund process. With these procedures, the TRA adopted a Risk Profiling System that categorises claimants for VAT refunds in three risk groupings: Gold Claimants, Silver Claimants and Other Claimants. Gold Claimants are those who are low risk with a good VAT payment and claim record. The compliance record relied on must include the past 2 years without any blemish in the regularity and quality of VAT returns and tax payments. Refund claims for this group are not audited and are paid within 30 days of being lodged. Audits for Gold Claimants are done only once a year.[161] Silver Claimants are those who fail to meet the Gold Claimant criteria. For this category, the first two VAT refund claims are paid within 30 days and without being audited. However, before the third claim is paid, the claimant is audited with respect to both current and previous claims. VAT refund claims falling into the Other Claimants group are those perceived by the TRA to be high risk. These are routinely audited. Understandably, VAT refunds for such claims are usually delayed depending on how quickly the audit process is completed. It is surprising that, according to the taxpayer survey by PricewaterhouseCoopers, there was very little awareness of this VAT refund system. The fact that many of those who were aware of it thought it would not work is evidence of the lack of confidence in the TRA as an institution. To a large extent, their fears have been confirmed, because, by June 2010, there was a substantial backlog of unpaid VAT refund claims.

Given the concerns expressed on the sluggish clearance of goods by customs, the PricewaterhouseCoopers Report recommended that the integration between the Tanzania Inspection Service Company Ltd (TISCAN) and the Automated System for Customs Data

---

160 Tanzania Revenue Authority "VAT General Guide" 2007.
161 If the end of the year audit discovers significant irregularity, the Gold claimant will be demoted to the Silver or Other Grouping.

(ASYCUDA++)[162] should be fast tracked to enhance customs clearance processes. PricewaterhouseCoopers recommended that the complaints procedures should be improved by providing more explicit information in the Taxpayer's Charter.[163] The TRA can try to ensure the timely dissemination of changes or amendments to tax laws. Other recommendations include development of taxpayer education programs tailored to meet large taxpayers' needs and to revise arrangements on refund claims.

To summarise, the points of complaint by taxpayers against the TRA and against tax administration in general, are the following: multiplicity of taxes, high tax rates, uncaring tax administration, high cost of tax administration, inconsistencies between tax policy and tax administration, unjust administration procedures and irresponsible use of tax revenue.

A good number of taxpayers complain about the numerous taxes they have to pay which leave them confused and unable to comply. The First Schedule of the Tanzania Revenue Authority Act[164] lists 24 tax laws which are administered by the TRA, each imposing a tax. There are also rates and local government taxes provided for under four separate statutes: the Local Government (District Authorities) Act,[165] the Local Government (Urban Authorities) Act,[166] the Local Government Finances Act,[167] and the Urban Authorities (Rating) Act.[168] In addition, local governments and urban authorities have rule making powers which enable them to make by-laws for the imposition of ad-hoc charges to fund their activities.

In addition to taxes and rates, there are numerous compulsory institutional levies and quite a few compulsory civic contributions are

---

162 ASYCUDA++ is the later version of ASYCUDA. ASYCUDA was developed by UNCTAD (United Nations Conference on Trade and Development) and made available to member countries of UNCTAD to assist their customs administration in improving revenue collection through electronic processing of customs data. ASYCUDA is in use only in developing countries. Countries which showed proficiency in the use of the original version of ASYCUDA were upgraded to ASYCUDA+ and thereafter to ASYCUDA++. ASYCUDA++ has the ability to allow clearing and forwarding agents interfaced with the Customs Department to input import/export data directly into the Customs Department data system which speeds up the processing of customs information and the clearance of goods.

163 The Taxpayer's Charter is probably not the right place; such information could be more effectively disseminated in taxpayer education leaflets or booklets.

164 Tanzania "Tanzania Revenue Authority Act No. 11" of 1995.

165 Tanzania "Local Government (District Authorities) Act No. 7" of 1982.

166 Tanzania "Local Government (Urban Authorities) Act No. 8" of 1982.

167 Tanzania "Local Government Finances Act No. 9" of 1982.

168 Tanzania "The Urban Authorities (Rating) Act No. 2" of 1983.

encouraged by government. For example, patients going to government hospitals are required to pay money before being attended to. This payment is not a charge for services or a user pay fee; it is dubbed a 'contribution' to assist with the cost of running the public institution. Similar payments are required from parents towards the running of public schools owned and funded by the government.

Apart from the many taxes, there is also a feeling that some of the numerous taxes levied are driven by a desire to raise more revenue without regard to the paying ability of the persons against whom the tax demands are made. Wages in Tanzania are generally low. The minimum wage for the public sector announced in December 2007 was Tzs 150,000[169] per month. This was increased to Tzs 180,000 in July 2010 (possibly motivated by the general elections held in October 2010). The minimum wage announced in 2007 was intended to apply to the private sector as well, but had to be suspended for the manufacturing enterprises because of alleged inability to pay.[170] For employees in the hospitality industry (waiters and waitresses) and for domestic employees, wages are as low as Tzs 30,000 per month and have proved impossible to regulate. An attempt in 2007 to raise wages for domestic employees and those of waiters and waitresses, to Tzs 65,000, led to mass terminations and had to be suspended.

The complaint against high tax rates noted in the two taxpayer perception reviews referred to above is now commonplace. The high band marginal rate is 30% (giving an effective income tax rate for individuals of about 27% of income). Although this rate may appear lower than, for example, the South African maximum income tax rate of 40%, it is still a significant portion of gross wages, considering the generally low wages in Tanzania.

The corporate rate is 30% (25% for companies listed on the Dar es Salaam stock exchange). The upper band for customs duty used to be 30% (until 1st January 2005, when it was reduced to 25% upon introduction of the EAC Customs Act), and on many goods it is coupled with *ad valorem* excise duty of 7%, 10%, 20%, 30% and 120%.[171] To this is added the VAT for every import transaction at 20% of the value of goods. VAT at the same rate also applies to all supplies of goods and services save for a few non-VATable transactions.

---

169 Around USD $125 at an average exchange rate of Tzs 1200.
170 *Daily News* of 6th January 2008: p.1.
171 The 120% is the excise on plastic shopping bags which clearly is a prohibitive tariff aimed at discouraging the importation and use of plastic bags; this prohibitive measure was accompanied by a government directive issued in 2006 to close down the manufacturing of plastic bags in Tanzania.

The perception that the TRA is an uncaring institution is said to stem from the manner in which it carries out its functions. It is accused of acting without regard to the effect of its actions on the productive activities of the taxpayers. Officers of the TRA are often accused of being robotic, vindictive, un-caring and highhanded. Taxpayers complain that there is a very low level of professionalism in the manner in which the officers administer taxes.

There is also another major perception problem. Allegations of corruption, bribery and extortion are rampant. Many of the incidents reported are blatant. Even the subtle ones leave the tax system choked with inefficiency, as many times tax decisions are made only upon incentives being given. It takes a long time to get an answer to written queries. It is not uncommon for a letter from a taxpayer to remain unanswered for over a year. Often, remarks showing negative perception of the TRA are heard in drinking and eating places.

In fairness to the TRA, part of this inefficiency is attributable to the fact that the tax administration in Tanzania is very small, inexperienced, unskilled and ill-equipped. As a result, its ability to process tax work is limited. The TRA's ability to assess everyone and enforce collection of tax assessed is severely limited. Similarly, the TRA's ability to undertake audits (specific or random) so as to assess the reliability of information received is also limited. Nevertheless, these inadequacies cannot fully account for the all-around inefficiency that the TRA as an institution exhibits. A large part of the TRA inefficiency stems from the static attitude of the staff. Whatever the reasons or justifications, the inefficiency of the TRA results in selective taxation, making the whole tax system unfair and unacceptable.

Another concern for taxpayers is the high cost of taxation. Relative to revenue returns, many people believe that the cost of administering taxes in Tanzania is too high. The public also complains about the official lifestyle of the TRA as an institution and the lifestyle of the tax officers, all of which is funded by taxpayer money. The posh buildings, the overly comfortable interior, the clearly superior salaries paid to the TRA officers and the expensive four-wheel drive vehicles used by the tax officers are seen as wasteful living in the face of other priorities competing for government funding.

There are substantial funds allocated to the TRA by government to fund the operations of the TRA. Looking at the budget allocation trend for 2001 to 2008, the requirement for money seems to grow every year. Table 1 below shows the TRA expenditure figures for that period.

TABLE 1: TRENDS IN BUDGET ALLOCATION FOR THE TRA
(IN BILLION TANZANIA SHILLINGS)

2001/02	2002/03	2003/04	2004/05	2005/06	2006/07	2007/08
34,77	37.43	44.31	47.09	63.63	74.33	84.38
Annual Increase	10.8%	11.8%	10.6%	13.5%	8.56%	8.80%

* Source: TRA Annual Reports 2001/02to 2007/08

An important point to note is that the budget allocation figures shown in Table 1 above do not include very substantial assistance funding and equipment donations from donor countries for the TRA under the Tax Administration Program (TAP), which in 2007 was replaced by the Tax Modernisation Program (TMP) through which all project funding by donors is now provided. Assistance funding from international agencies between 2000 and 2006 amounted to USD 75 million as shown in Table 2.

TABLE 2: TRA EXTERNAL SUPPORT UNDER TAP 2000-2006[172]

Type of Funding	Financier	USD $
(i) Credits	IDA Credit	40,000,000
(ii) Grants	European Union	7,000,000
	DFID UK	6,500,000
	SIDA Sweden	5,000,000
	DANIDA Denmark	2,500,000
	GTZ Germany	3,400,000
	USAID USA	2,500,000
	FINIDA Finland	800,000
	UNDP	300,000
(iii) Government		7,000,000
Total Project Funding		75,000,000

* Source: TRA " A decade of TRA Transformation 1996-2006"[172]

Additional grants from international agencies given to TRA under the TMP program amounted to USD 16 million ($9.116m for 2007 and $7.013m for 2008).[173] One needs to read the figures in Table 1 and Table 2 together to appreciate the substantial funding consumed by the TRA.

There is another dimension to the cost of tax administration. Often, tax collection obligations are imposed on members of the public and private institutions without regard to the cost to the person or institution for undertaking the tax collection/payment obligations for TRA.

Later it will be shown how withholding tax obligations, with regard to taxpayers who are only their employees, customers, or suppliers, are imposed on companies without regard to the cost of compliance to the company. These unacknowledged burdens on the public, together with perceived wastefulness in the TRA, compound taxpayer disillusionment with taxation.

Given the TRA's propensity for spending, taxpayers feel aggrieved by the TRA's reluctance to administer even the most beneficial tax incentives allowed by the tax laws or other legislation. Taxpayers, both corporate and non-corporate, are frustrated by the reluctance of the TRA to honour measures announced by the government giving benefit to taxpayers, and the partial manner in which tax credits and refunds are administered by the TRA.

---

172 Tanzania Revenue Authority *A Decade of TRA Transformation 1996-2006* 2007: p.35.
173 TRA *Annual Report 2006/07* and *Annual Report 2007/08*.

One such example is the package of tax incentives given to mining companies in order to encourage investment in and growth of the mining sector. Mining companies execute Mining Development Agreements with the government, stipulating clearly the tax exemptions or preferential rates to be used in relation to tax on mining operations, but the TRA to a large measure, frustrates the enjoyment of these tax breaks. Companies granted investment certificates[174] by the Tanzania Investment Centre (TIC) report similar frustration as tax holiday periods are at times ignored by the TRA, which pursues tax claims against the companies abrogating tax holiday provisions contained in the certificates. At times too, some tax relief entitlements are denied for frivolous reasons.

Additionally, there is a perception that the TRA is not consistent in its manner of administration. Actions taken against taxpayers in the same position are not always consistent. The treatment of the same transactions over time is also not consistent. Similarly, tax rules are not administered in a consistent and transparent manner. Officers and offices in various parts of the country do not act the same way in relation to the same matter.

The problem of inconsistency between tax policy and tax practice, and examples of attempts by the TRA to frustrate the enjoyment of tax relief provisions, are discussed further in Chapter Six.

Selective justice is another problem noted by taxpayers in Tanzania. The perception of selective justice is compounded by the inconsistent manner in which procedural requirements are enforced. It is often the case that procedures are used to frustrate substantive justice.

For example, the TRA often refuses to receive and determine objections against tax assessments if the format of the objection has not been complied with. Form requirements include such things as each assessment to be separately objected to and the grounds of objection to be presented in numbered paragraphs. One would think that the better approach is to receive the objection and deal with its substance, or if need be, allow the taxpayer to rectify the shortcomings if the format of objection has not been adhered to.

Another example of how the TRA frustrates justice for taxpayers is the refusal by the tax commissioners to use their statutory discretion to waive the requirement to pay one third of disputed tax in appropriate

---

174 These are investment charters issued under statutory authority, which serve as the blue print for the terms of investment and the entrenched protections relating to the investment.

cases so as to enable a disputed assessment to be reviewed. It is quite rare to have a waiver request accepted by the TRA. The TRA sees the requirement to pay one third of the disputed tax as a revenue collection measure and insists on it without regard to the merits of the assessment objected to. The TRA's attitude is that officers should not look at any objection until one third tax is paid, even if the objection to the assessment says there is a mathematical or accounting error to the tax assessment.

To demonstrate the negative approach by the TRA on use of administrative discretion, some data from the Tax Appeals Board is instructive. Between April 2002 and March 2010, 84 applications on administrative matters (not liability to tax) were filed against the TRA. More than half (44) were determined in favour of the taxpayer. Only 15 were refused. A few (8) were withdrawn, and the rest are pending decision. A majority of these proceedings could have been avoided.

Another perception problem against the tax system is that many taxpayers in Tanzania think that tax revenues are not properly used. The government's pattern of expenditure and the apparent lack of priority for social services, such as education, health and social welfare, is an area of complaint by many people. This perceived irresponsibility in government expenditure provides a good pretext for non-compliant tax behaviour, and makes it impossible for government to rely on the notion of 'benefits received' to justify tax payment claims, even from those who would otherwise have been willing to pay.

Perceptions of equity, or the lack of it, affect tax behaviour. Individuals normally respond more or less in the same manner as others do. Kahan[175] and Legreman[176] make the argument that trust, not only in the government, but also among taxpayers, is crucial in creating confidence in the tax system and in fostering voluntary taxpayer compliance. A taxpayer does not want to stand out as champion for the cause, paying taxes while aware that others are not doing so. Taxpayers will respond in a certain way if they are aware that others similarly placed will respond in like manner. Smith[177] appears to agree with Kahan and Ledreman that widespread tax compliance creates an all-around culture of compliance in society which is infectious among individuals. On the other hand, if

---

175 D. M. Kahan "The Logic of Reciprocity: Trust, Collective Action and Law" 2003: p.80-82.
176 L. Lederman "The Interplay between Norms and Enforcement in Tax Compliance" 2003: p.1453.
177 K. W. Smith "Reciprocity and Fairness: Positive Incentives for Tax Compliance" 1992: p.223.

some think they can get away with tax cheating, believing no harm will result to them and society will go on because others will pay, then such thinking begins to spread and the band of non-compliant individuals starts to grow.

Compliance will also increase under conditions of trust and reciprocity.[178] If a taxpayer feels that others comply with their tax obligations, he/she too will feel the need to comply.[179] If, however, the taxpayer believes that other taxpayers do not comply, or are unlikely to comply with their tax obligations, he/she will also feel no need to comply, unless driven by fear of discovery and punishment. There may be a few people who comply with taxation for moral or other reasons, but for many, the sense of morality will be undermined by the lack of reciprocity on the part of others. As a result, tax compliance will decrease amid distrust and suspicion that others are not complying.[180] The two taxpayer perception surveys carried out in Tanzania demonstrate that the lack of reciprocity and the belief that there is widespread evasion results in increased non-compliant behaviour.

Taxpayers may not feel the need to pay their taxes voluntarily when they believe that others in the society are cheating, or that the vice of cheating is not given the contempt it deserves.[181] However, reciprocity and inclusiveness does not end only with the assurance that everybody is paying tax. In addition, there must be a perception that the tax framework ensures that all taxpayers are paying their fair share of taxation. As many in Tanzania feel this is not the case, the TRA has the duty to ensure that every taxpayer pays their taxes.

There is also a responsibility on the part of the government to ensure that the tax system is designed in such a way as to enlist compliant behaviour, and taxpayers are able to see that everyone who ought to pay tax is doing so. Good governance in this respect not only requires tax payment by all, but also taxpayers to be recognized as important stakeholders who must participate in the designing of the tax system and in the adoption of important tax measures. The government of the day must have a participatory system whereby taxpayer consultation is a necessary component of the process of tax legislation. Taxpayers must be given an opportunity to air their views, and after the legislation

---

178 D. M. Kahan "The Logic of Reciprocity: Trust, Collective Action and Law" 2003: p.80-82, at 85.
179 Ibid.
180 Ibid.
181 L. Lederman 2003: p.1453.

is passed deliberate steps must be taken by both the government and the tax administration to educate taxpayers on their responsibility with regard to new tax measures. This is what inclusiveness and consensus-building entails.

Spicer and Lundstedt[182] argue that taxpayers will reciprocate with compliance to taxation if they are treated as important players and are accepted as partners in the tax system. Scholz[183] agrees, saying that when taxpayers are ignored, mistreated or merely used as a revenue source, they will respond with distrust and hatred for the tax administration. Such mistrust or hatred, as exhibited in the two taxpayer perception surveys carried out in Tanzania, is the result of bad personal experiences they have had with the tax administration. It may also have resulted from negative interaction with tax officers, or it could be the result of the experiences of others which have led the taxpayer to form a biased view based on norms and habits of a reference group.[184] A taxpayer's experience relating to a tax audit or a tax investigation which is poorly carried out, or such other intrusive behaviour on the part of the tax authority, will account for lasting resentment against taxation and may increase tax resistance.[185]

Good governance in this regard requires that there should be effective mechanisms in the tax system to compel tax administrators to treat taxpayers with respect and to respect taxpayer rights. Good governance also requires that any rights ascribed to taxpayers are effective because they can be enforced. This reciprocity between taxpayers and tax administrators promotes voluntary tax compliance.

The fairness required in the administration of laws in other branches of law applies equally to the administration of tax laws. In all branches of law, the question of justice is paramount, because justice is the objective of all law.[186] What makes society civilized is the belief that there are certain minimum standards which as human beings we must observe. These minimum standards are incorporated into the social contract and inform the legal system, establishing fair-play rules that govern members of society. When those disappear, lawlessness is unleashed. In the absence of justice, there is no place for law.

---

182 M. W. Spicer and S. B. Lundstedt "Understanding Tax Evasion" 1976: p.295-305. See also M. W. Spicer and L. A. Becker "Fiscal Inequality and Tax Evasion: An Experimental Approach" 1980: p.171-175.
183 J. T. Scholz "Trust, Taxes and Compliance" 1998: p.135.
184 *Ibid.*
185 *Ibid.*
186 T. R. Tyler 1990: p.41.

Jurists agree that one's perception of justice in the society affects one's compliance with laws.[187] When the common perception of what is just differs from the justice seen enshrined in the statutes, people lose confidence in the laws enacted and will deviate from compliance with those laws.[188] A perception that a law is unfair or unjust has the potential to make an individual less compliant with that law.[189] Such non-compliance may result in the domino effect, whereby non-compliance is not limited only to the law which is perceived to be unjust, but to others as well which are unrelated. The standing of the whole legal system is put at risk by some unjust laws. The perceived fairness of a law increases the likelihood of compliance with it. The extent to which people feel that the particular conduct prohibited by law is morally wrong and the extent to which people feel that the law prohibiting that conduct deserves respect and ought to be obeyed, plays a crucial role in peoples' deference to law.

Equally, administrative decisions which defy the common notion of what is just even though made according to law, will undermine the public confidence in the justice system. Judge Marshall succinctly summed up the concern with court decisions which undermine respect for the law. He said,

The jurist concerned with public confidence in and acceptance of the judicial system might well consider that however admirable its resolute adherence to the law as it was, a decision contrary to the public sense of justice as it is, operates, so far as it is known, to diminish respect for the courts and for law itself.[190]

Perceived injustice can also arise from criminal punishment schemes that do not accurately reflect commonsense notions of crime and punishment.[191] Legal scholars recognize the possibility that disproportionate punishments can promote lawbreaking among citizens.[192] Hart has argued that, in designing a morally acceptable system of criminal punishment, one should draw upon commonsense notions regarding appropriate punishment, given the gravity of the offense in question.[193] He observes that, if a legally defined gradation of crimes differs sharply from the commonsense consensus, there is the

---

187 M. Silberman "Towards a Theory of Criminal Deterrence" 1976: p.445-47.
188 *Ibid.*
189 H. G. Grasmick and D. E. Green "Legal Punishment, Social Disapproval and Internalisation as Inhibitors of Illegal Behaviour" 1980: p.334.
190 *Flood v Kuhn* 1972.
191 J. Nadler "Flouting the Law" 2005: p.1404.
192 *Ibid.*
193 H. L. A. Hart *Punishment and Responsibility* 1968: p.25.

risk of either contradicting common morality, or flouting it, bringing the law into contempt.[194]

Generally, therefore, people are more willing to comply with any law which they believe is fair in its content and is also fairly administered.[195] In the same way, people will generally be willing to pay taxes voluntarily if they believe that the laws governing tax payment are fair and are administered responsibly.[196]

In this regard, the role of good governance is to create the environment which influences positive responses from taxpayers. Good governance can create such conditions by imposing limits on those who are exercising statutory powers, by putting reasonable limits on what they can do and proscribing what they should not do. It means circumscribing the powers of those who administer taxation. The need to circumscribe taxing powers does not take away anything from the equally compelling need to give tax administrators sufficient powers to collect tax efficiently and to deal effectively with non-compliant taxpayers. Tax administrators need that power so as to reinforce attitudes against non-compliance and ensure that no taxpayer takes the chance to free ride.

As shown in the two taxpayer surveys conducted in Tanzania, perceptions that taxes are administered selectively, or that tax rates on various types of income do not reflect a fair distribution of tax burden, or reflect the different tax position of the payers, greatly undermine confidence in the tax system. Equally, where some people are not taxed at all, the spirit of voluntary tax payment evaporates.[197]

From a perception perspective, the overall fairness of the tax system does not require a complicated definition. The fairness of the tax system is simply what is just as perceived by a majority of the taxpaying public representing what can be accepted as the public view of the tax system in place.

In Tanzania, the feeling that tax laws are not fair, or are not fairly administered, is fuelled by the presence in the tax system of some tax exemptions which defy the common sense of fairness. Certain highly paid people such as ministers and parliamentarians are exempted from taxation on the many lucrative allowances they receive, while poorly paid people such as nurses and primary school teachers bear

---

194 *Ibid.*
195 D. M. Kahan "Signaling or Reciprocating?..." 2002: p.405.
196 *Ibid.*
197 *Ibid.*

the brunt of full taxation.[198] The feeling of selective taxation is much stronger among those who feel that the rich are not taxed in proportion to their wealth, but the poor are hounded for any little income they make. Where the tax framework exempts those who are better placed to pay taxes, but is stacked against those less fortunate, the feeling of the unfairness of taxation is hard to deny. This demoralizes many individuals who otherwise would have been willing to voluntarily meet their tax obligations. Such selective taxation greatly undermines voluntary compliance, as people will tend to associate tax with injustice.

In the preceding section, the need for accountability in public spending was presented both as a feature of good governance and also as an incentive to the tax-paying public to pay taxes. However, the accountability of government must go beyond accounting for what is collected and spent. It extends to the selection of priorities for government spending, and must extend as well to ensuring that all taxpayers meet their tax obligations so that compliant taxpayers do not feel they are being taken for a ride.[199] Cowell[200] argues that existing levels of non-compliance may generate resentment, eventually escalating to taxpayers undertaking more acts of non-compliance as a form of protest against the government and the tax administration, or as a means of equalizing the tax burden. There is a duty on the part of the government to reign in the unwilling taxpayers, so that their non-compliance does not affect the compliant attitude of willing taxpayers.[201] Where the government fails to do that, tax compliance could remain a matter of choice (driven by morality or other intrinsic factors).[202]

Accountability also extends to a duty on the part of government to identify and respond to taxpayer needs,[203] Where a government is elected on a platform of promises which have fired up the public, it must deliver on those promises. The way the government delivers to the electorate influences compliance patterns not only for tax laws but for all laws. By so doing, the government justifies or vindicates itself in its right to tax its citizens.[204] Unfortunately for Tanzania, election promises are largely forgotten soon after the elections.

---

198 Section 10 of the Income Tax Act No. 11 of 2004, read together with the Second Schedule paragraph 1(s).
199 A. Raskolnikov "Crime and Punishment in Taxation: Deceit, Deterrence and Self-Adjustment Penalty" 2006: p.574.
200 F. A. Cowell *Cheating the Government: The Economics of Tax Evasion* 1990: p.101-124.
201 *Ibid.*
202 *Ibid.*
203 J. S. Carroll 1989.
204 M. Levi *Consent, Dissent and Patriotism* 1997: p.67.

Taxpayers accept that taxes have a purpose to serve in the society. Even those who are not motivated by patriotism in paying tax know that taxes serve a good purpose in society. Taxes are not nondescript donations thrown away to the state. Thus, as the state responds to the taxpayers' needs, it proves to them that taxes are meant to serve them and not otherwise.

Taxpayers also have expectations that the government will supply certain services in return for taxes paid.[205] Many taxpayers are aware, though, that they cannot receive equal benefits in exchange for the amount of taxes paid.[206] However, they expect that the government will provide some services.[207] Where the government fails to deliver at the expected level, there must be good reason.[208] If no plausible explanation is given for failure to deliver, taxpayers will feel betrayed,[209] a feeling that may well reflect itself in tax resistance.

Taxpayers view the government as an investor.[210] As investor it is expected to invest in human capital and social infrastructure like health services and education. It is also expected to invest in physical infrastructure such as roads, railways, power systems and communication. Government's claim to taxation is legitimised by the extent to which it discharges its role as investor.[211] Where the government fails to carry out investments in society, taxpayers may well say to the government, 'you did not play your part, so we will not play our part in payment of tax'.[212] In other words, the government's failure to discharge its role as investor puts its claim to tax in question, puts its people's trust in doubt, and drives taxpayers to tax avoidance and tax evasion.[213] There lies the link between governance and tax compliance.

Conclusion

This chapter has attempted to demonstrate that compliance theories which rely only on enforcement and an economic perception of tax compliance fail to appreciate the crucial influence which the legitimacy of government, the trust people have of the government, and the

---

205 *Ibid.*
206 *Ibid.*
207 *Ibid.*
208 J. G. Cullis and A. Lewis "Why People Pay Taxes: From a Conventional Economic Model to a Model of Social Convention" 1997: p.318; also M. Levi "A State of Trust" 1997: p.56.
209 *Ibid.*
210 *Ibid.*
211 I. Budge *The New Challenge of Democracy* 1996: p.121.
212 *Ibid.*
213 *Ibid.*

existence of good governance, have on tax compliance. Equally, theories that rely on fear of detection and punishment alone as the driving forces behind tax compliance cannot explain why some compliance exists even where there is no risk of discovery and punishment. Sanctions alone do not drive tax compliance. The severity of sanctions against deviant tax behaviour cannot fully remove the non-compliance syndrome which is so multifaceted.

Non-economic factors such as social norms, the sense of fairness, the legitimacy of government, the trust people have in their government, the manner in which the government is accountable to its people, moral considerations and other factors, must all be recognized as influencing taxpayer behaviour.

3

Taxpayer Rights and Compliance

Introduction

In one his writings, Professor Bentley has argued that, "a tax authority intent on reducing tax avoidance and increasing voluntary taxpayer compliance should move away from the traditional strong-arm tactics ... (because) taxpayers respond favourably to a positive and helpful approach by tax authorities."[214]

In the previous chapter, a general proposition was put forward that good governance (rule of law and constitutionalism) is a prime foundation for better tax compliance. Building on that premise, this chapter advances the view that a tax system built on observance of the rule of law is better placed to offer recognition and protection of taxpayer rights in the administration of taxes, and that such recognition in itself provides an even better foundation for tax compliance. This chapter is also premised on the view that taxpayers who are aware of their rights, who expect, and in fact receive, fair and efficient treatment, are more

---

214 D. Bentley "Definitions and Development" in D Bentley (ed) *Taxpayers' Rights: An International perspective*, The Revenue Law Journal, School of Law, Bond University, 1998: p.11.

willing to comply with taxation.[215] It is in this regard, that Professor Bentley's words above provide a sound starting point for a discussion of the protection of taxpayer rights and how this protection impacts on taxpayer compliance.

A 1990 survey of OECD[216] countries noted that tax administrations are given wide powers to determine the tax base, to verify information provided by taxpayers and third parties, and to collect the tax due. There may be a potential conflict between the use of these powers to minimise tax evasion and avoidance, and to ensure that all taxpayers are fairly treated, with the need to respect the rights of individual taxpayers.

The rights to privacy, to confidentiality, of access to information, and to appeal against decisions of the tax administration, for example, are fundamental rights in democratic societies. A high degree of cooperation from taxpayers is required if complex tax systems are to operate efficiently. Cooperation is more likely to be forthcoming if taxpayers perceive the system as fair and if their basic rights are clearly set out and respected. Croome[217] proceeds from this premise in discussing how South African taxpayers have used the South African Bill of Rights to protect specific rights.

Professor Bentley[218] notes that with most tax systems, protection of taxpayer rights has for long depended largely on the general legal and constitutional protection afforded to citizens. It is only in recent times that a rights protection approach specific to taxpayers has emerged. Even then, there is still a lingering link between statute based and/or constitution based taxpayer protection and the emerging set of rights distinct to taxpayers, which are not necessarily founded in general statutes, but are internalised in laws specific to taxation. These distinct taxpayer rights are now found in documents such as taxpayer charters, which are not founded on statute law, but are evolving from the interaction between taxpayers and tax administrators and are internalised into tax administration.

Classification of Taxpayer Rights

In his previously cited work, Professor Bentley[219] suggested that there

---

215 D. Bentley *Taxpayers' Rights* 2007: p.50.

216 OECD *Taxpayers Rights and Obligations: A Survey of the Legal Situation in OECD Countries* 1990.

217 B. Croome, Taxpayers' Rights in South Africa (2010) Juta & Co. Ltd. Clairemont, South Africa

218 D. Bentley "Definitions and Development" in *Taxpayers Rights* 1998: p.12.

219 See note 219 at 4-6. In this book Professor Duncan Bentley teamed up with a group of twelve international authors for a publication dedicated to various aspects of taxpayer rights.

are two categories of taxpayer rights.[220] The first type of rights, referred to as 'primary rights' or 'statutory legal rights', encompasses those rights which relate to the specific validity, operation and application of tax laws. Rights of this kind mostly arise at the interface between the tax law and the taxpayer.

The second type, referred to as 'secondary rights' or 'administrative rights', encompasses the ordinary rights of most taxpayers who attempt to comply with the law and want to see fairness and efficiency in the daily operation of the tax administration, tax collection and tax enforcement process.[221] These rights tend to occur at the interface between the tax authority and the taxpayer and focus on the process of administration.

A suggestion that there is a third type of rights encompassing the right to a standard of service and treatment by the tax authority has been dismissed, because these so-called 'rights', when examined closely, encompasses things which are no more than goals, expectations or promises. Notwithstanding, Professor Bentley notes that these 'expectations or promises', which translate into norms of behaviour or service standards, are themselves assuming great importance in changing the culture of tax administrations, especially now that the service-oriented culture of private enterprise has come to be applied to public administration.[222] Braithwaite[223] sees the same trend emerging whereby the traditional command and control approach to enforcement of taxation obligations is giving way to a responsive approach designed to motivate taxpayers to comply with their tax obligations.

Primary rights (statutory legal rights) include such things as the right not to be taxed, except in accordance with the law. This right, written into many constitutions, translates itself into several sub-rights. The first is the taxpayer's right to pay no more than the law requires. This is a controversial right and the extent to which it should be entrenched has been contested. Those who support its entrenchment point to such things as the desirability of interpreting the grey areas in tax laws in favour of the taxpayer. Those who oppose its strict entrenchment decry the avenues it opens for wide-scale tax avoidance schemes. The second sub-right is the prohibition against retrospective taxation. For example, the Swedish Constitution contains a specific prohibition against the

---

220 D. Bentley "Chapter 1: Definitions and Development" in *Taxpayers' Rights* 1998: p.4-6.
221 D. Bentley "Formulating a Taxpayer's Charter of Rights: Setting the Ground Rules" 1996: p.100.
222 D. Bentley *Taxpayers' Rights* 2007: p.15.
223 V. Braithwaite "A New Approach to Tax Compliance" 2003: p.1.

retrospective effect of tax statutes.[224] However, the existence of such prohibition when posted as a specific right attracts controversy. In many countries, it is not uncommon that new tax measures are announced either in parliament (or outside) and take effect immediately, long before the legislative process for them is completed. The justification for immediate application is often that the delay required to complete the legislative process affords opportunity for taxpayers to re-organise their affairs such that the effect of the new tax measure on them is minimized or nullified, resulting in the loss of tax revenue. There is another problem as well. For many countries, it is permissible for the tax authority to change its view as to the meaning and effect of a taxing provision. When this happens, those affected by the change of view are effectively being taxed retrospectively. This can be prevented if an administrative arrangement is agreed not to review transactions which occurred before the change of view.

A second type of primary right is the right to equality (equal treatment before the law). In taxation terms, this often means that those with equal ability should bear the same burden of tax. However, this is not the same thing as saying that tax laws should affect all taxpayers in the same way. In a rather extreme application of the equality principle, a German Court ruled that a tax on real estate breached the equality principle as it placed a heavier tax burden on some taxpayers than they would have borne had they invested in other forms of property.[225]

There is bound to be some discrimination in the manner in which various taxpayers are affected by a particular tax. When considering the constitutionality of a differing treatment of taxpayers, the Supreme Court of Canada, in *Thibaudeau v Canada*,[226] took the view that the essence of the income tax law is

> to make distinctions, so as to generate revenue for the government while equitably reconciling a range of necessarily divergent interests.

The third primary right is the right to privacy. The enforcement of this right has witnessed the restriction of the powers of search and seizure in income tax statutes and other laws in several jurisdictions. Canada and South Africa provide good examples.[227] The right to privacy often goes hand in hand with the right to confidentiality and secrecy

---

224 See Chapter 2, Paragraph 10, *Regeringsformen*.
225 (2Bvl 37/91 of 22 June 1995, BStBL II 1995 at 655).
226 [1995] 1 CTC 212 at 392.
227 Canadian cases include *MNR v Kruger Inc* [1984] CTC 506 and *Baron v Canada* [1993] 1 CTC 111. For South Africa see *D A Park-Ross v The Director, Office for the Investigation Serious Economic Offences* (1995) (2) SA 198 (C).

over information given or held by the tax authority relating to taxpayers, which is examined at some point in this chapter.

The right to information is the fourth primary right. It relates both to an obligation on the tax authority to provide adequate information as to taxes and tax compliance matters and to the right of access to information held by the tax authority relating to the taxpayer.

The fifth right is the right of appeal against assessments or other taxing decisions made by the tax authority. A right of appeal is, in many countries, specifically provided for by statute.

The sixth primary right is the right to a fair trial. In *Funke v France*,[228] the European Court of Human Rights invoked Article 6 of the European Convention on Human Rights relating to the right to a fair trial and held that the right to silence and the right against self-incrimination were a necessary part of the right to a fair trial in the context of a customs investigation. It held that the customs law must provide adequate and effective safeguards against abuse in the exercise of the powers of entry, search and seizure. The court stated:

in the absence of any requirement of a judicial warrant, the restrictions and conditions provided for in law ... appear too lax and full of loopholes for interferences in the applicant's rights to have been strictly proportionate to the legitimate aim pursued.[229]

Professor Bentley[230] has noted, though, that for many countries there is no requirement for a warrant in the exercise of powers of entry, search and seizure given under tax statutes, nor is there provision for a taxpayer to claim the right to silence, or the privilege against self-incrimination as exist in criminal law investigations.

On the other hand, secondary legal rights or administrative rights have as their main objective to eliminate the arbitrariness of officers and to ensure fairness of the processes that go with tax administration.

Secondary legal rights or administrative rights include such rights as the right to receive timely decisions or timely responses to tax inquiries, the right to certainty in taxation decision-making (typified in advance rulings or clear administrative guidelines for officers), the restriction of entry and search powers to working hours or other reasonable times and the limitation on the use of information gathered during audit and investigation.

---

228 European Court of Human Rights judgment of 25 February 1993 Series A No 256-A
229 *Funke v France, op cit.* at paragraph 57.
230 D. Bentley "The Commissioner's Powers: Democracy Fraying at the Edges?" 1994: p.101.

Secondary legal rights have developed on the recognition that a tax system relies on the underlying support of the community. A tax administration will only perform its role effectively if it has the confidence of the community in the way it goes about its job.[231] Taxpayers respond positively to a good relationship with tax authorities.

Taxpayer Rights and Procedural Justice

Torgler[232] and Frey[233] have argued that there is a psychological contract between the taxpayer and those who collect taxes. This contract hinges on justice (fairness) cutting across the breadth of interaction between tax administrators and taxpayers. Procedural justice which, in essence, embodies the fairness of the system, is a central pillar of the psychological contract which exists between taxpayers and tax administrators. Procedural justice manifests itself in various factors. One of them is the extent to which taxpayers are effective players in the taxing game. Taxpayers must be given the opportunity to challenge tax decisions and to correct the mistakes of tax officers. To a large extent too, taxpayers, as stakeholders in the tax system, must play a part in designing or introducing new taxes.

Smith[234] points to the need for consistency in decision-making. Procedural justice requires consistency in the making of tax decisions and in the actions of officers. Fairness requires that individual discretion plays a minimal part in tax administration so that all elements of arbitrariness are removed. It also requires that tax officers be considerate and even-handed as they go about extracting taxes from taxpayers.

Taxpayers respond to the tax system depending on the way they are treated by the tax authority. Barzel[235] has argued that taxpayers may use tax compliance to signify their co-operation with the system. Their actions will depend on the treatment they are given by the tax authority. Taxpayers will respond to enforcement which they perceive as overzealous by protesting or rebelling against the impending tax

---

231 These comments were made by Michael Carmody, the Australian Commissioner of Taxation in his paper 'Future Directions in Tax Administration of Community Confidence: The Essential Building Block' (Chapter 16) in C Evans and Greenbaum (eds) *Tax Administration: Facing the Challenge of the Future*, Prospect Media, 1998

232 B Torgler *Tax Compliance and Tax Morale: A Theoretical and Empirical Analysis*, Cheltenham United Kingdom, 2007, at 270.

233 B. S. Frey and L. P. Feld *Tax Compliance as the Result of Psychological Contract: The Role of Incentives and Responsible Regulation* 2005.

234 K. W. Smith "Reciprocity and Fairness: Positive Incentives for Tax Compliance" 1990: p.311-329.

235 Y Barzel *A Theory of the State: Economic Rights, Legal Rights, and the Scope of the State* Cambridge University Press, 2002.

collection.[236] Taxpayers are also quick to respond to what they see as violations of a performance standard they expect from a well run tax administration. The survey reports on the TRA by the National Bureau of Statistics (2003),[237] and by PricewaterhouseCoopers (2006),[238] suggest that the TRA's unresponsiveness, unfair treatment of taxpayers and a perceived uncaring attitude engenders disrespect for and rebellion against the tax authority and tax laws.

Taxpayer Rights in Tanzania

In Tanzania, taxpayer rights are embedded in both the Constitution[239] and the various tax statutes in force. Tanzania also has a Bill of Rights in the Constitution. The Bill of Rights contains basic rights and duties such as the rights to equality,[240] to life,[241] to personal freedom,[242] to privacy and personal security,[243] to freedom of movement,[244] to freedom of expression,[245] to freedom of thought and conscience,[246] to freedom of religion,[247] to freedom of association,[248] to freedom to participate in public affairs,[249] to work,[250] to just remuneration,[251] and the right to own property.[252]

The recognition and protection of the right to property is especially important because the right to tax is founded on recognition of the property rights of individuals.[253] It is this recognition which sets taxation apart from other forms of government confiscation. Equally, it is this recognition which has placed legal limits on the manner of extraction of taxes and dictated the legal content for the extraction of taxes as

---

236 *Ibid.* at 121.

237 National Bureau of Statistics 2003.

238 PricewaterhouseCoopers "Stakeholders Perception Survey Report 2006", Large Taxpayer Department, the TRA, Dar es Salaam.

239 The Constitution of the United Republic of Tanzania provides in Article 138 (1) that no tax shall be imposed save in accordance with a law properly enacted by Parliament.

240 *Ibid.* Article 12.

241 *Ibid.* Article 13.

242 *Ibid.* Article 14.

243 *Ibid.* Article 15.

244 *Ibid.* Article 16.

245 *Ibid.* Article 17.

246 *Ibid.* Article 18.

247 *Ibid.* Article 19.

248 *Ibid.* Article 20.

249 *Ibid.* Article 21.

250 *Ibid.* Article 22.

251 *Ibid.* Article 23.

252 *Ibid.* Article 24.

253 D. Bentley *Taxpayers' Rights: Theory, Origin and Implementation* Series on International Taxation, Kluwer Law International, 2007: p.12.

reflected in the requirement to observe laws and the constitution. Taxation is intrinsic to the overall system of property rights designed to fund the maintenance and development of the social order and to promote beneficial economic results.[254]

The right to privacy and protection of private communications afforded by Article 16 of the Constitution has assumed great significance in the taxation field because of the powers given to the tax administration to access personal information for tax purposes. Relying on Article 16, it is possible to challenge actions of entry, search and seizure of documents, undertaken by tax officers in connection with tax investigations or audits. It is notable, however, that while the TRA has intensified its investigation and audit functions, there is still no case that has been taken in reliance on the protection of privacy provisions in the constitution.[255]

In any case, the laws in Tanzania embody basic taxpayer rights by extension only. There are no specific protections for taxpayer rights. In order to benefit from the protection of law, the taxpayer must find a provision in the general laws which he/she is able to apply to the specific breach that has occurred, or threatens to occur. But the tax laws do have some provisions which reiterate basic rights as protected in the constitution of Tanzania.

For instance, Article 13 of the Constitution, which entrenches equality before the law and the right to protection of the law, also makes detailed provision of sub-rights which find expression in tax statutes. Article 13, sub-article (6) provides,

> (6) To ensure equality before the law, the state authority shall make procedures which are appropriate or which take into account the following principles, namely:
>
> a. when the rights and duties of any person are being determined by the court or any other agency, that person shall be entitled to a fair hearing and the right of appeal or other legal remedy against the decision of the court or of the other agency concerned;
>
> b. no person charged with a criminal offence shall be treated as guilty of the offence until proved guilty of that offence;
>
> c. no person shall be punished for any act which at the time of its commission was not an offence under the law and also no

---

254 J Finnis *Natural Law and Natural Rights*, Oxford University Press, 1980, at 155, and 256-257.
255 See discussion in Chapter Seven.

penalty shall be imposed which is heavier than the penalty in force at time the offence was committed;

d. for the purposes of preserving the right or equality of human beings, human dignity shall be protected in all activities pertaining to criminal investigations and process and in any other matters for which a person is restrained on in the execution of a sentence;

e. no person shall be subjected to torture or inhuman or degrading punishment or treatment.

The sub-rights stipulated in sub-article (6) in relation to (a) fair hearing and right of appeal, (b) presumption of innocence, (c) prohibition of retrospective punishment, (d) dignified investigation, search and arrest, and (e) prohibition of degrading treatment, all find expression in tax statutes.

Section 6 of the Tanzania Revenue Act[256] provides for the right of appeal in the following terms:

6. Any person who is aggrieved by the decision of the Commissioner General in relation to any act or omission in the course of discharge of any function conferred upon him under the law set out in the First Schedule to this Act (tax laws), may appeal to the Board in accordance with the provisions of the Tax Revenue Appeals Act.

The Tax Revenue Appeals Act[257] entrenches in Section 12 the right to dispute a tax assessment. Section 12 (1) provides,

Any person who disputes an assessment made upon him may, by notice in writing to the Commissioner General, object to the assessment.

In Section 16 (1), the Tax Revenue Appeals Act entrenches the right of appeal against tax decisions. It provides,

Any person who is aggrieved by the final determination of the assessment of tax by the Commissioner General may appeal to the Board.

Section 7 of the Tax Revenue Appeals Act created the Board as a judicial body with exclusive jurisdiction[258] to hear and determine disputes relating to taxation. Appeals from the Tax Appeals Board go to the Tax Appeals Tribunal, which is chaired by a judge of the High Court of Tanzania. A final appeal lies with the Court of Appeal of Tanzania, but only on matters of law, not fact. Normal courts have no jurisdiction to hear tax disputes, except by way of judicial review.

---

256 Tanzania Revenue Authority Act No. 11 of 1995 (Revised Edition 2006) Chapter 399.
257 Tax Revenue Appeals Act No. 15 of 2000.
258 Section 25 Tax Revenue Appeals Act.

Some sections of society criticize the government for giving exclusive jurisdiction to quasi judicial bodies especially created, rather than the ordinary courts. This criticism is not entirely justified. As will be shown later, both the Tax Appeals Board and the Tax Appeals tribunal have managed to operate with an acceptable degree of independence and have shown reasonable competence. In addition, removing tax disputes from the ordinary courts (which are clogged with cases) has expedited the determination of tax cases. So the criticism is only true to the limited extent that special tribunals encroach on separation of powers and the institutional independence of the judiciary. It is not always the case that the operational independence of the tribunal will be affected simply because it is a special tribunal.

Another right entrenched in the tax statutes is the right to a fair hearing, as reflected in provisions which recognize the right to legal or professional representation[259] and the right to prove a case by evidence.[260] However, it will be shown later that the constitutional right to be presumed innocent and the normal rules relating to proof are not fully respected in tax statutes.[261]

The TRA has, in addition, adopted a Taxpayer's Charter[262] which covers a wide range of both secondary and primary taxpayer rights. The Taxpayer's Charter also incorporates service standard pronouncements which act as a benchmark for customer service expectations.

It is clear from the statements accompanying the Taxpayer's Charter that the Charter is premised on both the Constitution and the tax laws administered by the TRA. The TRA states in the background to the Charter that,

> The Constitution of the United Republic of Tanzania among other things guarantees the right to equal treatment before the law, the right to privacy, the right to information, the right to fair treatment and the right to possess property.

> The Tanzania Revenue Authority (the TRA) was established by Act No. 11 of 1996, and has been given by law the responsibility of assessing, collecting and accounting for all Central Government taxes. In performing this responsibility, the TRA and the Government recognize the need to develop a productive partnership between the TRA and the taxpayer by ensuring that

---

259 Sections 18 (2) (a) and 22 (3) of the Tax Revenue Appeals Act.
260 Section 22 (5) of the Tax Revenue Appeals Act.
261 See part 5.5.3 of Chapter 5.
262 The TRA, Taxpayer's Charter, prepared by the Taxpayer Services and Education Department, Tanzania Revenue Authority Head Office, Dar es Salaam. The Charter was issued in October 2006 as part of the Tenth Anniversary celebrations for the TRA.

the administration of taxes is carried out in accordance with the Constitution of the United Republic of Tanzania and the various revenue laws enacted by Parliament and administered by the TRA.

The TRA, in carrying out its mandate, has adopted a corporate plan which underscores the fundamental strategies for effective tax administration among which is to ensure there is in existence a robust taxpayer education and customer care program, improved access to information, improved data keeping, and simplifying information filling.

In order to ensure that taxes are administered responsibly and fairly and that the tax practices adopted by the TRA are consistent with the Constitution and the laws of the country, the TRA has put forward this Taxpayers' Charter as a pronouncement of the commitment by the TRA to forging a good partnership with the taxpayer and to adopting tax administration practices which allow the partnership with the taxpayer to grow and thereby improve tax administration.

The Taxpayers' Charter sets out the rights and obligations of the taxpayer on the one hand and on the other, the duties and service standards of the TRA in dealing with the taxpayer. As such the Charter is a performance standard only, it is not a legally binding instrument. Both the taxpayer and the TRA must ultimately invoke the relevant laws in acting against, or seeking to prevent, an action which is inconsistent with the Charter and the laws.[263]

The Taxpayer's Charter does not replace or stand in tandem with the statutory provisions which prescribe enforceable rights. Only statutory provisions stipulating rights may be relied upon in acting against, or seeking to prevent actions which are inconsistent with, the TRA Taxpayer's Charter.

It is to be noted too that TRA Taxpayer's Charter is a work in progress which will keep changing. It is declared at page 2 that,

"This Taxpayers' Charter is not a static instrument and will be reviewed and improved from time to time along with the changing economic development and changing tax practices."[264]

Although the TRA Taxpayer's Charter is not a legally binding instrument, its importance should not be discounted. It embodies the vision of the TRA, which is to build "a modern tax administration".

---

263 *Ibid.*
264 *Ibid.* at 2.

The first, second and third TRA Five Year Corporate Plans[265] all state that the "TRA is committed and dedicated to becoming a modern tax administration by the end of the Plan period."[266] According to the two earlier corporate plans,

> ... a modernized tax administration is one that has a strong enforcement capacity delivered by highly qualified, motivated and committed staff; has an integrated approach to the administration of taxes; is computerized; uses modern practices and processes; and enjoys high levels of tax compliance by creating a taxpayer-friendly environment.[267]

The Third Corporate Plan, running from 2008/2009 to 2012/2013, states the features of a modern tax administration as being an ability to meet collection targets, to deliver services that meet customer expectations, a fair and consistent application of laws, and skilled and qualified staff with high levels of integrity.

Corporate strategic plans have become important documents against which the performance of an organization over time is measured. The issuance of the TRA Taxpayer's Charter by the TRA and its observance by the TRA staff is an important milestone in meeting the TRA expectations under the Corporate Plans.

As a service standard, the TRA Taxpayer's Charter also embodies the TRA's Mission Statement by which the TRA strives

> ... to be an effective and efficient tax administration which promotes voluntary tax compliance by providing high quality customer service with fairness and integrity through competent and motivated staff.[268]

In addition, the Charter embodies the stated core values of the TRA and its employees, who are expected to be business oriented and professional in appearance and approach, to be fair and accountable for the decisions they make in their areas of responsibility, to be prompt in the delivery of services, to be accessible, to treat taxpayers colleagues and stakeholders with dignity and respect, to be honest and have integrity in their dealings, and to be committed and motivated to achieve TRA goals and objectives.

---

265 The TRA, First, Second and Third Five Year Corporate Plans (1998/1999 to 2012/2013, Tanzania Revenue Authority, Head Office, Dar es Salaam.
266 *Ibid.*
267 *Ibid.*
268 This Mission Statement is contained in the First and Second Corporate Plans of the TRA. The first Corporate Plan was for the years 1998/99 to 2002/03. The second, was for the years 2003/04 to 2007/08.

The taxpayer 'rights' proclaimed in the TRA Taxpayer's Charter are examined below.

Taxpayer Rights in the TRA Taxpayer's Charter

The TRA Taxpayer's Charter proclaims that, in its dealings with the taxpayer, the TRA will observe and respect the following rights of the taxpayer:

i. Right to receive tax forms, returns and information written in plain language;

ii. Right to impartial treatment;

iii. Right to courtesy and consideration;

iv. Right to privacy and confidentiality;

v. Right to presumption of honesty;

vi. Right to impartial review of tax assessment;

vii. Right to tax benefits under the revenue laws;

viii. Right to quality service; and

ix. Right to an internal complaints procedure;

Through the Taxpayer's Charter, the TRA commits itself, and, by doing so, creates a duty upon itself to provide tax forms, returns and information written in plain language. The taxpayer acquires a right to receive from the TRA complete, simple and accurate tax information through the print and electronic media (i.e. newspapers, pamphlets, leaflets, website, radio and television), so as to assist him/her to comply with the tax laws administered by the TRA. The declaration of this duty by the TRA to provide information, as a taxpayer right, is problematic. On the one hand, the TRA's declaration of a taxpayer right to information on tax laws and compliance obligations is unlikely to affect the now established common law principle that every person is presumed to know the law.[269] This presumption, represented in the maxim *ignorantia juris non excusat*, is widely accepted by the courts in Tanzania[270] and applies as well to taxation. On the other hand, there is no statutory basis on which the right to receive information on taxation laws can be

---

269 Under English law every person is presumed to know the law, in other words ignorance of law is no defence to liability for an offence. See *Bilbie v Lumley* (1802) 2 East 469; see also P Mathews 'Ignorance of the Law is No Excuse?' (1983) 3 *Legal Studies* 174; and A T H Smith 'Error and Mistake of Law in Anglo-American Criminal Law' (1985) 14 *Anglo-American Law Review* 3.

270 For example *Yero Transport Services Ltd v Attorney General & 2 Others*, Civil Application No. 58/2001, Court of Appeal of Tanzania (unreported); and *Calico Industries v Pyaraliesmail Premji* [1983] TLR 28.

enforced, because it is not one of the rights recognized under statute, or by the Constitution. With this in mind, it is proper to see "the right to information" as a performance standard only, desired to be achieved by the TRA as a tax administration, but not as a duty binding on the TRA as a matter of law. Therefore, for the taxpayer who does not receive information regarding liability to tax, the obligation to comply will not abate simply due to failure by the TRA to provide information.

The right to impartial application of tax law is indeed a legal right.[271] The taxpayer has a right to impartial application of the tax laws so that the TRA collects no more than the correct amount of tax. However, even this right is not without controversy.

In contesting an assessment or a tax decision, the person objecting is required to demonstrate that the law has not been applied correctly to his/her circumstances. It is not enough to merely say that the same law has not been enforced on others, or that it has been applied differently. This will not of itself make what is done wrongful in terms of the tax statutes. It is possible, however, to mount a challenge against the validity of the officer's discriminatory application of law and have that quashed. But if the application of law is itself correct, the fact that it has not been applied to others in the same way will not render the tax illegal. It is also accepted that the tax administration can change its view as to the interpretation and application of any tax provision.[272] This position may also impair the realization of the right against discrimination in taxation, because, as the tax administration changes its view on a tax provision, new cases will be treated differently.

The Taxpayer's Charter states that a taxpayer has a right to receive courteous and considerate treatment in dealing with the TRA, whether the TRA is requesting information or arranging for an interview or an audit of his/her business records. This too is a performance standard only. It cannot be enforced as a legal right.

The Taxpayer's Charter also declares that the taxpayer has a right to privacy and confidentiality over personal and financial information supplied to the TRA, unless such privacy and/or confidentiality

---

271 The right to equality before the law is provided in Article 13 (2) of the Constitution which proclaims that "No law enacted by any authority in the United Republic of Tanzania shall make any provision that is discriminatory either of itself or in its effect."
272 In Australia positions taken by the Australian Taxation Office as to the application of a taxing provision only became binding on the tax administration after the enactment of the Freedom of Information Act 1982. Section 9 thereof requires copies of documents used by tax officers in making decisions to be made available to the public. This is not the case in many other countries and is certainly not the case in Tanzania.

are derogated by law. While the right to privacy and confidentiality is provided for by law, the extent of this protection is tempered by a number of factors. The first is that the tax statutes themselves contain many areas which erode confidentiality and secrecy of information given by the taxpayer or gathered from him/her. Secondly, even when it is proven that confidentiality and secrecy have been breached by an officer, there is no financial remedy for the taxpayer as the immunities placed on public officers will protect the officer from a civil claim for monetary compensation.[273] The only remedy available is prosecution and punishment of the offending officer as a matter of criminal law. This is not a remedy for the taxpayer, but an action by the state to preserve the integrity of the system.

The taxpayer's right to privacy is also undermined by the wide powers given to the TRA for information gathering and for audits and inspections. These powers are discussed in the following sections.

Looking at it from the perspective of Article 16 of the Constitution, which guarantees the right to privacy, the inspection powers of the TRA are inimical to the protection afforded by the Constitution. A person's premises should be protected from intrusion, except in relation to an investigation for a criminal offence. Tax laws need to limit the scope for which access to premises is permitted.

The intrusion on privacy is compounded by the failure to require notice to the occupier of premises where entry is required. No notice or warrant is required to enter and inspect premises if entry is made between 9 am and 6 pm.[274] Failure to require notice is a significant erosion of the right to privacy. It also undermines the right to the protection of the law and respect for the due process of law.

The Taxpayer's Charter recognizes that the taxpayer has a right to be presumed honest, unless previous conduct derogates from that presumption, or evidence to the contrary exists. The TRA's formulation of the right to the presumption of innocence departs from the understanding of that right under common law and also under the Constitution of Tanzania. As a common law principle and also as a basic right under the Constitution of Tanzania, the presumption of innocence

---

273 There is, however, an arguable case for a civil remedy against the government in its vicarious capacity, subject to the rules governing tortuous claims.
274 Section 138 ITA 2004.

is not qualified.[275] Rules of evidence applicable to criminal prosecutions generally exclude evidence of character or previous conduct (criminal record), unless the accused has held himself to be a person of good character.[276]

It is, therefore, fair to say that the presumption of innocence as embodied in the TRA Taxpayer's Charter is also a performance standard only. But, even as a performance standard, it falls short of the requirements of some provisions of the general law in Tanzania. It may indeed be reflecting the position of the tax statutes in Tanzania, as many statutes shift the burden of proof to the taxpayer and lower the standard of proof for the tax administration.

The right to an impartial review of a tax assessment is truly a legal right. Tax statutes give the taxpayer a right to object to an assessment or other determination by the TRA,[277] unless that right is circumscribed by other law. Where an objection is lodged by the taxpayer, the TRA has a duty to conduct an impartial review of the disputed assessment, acting as expeditiously as possible and notifying the taxpayer of the review decision made. If the review decision does not fully resolve the dispute, the taxpayer has a right of appeal to an impartial body as provided by law, and the TRA has a duty to explain that right of appeal to the taxpayer. This, indeed, is a taxpayer right and the laws in existence sufficiently provide for its realization.

The taxpayer has a right to plan his/her tax affairs so as to reap the maximum benefit allowed under the revenue laws. The TRA has a duty to apply the tax laws in a consistent and fair manner to every taxpayer. The right to pay no more than the law requires, or to take optimum advantage of the tax laws, is glorified in its history only[278] Provisions in modern tax legislation, which aim to counteract tax avoidance,

---

275 Cross says "When it is said that an accused person is presumed to be innocent, all that is meant is that the prosecution is obliged to prove the case against him beyond reasonable doubt. This is the fundamental rule of our criminal procedure, and it is expressed in terms of a presumption of innocence so frequently as to render criticism somewhat pointless…." R Cross and C Tapper *Cross on Evidence* (6th ed) Butterworths, London, 1985, at 114-115.

276 *R v Butterwasser* (1948) 1 KB 4, (1947) 2 All ER 415.

277 Section 21 (1) of the Tax Revenue Appeals Act No. 15 of 2000.

278 *IRC v Duke of Westminster,* 1936, AC 1 continues to be cited as putting forward a sound principle of law, but the observance of this principle is now severely eroded. More recent cases decided on tax avoidance have recognized the legitimacy of striking down tax avoidance schemes. The House of Lords made it clear in *Ramsay v IRC,* 1982, AC 300 (HL) and in *Furniss v Dawson,* 1984, 1 All ER 530 (HL), that transactions which have no legitimate commercial purpose except the minimization of tax will be struck down.

have ensured that this right is a pale shadow of what it used to be.[279] In Tanzania, both the income tax law and the value added tax law contain provisions which make it difficult to realize this taxpayer right.[280]

The taxpayer has a right to receive quality service from the TRA officers. This right is clearly a performance standard only. However, even as a performance standard, this vaguely stated right is hard to enforce and breaches of it will not lead to a legal remedy.

The right to an internal complaints procedure, even though it is not a statutory legal right, is an important one. A taxpayer who believes that he/she has not been fairly treated by an officer of the TRA has a right to lodge a complaint administratively at a higher level. Where a complaint is made to an officer at a higher level, the officer has a duty to investigate the complaint and deal with it to the satisfaction of the taxpayer. As an addition to the right of objection to assessment and tax decision, the introduction of this right under the Charter is indeed welcome. Its value is limited by the fact that it is largely a concession by the tax authority, but has no basis in law.

By embodying such principles as the right to information, the right to be presumed compliant, the duty of privacy and confidentiality, and the right to courteous treatment, the Charter sets a performance standard which, if adhered to in the day to day administration of taxation, will lead to a public belief that taxes are administered fairly and impartially.[281] This belief will improve taxpayer acceptance of the tax system[282] and lead to higher levels of voluntary compliance.[283]

In accordance with the Mission Statement of the TRA, the Taxpayer's Charter commits the TRA officials to be courteous, polite and service oriented. They are to refrain from any form of arrogance, harassment

---

279 The United Kingdom, Canada, Australia and United States of America all have statutory provisions which aim to counteract tax avoidance schemes. Modern tax literature premised on fair distribution of the tax burden also urge that tax avoidance be treated with the same stigma as tax evasion because both have the same effect on the economy.

280 Income Tax Act 2004 (Sections 33 against transfer pricing; 34 against income splitting; and 35 aimed generally against tax avoidance schemes); the Value Added Tax 1997 (Section 67 aimed against schemes for obtaining undue tax benefit).

281 The preamble in part declares that "to ensure that taxes are administered responsibly and fairly ... the TRA has put forward this Taxpayer's Charter as a pronouncement of the commitment by the TRA to forging a good partnership with the taxpayer and to adopt tax administration practices which allow the partnership with the taxpayer to grow and improve tax administration".

282 Clause 2 on taxpayers' rights.

283 Clause 2.9 of the Charter.

or authoritarian behaviour towards taxpayers.[284] Officers are urged by the Charter to respond to phone calls expeditiously and to deal with all enquiries in a timely manner.

By way of comparison, the Uganda Revenue Authority (URA) Client Service Standards, published in 2006, go much further in setting down a behaviour code for tax officers. In the foreword to the booklet containing the Standards, Mr. Allen Kagina, the URA Commissioner General, succinctly captures the need for a new mind-set for tax officers. He writes,

> In Uganda Revenue Authority, we recognize that we can only fulfill our mandate if we put the client first. URA has been engaged in various initiatives that were aimed at transforming ourselves into a professional tax administration agency providing quality service to all our clients. As we embark on the process of modernizing our services, we must do so with the client in focus.[285]

The Client Service Standards of the URA are in two parts, starting with a General Standard dealing with very mundane things such as the need for officers to maintain eye contact when speaking to taxpayers and good telephone etiquette, for example, answering calls within three rings and calling back immediately in case of inability to take the call when the phone rings. It also covers such professional behaviour as the requirement to wear identity cards, no jeans, tight fitting dress or provocative micro minis that enhance sex appeal, and the need for general neatness of the person and place of work.

In the second part are Service Standards. They deal with such things as limiting the duration of queuing to a maximum of thirty minutes, an obligation to provide tax information, a prohibition against exploiting taxpayer ignorance of the law, imposing a ten day notice requirement for undertaking audits, an obligation to renew road licenses within twelve hours of payment, registration of motor vehicles within three hours, and the obligation to explain tax assessment.

Although these requirements impose on URA officers a performance standard only and do not create enforceable legal rights, the mere existence of such taxpayer focused performance requirements makes the taxpayers feel valued. With this in mind, when slogans like "Developing Uganda Together" are used by the URA, or as in the case of the TRA "From Tax Collector to Partner in Development", the taxpayer can relate to those expressions and feel part of the tax system.

284 Clause 4.1 on the TRA Officers Service Standards.
285 URA Client Service Standards, URA 2006 at ii.

Enforceability of Taxpayer Rights in Tanzania

While the TRA Taxpayer's Charter is not a legally binding instrument, it is possible to isolate those taxpayer rights it deals with which are also entrenched in the tax laws (or other laws) and are capable of enforcement by taxpayers.

The right of appeal against taxing decisions by the TRA is provided in both the TRA Act and the Tax Revenue Appeals Act, and is capable of enforcement in a court of law. Section 6 of the TRA Act provides that any person aggrieved by a decision of the Commissioner General (which includes all other officers of the TRA) may appeal to the Appeals Board established under the Tax Revenue Appeals Act 2000. Section 16 (1) of the Tax Revenue Appeals Act 2000 provides for a general right of appeal. Section 16 (1) also provides for the right of a second appeal to the Appeals Tribunal (16 (5)), with a third and final appeal lying with the Court of Appeal (Section 25).

The right of appeal to an independent judicial body or tribunal is a basic right. It ensures there is an effective check on arbitrary taxation; as Professor Bentley says, "without justice and rule of law, taxation becomes an arbitrary exaction at whim."[286] The right of appeal is also an important remedy against injustice that may result from a tax administration vested with enormous powers, which, if exercised without challenge, can very easily be misused.

The right of appeal and the right of objection against an assessment to tax are fundamental to the tax system. They give the taxpayer an opportunity to challenge tax decisions. At times the right of objection and appeal has been attacked because it is capable of being used by taxpayers to delay payment of tax which is properly due. However, the value of such a right in protecting the observance of law in the administration of taxes cannot be questioned.

The existence of the right of objection and appeal confers on the tax administration the required legitimacy and sense of fair play in its dealings with taxpayers. A taxpayer, who has the opportunity to challenge a tax decision, does so and loses, or chooses not to exercise that right, cannot complain that the taxation imposed on him/her is unfair. The right also underscores the transparency which must exist in the decisions of the administration. Perceived transparency promotes voluntary tax compliance.

Nonetheless, the right of appeal with respect to taxation is not unique. It is part of the general law of Tanzania and applies with respect

286 D. Bentley *Taxpayers' Rights* 2007: p.2.

to decisions made under other laws. The right of appeal is guaranteed under Article 13(6)(a) of the Constitution of Tanzania.[287] It is ancillary to the right to the protection of the law under Article 13(1),[288] which in paragraph 13(6)(a) extends to the right of a fair hearing.[289] It has been said that the right to a fair hearing involves not only the opportunity to be heard, but includes as well the right to be heard by an independent and impartial body.[290] As correctly recognised by courts in Australia, liability to tax cannot be imposed upon citizens without leaving open to them some judicial process by which they may show that they are not in fact liable to tax or not liable in the amount assessed.[291]

The realisation of the right of objection and the right of appeal in Tanzania is surrounded by certain impediments. A taxpayer who is aggrieved by a tax assessment must issue an objection and seek review from the same office which made the assessment.[292] It is often the case too that, when an objection is lodged, the assessment is reviewed by the same officer who made the assessment. This practice reduces the value of the objection procedure as a way of impartially reviewing tax decisions and disputes relating to the correctness of tax. This impediment in the objection procedure is compounded by the requirement that, for an objection to be entertained, the taxpayer must pay one third of the tax assessed.[293] Such provisions have led courts in the United States of America to say that the power to tax may equal the power to destroy.[294]

---

287 Article 13(6)(a) provides that: "(6) To ensure equality before the law, the state authority shall make procedures which are appropriate or which take into account the following principles, namely (a) when the rights and duties of any person are being determined by the court or any other agency, that person shall be entitled to a fair hearing and to the right of appeal or other legal remedy against the decision of the court or of the other agency concerned;" Constitution of Tanzania 1977 (as amended up to 2005).

288 Article 13(1) provides that "(1) All persons are equal before the law and are entitled, without any discrimination, to protection and equality before the law."

289 Ibid.

290 Article 10 of the Universal Declaration of Human Rights provides that: "Everyone is entitled in full equality to a fair and public hearing by an independent and impartial tribunal in the determination of his rights and obligation and of any criminal charge against him." UN General Assembly (adopted 10 December 1948).

291 DFCT v Brown (1958) 100 Commonwealth Law Report 32 at 40-41.

292 Section 12 (1) of the Tax Revenue Appeals Act No. 15 of 2000.

293 Section 12 (2) of the Tax Revenue Appeals Act.

294 Bull versus United States, 259 U.S. 247, 259 (1935) where the Court observed that "taxes are the life blood of the government, and their prompt and certain availability an imperious need"; while in McCulloch versus Maryland, 17 U.S. 316, 431 (1819), it was observed that "the power to tax involves the power to destroy".

It is arguable that circumscribing the right of appeal against tax assessments in the manner done by the Tax Revenue Appeals Act runs contrary to the spirit of the Constitution because the Constitutional right of appeal envisages an appeal to an impartial and un-inhibited appellate tribunal. The gravity of this limitation is best appreciated in the context that a combination of the incompetence that permeates the TRA, together with a tendency towards overzealousness shown by some officers has led to inflated tax assessments. It can also be said that the requirement for payment of one third of the disputed tax, even though well intentioned,[295] goes against the well established principle of the presumption of innocence. Similarly, from a taxpayer rights standpoint, the requirement to prepay a substantial part of disputed taxes undermines the protection of the right not to be deprived of property without a hearing before an impartial tribunal. The problem with this provision is that, rather than encourage voluntary tax compliance, it undermines it. With such a provision in place, it is difficult to convince taxpayers that the tax system is fair.

As indicated previously, the right to organise one's affairs so as to optimise tax benefits under the law is problematic. Likewise, "the right to pay no more than is provided by clear law" (as stated in the Taxpayer's Charter) is equally problematic. To appreciate the problem, one needs to start with the Constitution. In stating that no person shall be taxed except in accordance with law,[296] the Constitution implicitly entrenches the right of the taxpayer to order his/her affairs in such a way that he/she takes maximum advantage of the tax law. In administering tax laws, no person is to be taxed because he/she "ought to be taxed"; a person is taxed because there is a clear law providing for the tax imposed on him/her. In saying this, one ought to be mindful of the fact there are, in nearly all tax statutes in Tanzania, clear provisions which give power to the TRA to nullify schemes for minimisation of tax.[297] Therefore, while in terms of the Constitution and the Taxpayer's Charter, one may claim an entitlement to pay no more than is required by law, the operation of

---

295 Prepayment of part of disputed taxes has been justified on the premise that there is an equally compelling public interest in ensuring that the collection of tax revenue does not stall in litigation, and that taxpayers do not use the appeal procedure to delay tax payment that is rightly due.

296 Article 138 (1) of the Constitution of Tanzania 1977 (2005 edition).

297 Sections 34, 35, and 57 of the Income Tax Act No. 11 of 2004 empower the TRA to counteract transfer pricing, income splitting, dividend stripping and other schemes to reduce tax. Section 67 of the Value Added Tax Act No. 24 of 1997 empowers the TRA to nullify schemes which seek to enable the taxpayer to obtain an undue tax benefit.

the anti-avoidance provisions in the tax laws make this right elusive and virtually un-enforceable.

The right to information is a limited one and is difficult to enforce. The presumption of knowledge of the law absolves the TRA from any legal duty to provide information. Therefore, the duty to provide information as presented in the Taxpayer's Charter is only a performance standard. No sanction can attend the TRA's non-compliance with this objective. From the TRA perspective, giving concise and clear information in simple language enables the taxpayer to comply with what is expected of the taxpayer.

There are two types of information taxpayers have a right to receive. The first type is general information regarding various taxes and how to discharge the compliance obligations placed on taxpayers. This information comes in the form of the tax statutes, subsidiary legislation and Government Notices. In addition, however, the TRA disseminates to the taxpayers ad-hoc publications in the form of booklets, leaflets and fliers, explaining the various taxes and the compliance procedures.

General information is also given to taxpayers in the form of Practice Notes issued by the TRA, outlining how the TRA, in relation to any matter, will interpret and apply a particular tax provision. Section 130 of the Income Tax Act provides as follows:

(130)(1) To achieve consistency in the administration of this Act and to provide guidance to persons affected by this Act, including officers of the Tanzania Revenue Authority, the Commissioner may issue in writing practice notes setting out the Commissioner's interpretation of this Act.

(2) A practice note shall be binding on the Commissioner until revoked.

(3) A practice note shall not be binding on other persons affected by this Act.

(4) The Commissioner shall make practice notes available to the public at offices of the Tanzania Revenue Authority and at such other locations or by such other medium as the Commissioner may determine.

Practice Notes serve two purposes. They set a common framework for decision making among officers of the TRA. Practice Notes also create certainty in tax planning, because taxpayers are able to predict the tax consequences of their actions with a reasonable degree of certainty.

A position expressed in a Practice Note is binding on the TRA until the courts express a contrary view of the statute, or until revoked by the TRA.[298]

Although Section 130 (2) says that a Practice Note is binding on the TRA, the fact that this operates only until the Practice Note is revoked effectively means the Practice Note may be modified at any time if the Commissioner changes his/her view of the provision for which the Practice Note was issued. In any case, Practice Notes are not binding on taxpayers.[299] Taxpayers retain the right to challenge the correctness of the view the TRA takes in a Practice Note. Nonetheless, Practice Notes are an effective guide as to how the law will be implemented by the TRA. A taxpayer relying on the position expressed in a Practice Note is protected from penalty or other adverse action by the TRA.

The second type of information which a taxpayer has a right to receive is of a more specific nature and relates only to proposed transactions or transactions already undertaken. Under Section 131 of the Income Tax Act 2000, a taxpayer has the right to seek and obtain a ruling as to what view the TRA will take on a particular transaction which is proposed or has happened. Rulings issued under Section 131 are called Private Rulings. Section 131 provides that,

131 (1) The Commissioner may, on application in writing by a person, issue to the person, by notice in writing served on the person, a private ruling setting out the Commissioner's position regarding the application of this Act to the person with respect to an arrangement proposed or entered into by the person.

(2) Where prior to the issue of a ruling under subsection (1), the person makes:

(a)   a full and true disclosure to the Commissioner of all aspects of the arrangement relevant to the ruling; and

(b)   the arrangement proceeds in all material respects as described in the person's application for the ruling, the ruling shall be binding on the Commissioner with respect to the arrangement.

(3) A ruling shall not be binding on the Commissioner under subsection (2) to the extent to which the Act as in force at the time the ruling is issued is changed.

---

298 Section 130 (2) of the Income Tax Act.
299 Section 130 (3) of the Income Tax Act.

A Private Ruling is binding on the TRA, if the taxpayer has disclosed to the Commissioner all relevant information and the taxpayer has carried out the transaction in all material respects as disclosed to the TRA.[300] Private Rulings are administrative guidelines which provide advice to taxpayers on the application of the tax law in particular situations. They guide taxpayers as to the tax consequences of a proposed transaction, or one that has just been undertaken.

In binding the TRA, Practice Notes and Private Rulings are an important feature in enhancing taxpayer rights and in ensuring desirable transparency in tax decision making. The downside, though, is that, if the TRA takes the wrong view and is corrected by court, the taxpayer must pay tax according to the view taken by the court. However, no penalties or interest will be payable by the taxpayer in respect of actions which have relied on Practice Notes or Private Rulings issued by the TRA.

The right to internal (administrative) review of taxing decisions is a right which is partly entrenched in the tax laws. All the tax statutes in Tanzania[301] provide for the right of objection against assessments or other decisions of the TRA affecting the tax position of the taxpayer. But the Taxpayer's Charter appears to go beyond the objection procedures and contemplates an administrative remedy which enables taxpayers to lodge complaints with senior officers in respect of the actions of subordinate officers. This extended right is not enforceable, and may only be available as a matter of good administration.

The TRA Taxpayer's Charter proclaims a right to secrecy for tax information provided to the TRA. However, in order to appreciate how this right has become unrealisable, one needs to look beyond the Taxpayer's Charter.

The TRA duty to keep taxpayer information secret is akin to the duty of confidentiality imposed on banks and financial institutions. The only difference is that, for banks, the duty arises either from contract only, or from both contract and statutes which regulate financial institutions. For the TRA, the duty of secrecy is purely statutory. For instance, the Income Tax Act No 11 of 2000 requires that all taxpayer information supplied or obtained in connection with taxation must be kept secret

---

300 Section 131 (2) of the Income Tax Act.
301 For example, the Income Tax Act, the VAT Act, the EAC Customs Management Act and the Stamp Duty Act all provide for the right of objection, which triggers an internal review of the taxing decision made, which may well lead to vindication of the taxpayer position.

and may not be divulged.[302] Section 140 of the Income Tax Act 2004
provides that,

140 (1) Every officer authorised under or instructed with the
administration of this Act or person who was formerly so authorised or
instructed shall

> (a) regard and deal with all documents and
> information coming into the officer's possession
> or knowledge in connection with the performance
> of duties under this Act as secret; and

> (b) not disclose such documents or information
> to a court, tribunal, or other person except as
> provided for in subsections (2) and (3).

In Tanzania, tax officers have always had powers of access to
information with the ability to inspect and seize records for tax
purposes. Sections 126 and 127 of the Income Tax Act No 33 of 1973[303]
were the first tax provisions to give tax officers "full and free access"[304]
to buildings or any other place where information is held. These powers
included a power to compel production of information, and a power
to search and seize documents.[305] While for a long time the inspection
and audit powers were confined to income tax only, this changed in
1997 when VAT was introduced,[306] and VAT officials were given powers
similar to those enjoyed by income tax officers.[307] Sections 138 to 140
of the Income Tax Act 2004, which replaced the Income Tax Act 1973,
give wide ranging powers to the Commissioner to access information
for income tax purposes. Similar amendments were made in the Stamp
Duty Act No 20 of 1972,[308] the Hotel Levy Act No 23 of 1972,[309] and the
Customs and Excise Tariff Ordinance,[310] before that law was replaced
by the East African Community Customs Management Act No. 1 of
2005, which maintained the information access powers.[311] The EAC

---

302 For example Section 140 (1) of the Income Tax Act.
303 Act No. 33 of 1973. This Act has now been repealed and replaced by the Income Tax
Act 2004.
304 Section 127 of the Income Tax Act 1973.
305 Section 126 of the Income Tax Act 1973.
306 The Value Added Tax Act No. 24 of 1997 re-issued in 2006 as The Value Added Tax
Act Chapter 148.
307 Sections 37, 38, and 39 of the Value Added Tax Act No. 24 of 1997.
308 Section 77 of the Stamp Duty Act No. 22 of 1972
309 Section 7 of the Hotel Levy Act No. 23 of 1972.
310 Section 138 of the EAC Customs Management Act No. 1 of 2005.
311 Section 236.

Customs Management Act limits the information gathering powers of the Commissioner for Customs to auditing and inspecting documents associated with goods which are, or have been, the subject of customs action.[312] Even with that limitation, it is still a fairly wide power, allowing unlimited examination of books, records, computer stored information, business systems, customs documents, commercial documents, and other data related to the goods.[313] It also extends to a power to question any person involved directly or indirectly in the business, or any person in the possession of documents and data relevant to the goods.[314]

Relying on its information gathering powers in the tax statutes, the TRA has increased tax inspection and audit capacity by expanding its statutory power to access information and by making the sanctions for non-cooperation more stringent.

A good example of how extensive this power has become is found in Section 138 of the Income Tax Act of 2004 which provides that,

> 138(1) For the purposes of this Act, the Commissioner and every officer who is authorized in writing by the Commissioner
>
> > (a)   shall have
> >
> > > (i)   at all times during the day between 9 am and 6 pm and without any prior notice; and
> > >
> > > (ii)   at all other times as permitted by a search warrant granted by a District or Resident Magistrate's Court, full and free access to any premises, place, document or other asset;
> >
> > (b)   may make an extract or copy, including an electronic copy, of any document to which access is obtained under paragraph (a);
> >
> > (c)   may seize any document that, in the opinion of the Commissioner or authorized officer, affords evidence that may be material in determining the tax liability of any person under this Act; and
> >
> > (d)   may, where the document is not available or a copy is not provided on request by a person having access to the document, seize an asset

---

312 Section 236 EAC Customs and Management Act of 2005.
313 Section 236 (a).
314 Section 236 (b).

> to which access is obtained under paragraph (a) that the Commissioner or authorized officer reasonably suspects contains or stores the document in any form.

Under Section 139 of the Income Tax Act 2004, the TRA officers may choose not to come to the taxpayer's premises, but instead, compel the taxpayer to bring the information required to them. What is of interest is the fact that the power of access to information and the carrying out of audits by tax officers is not limited to accessing information from the taxpayer. It extends to accessing information from any person in relation to the taxation of another person.[315]

It is notable that under the Income Tax Act there is no limit on the type and scope of information which may be seized or requisitioned by the TRA. It is enough for the TRA to allege that the information is for the purposes of the Act. There is no obligation under the statute to disclose the particular purpose for which the information is accessed or requisitioned. In two recent incidents, the TRA investigation officers raided the operational offices of the Geita Gold Mine and Bulyanhulu Gold Mine. With lately acquired forensic software capable of accessing several servers at once, they copied information from all the servers used by the two taxpayers.

> In addition to expanding the statutory powers which enable tax officers to inspect the affairs of the taxpayers and undertake audits of any type, the TRA has vastly increased its technical capacity to carry out checks, especially in the area of customs enforcement. Recently, the Customs Department has acquired and deployed a sophisticated scanner capable of scanning the contents of imported and containerized goods, which aims at increasing officers' capacity to detect and deter the mis-declaration of goods.

> These extremely wide powers are now seen by taxpayers as too intrusive and are resented. They are enormous powers and, if not properly controlled, can easily be misused. It is in this context that the right to have tax information kept secret becomes a very important right.

Secrecy of information serves more than one objective. Firstly, it aims at protecting the financial and commercial privacy of the taxpayer in his/her business or activity. Without the secrecy, sensitive information obtained from a taxpayer could easily fall into the hands of competitors and damage the taxpayer's business. Secondly, requiring secrecy of

---

315 Sections 138 and 139 ITA (read together).

taxpayer information and limiting its use to taxation purposes only encourages taxpayers to give information to tax officers.

However, the secrecy of information provided for tax purposes has never been absolute. Numerous exceptions have been enacted in the secrecy provisions, which now undermine almost completely the objectives of secrecy provisions in tax statutes.

Under Section 140 (2), disclosure of taxpayer information is permitted in the following cases:

140(2)   An officer may disclose a document or information referred to in subsection (1)

     (a)   to the extent required in order to perform the officer's duties under this Act;

     (b)   where required by a court or tribunal in relation to administrative review or proceedings with respect to a matter under this Act;

     (c)   to the Minister or the Chief Secretary of the President's office;

     (d)   where the disclosure is necessary for the purposes of any law administered by the Tanzania Revenue Authority;

     (e)   to any person in the service of the Government of the United Republic or the Revolutionary Council of Zanzibar in a revenue or statistical department where such disclosure is necessary for the performance of the person's official duties;

     (f)   to the Auditor General or any person authorised by the Auditor General where such disclosure is necessary for the performance of official duties; or

     (g)   to the competent authority of the government of another country with which the United Republic has entered into an international agreement, to the extent permitted under that agreement.

Section 140 does not prevent disclosures between/among officers of the TRA. There is no requirement that the officers to whom disclosure is made must be working on the taxpayer's file. Therefore, disclosure between/among tax officers could be for other purposes, or for no purpose at all, just idle conversation.

Section 140 (2) also allows officers of the TRA to share taxpayer information with other sections or departments of the TRA so that information given to the VAT Department in a VAT monthly return may be passed-on to income tax officers or customs officers and be used for tax purposes other than VAT.

The exceptions to secrecy as contained in Section 140 (2) extend to divulging information to a court or tribunal. The TRA is also allowed to share the information it obtains for taxation purposes with other government departments such as the Anti-Corruption Bureau and others.[316] This erosion of secrecy can have far-reaching implications for taxpayer compliance and may fuel taxpayer resistance.[317]

In conclusion, it can be said that these provisions, namely Section 138 on the TRA's power to enter and inspect premises; Section 139 on the power to require production of information; and Section 140 on the derogation from the requirement of secrecy; and similar provisions in other tax statutes, all result in too much power being given to the TRA. Such powers infringe unjustly on the protection of taxpayer rights afforded elsewhere. It is questionable whether there is a compelling enough public interest to warrant these derogations. To the contrary, the public interest in promoting voluntary taxpayer compliance requires such powers, when given, to be measured and to be better regulated.

The right to protection of property, recognised in the TRA Taxpayer's Charter and also entrenched under the Constitution, also requires discussion as to how the protection is achieved in the Tanzania tax statutes.

Article 24 of the Constitution of Tanzania provides that, subject to the provisions of the relevant laws of the land, every person is entitled to own property and has a right to the protection of his property held in accordance with the law.[318]

From the wording of Article 24, the right to protection of personal property is not absolute; it is subject to what the laws of the land allow. Looking at tax laws, the right to the protection of personal property is eroded by the tax collection powers given to the TRA. Understandably, a tax collecting authority ought to be given sufficient powers to enable it to discharge its duties, but such powers should be no more than is necessary to enable the authority to perform its function. It is also

316
317 Section 140 (1) of the Income Tax Act.
318 The Constitution of Tanzania of 1977 (as amended), Article 24 (1), 25.

important that powers are given in moderation and are well regulated to prevent abuse.

The tax statutes impose obligations on taxpayers so that taxes are paid promptly. Where taxpayers become tax debtors, the TRA has substantial powers to ensure that tax is paid. Firstly, the TRA has the general common law right available to creditors, as well as specific statutory powers of collection given under each taxing statute, giving the TRA a substantial advantage over other creditors.

Taxes become due and payable immediately the notice of assessment is issued. Most notices are issued with an 'immediate payment' endorsement.[319] For those taxpayers who are under the withholding system, the tax payable is withheld at source even before the payee receives the amount due to him/her.[320] Taxpayers, who pay their taxes under the instalment procedure, are supposed to pay their taxes on a quarterly basis, whether their accounting is on a calendar year basis or some other basis.[321] This system denies access to money which they otherwise would have had for the rest of the year. On the due date for payment, the tax becomes a debt due to the TRA and may be sued for in any court of competent jurisdiction.[322]

Where a corporate body fails to pay tax on the due date for which tax is payable, every person who is an officer of that company, or was an officer within the previous six months, is jointly and severally liable for the payment of the overdue tax.[323] Where the company is put in receivership, the receiver must notify the TRA within 14 days of his/her appointment as receiver, whereupon the TRA will notify him/her of the company's tax debt. Following this step, a notice by the TRA will instruct the receiver to sell sufficient assets under his/her possession to pay off the outstanding tax.[324] To the extent that the receiver fails to pay the tax liability, the receiver becomes personally liable to the TRA on account of the tax debtor's tax liability.[325]

---

319 Section 97 (d) of the Income Tax Act provides that the notice of assessment should specifically inform the taxpayer of the date by which the tax payable on the assessment must be paid.

320 Sections 81, 82 and 83 require that withholding taxes shall be extracted at source before salaries, or dividends or service fees are paid.

321 Section 88 (2) of the Income Tax Act.

322 Section 110 of the Income Tax Act.

323 Section 115 (2) of the Income Tax Act.

324 Section 116 (3) of the Income Tax Act.

325 Section 116 (4) of the Income Tax Act.

The TRA also has power to recover unpaid taxes from third parties owing money to the tax debtor.[326] The TRA may issue notice to any person owing money to the tax debtor,[327] holding money on account of the tax debtor,[328] holding money on account of another person for payment to the tax debtor, holding money on account of a third party for payment to the tax debtor,[329] or to a person having authority from a third party to pay money to the tax debtor.[330] Finally, the TRA can recover unpaid tax from an agent of a non-resident person who has not yet paid his/her taxes.[331]

In circumstances where the TRA has reason to believe that a person liable to pay tax may leave the country before the tax is due and payable, the TRA has power to bring forward the due date for payment of tax, in which case the tax becomes due and payable on the date specified by the TRA, usually immediately on issuance of the notice to pay. Under the law,[332] the TRA may issue notice to the Immigration Office requiring it to prevent the departure of a person until he/she has discharged the tax due for payment.[333]

Conclusion

The discussion in this chapter has shown how immensely important the recognition and protection of taxpayer rights is to general tax compliance. It has also been argued that taxpayer charters, proclaiming lofty taxpayer rights are, in themselves, not enough to lead to enjoyment of effective taxpayer rights. The tax laws must be aligned to give effect to what is said in the taxpayer charters and to the protection of taxpayer rights. The case of Tanzania shows that the protection of both primary and secondary taxpayer rights is, to a large extent, nullified by the tax statutes governing the administration and payment of tax. Although the basic tenets of constitutionalism and rule of law do exist and many taxpayer rights are incorporated in the tax statutes, other laws and the Constitution, the numerous derogations from full enjoyment of those taxpayer rights as found in tax statutes significantly erode the foundation on which taxpayer rights would otherwise be effectively enjoyed.

---

326 Section 117 of the Income Tax Act.
327 Section 117 (2) (a) of the Income Tax Act.
328 Section 117 (2) (b) of the Income Tax Act.
329 Section 117 (2) (c) of the Income Tax Act.
330 Section 117 (2) (d) of the Income Tax Act.
331 Section 118 of the Income Tax Act.
332 Section 114 of the Income Tax Act.
333 Section 114 (2) of the Income Tax Act.

Equally, the institutional culture of the tax administration has not changed sufficiently. Its officers must espouse more the new service-oriented culture proclaimed in the working documents of the TRA cited in this study. Continuing with the high-handed approach and relishing the derogations to taxpayer rights, as is the case with tax officers, will only deepen the taxpayer perception that the tax system is not fairly structured and is not fairly administered. When taxpayers feel that the tax system is not fair, it is difficult to achieve the high levels of voluntary taxpayer compliance the TRA desires.

4

Tax Administration and Compliance

Introduction

This chapter discusses the efforts being undertaken to modernise tax administration in Tanzania. It examines the overall objectives driving the transformation, and, at the same time, assesses the performance of the new tax authority. The discussion is both specific to the TRA and general, touching on the regional and continental trend for reforming tax administration in Africa. Finally, the discussion turns to how the new tax administration has approached the vexing question of tax compliance, and how the tax administration reforms undertaken have helped or hindered the tax compliance drive.

A book published by the TRA and launched on the occasion of its Tenth Anniversary in October 2006, notes that,

> Government finance in developing countries is often constrained by the ability to collect taxes. Domestic revenue mobilization in these countries is often hindered by the lack of information on informal businesses, the difficulty in imposing income tax withholdings on millions of self-employed people in agriculture

and services and extensive tax evasion. Such shortcomings have widespread socio-economic ramifications. Creating reliable, efficient and sustainable tax administrations has thus become an urgent and noble preoccupation of many governments.[334]

In the mid-nineties, acting on the need to create more effective tax administrations, the three East African countries (Kenya, Tanzania and Uganda) simultaneously embarked on the modernisation of their tax administrations. In each case, the process started with the setting up of a semi-autonomous government agency with responsibility for all government taxes, and, as well, non-tax revenue. The new tax authorities amalgamated and took over the functions of the former Customs Department, the Income Tax Department, and the Sales Tax/Goods and Services Tax Department, which, in each of these three countries, previously operated as singular government units reporting separately to the Ministry of Finance.

The tax administration modernisation efforts of the East African countries were replicated in nearby countries. Zambia and Rwanda both set up new and far improved tax administrations to replace the tax departments, existing for many years, which both had inherited from their colonisers.

The tax administration modernisation trend spread beyond the East Africa region. A report by the USA Agency for International Development (USAID)[335] shows that by mid-2004 the following African countries had embraced tax administration reform and created new modern tax administrations: Botswana (2004/05), Ethiopia (2002), Ghana (1986), Kenya (1995/96), Lesotho (2001/02), Malawi (1995/96), Rwanda (1999/00), Sierra Leone (2002), South Africa (1996/97), Tanzania (1995/96), Uganda (1991/92), Zambia (1993/94) and Zimbabwe (2000).

---

334 The TRA *A Decade of TRA Transformation 1996-2006*, Tanzania Revenue Authority, Dar es Salaam, 2006, at 3.

335 United States Agency for International Development (USAID), 'Are Semi-Autonomous Revenue Authorities the Answer to Tax Administration Problems in Developing Countries? A Practical Guide' Paper Prepared by A J Mann of Development Alternatives Inc, August 2004. Internet source http://ideas.respec.org/p/dai/wpaper/ accessed 26/01/2007.

Modernising Tax Administration

Dhillon and Bouwer[336] have put forward the following reasons for tax administration reform in developing countries:

Many developing nations inherit tax laws that have long since been reformed in developed nations. These laws can be complex, inelastic, inefficient and inequitable, generating undesirable outcomes in the economy and limiting the community's acceptance of the tax system as a whole. Tax reforms have become an increasingly important element of adjustment programs in developing countries, supported by the World Bank and the International Monetary Fund.

Along with tax reform, the community's experience of the tax administration system can be substantially improved, leading to improved acceptance of the wider tax system and improved collections. As the community's expectations of service from private sector organizations have grown, there is a corresponding increase in their expectations of the public sector. This has played out over several years in developed nations, but there are signs this is happening faster in developing nations. The paradigm that a revenue agency will maximize compliance just by cultivating a fear of being caught is not sustainable into the future. Modern revenue agencies seek to maximize voluntary compliance by making it easy to comply, while operating an insightful compliance program to treat noncompliance. An equitable tax system where everyone is seen to pay their fair share increases the likelihood of voluntary compliance.[337]

Establishment and Reform of the Tanzania Revenue Authority (TRA)

For Tanzania, tax administration modernisation was premised on a number of concerns. There was great weakness in tax administration and tax policy formulation. This weakness resulted in widespread tax evasion. There was also undesirable political interference in the operations of the tax departments (especially by the Ministry of Finance). This situation created a need to limit political interference and to free tax administration from civil service constraints. The tax revenue/GDP ratio, at an average of 11.3 for 1995 and 1996, was very low (one of the lowest in Sub-Saharan Africa). Tanzania had a fiscal deficit of between 5% to 7.9% of GDP in 1994 and 1995. These budget shortfalls,

---

336 A Dhillon and J G Bouwer 'Reform of Tax Administration in Developing Nations' Occasional Paper, Montgomery Research Institute, Tax Volume 1, 6/7/2005, Internet source http://www.revenueproject.com/document accessed 26/1/2007.
337 *Ibid.* at 1.

combined with fiscal deficits, generated a money supply expansion of
25% between 1994 and 1996, leading to high inflation and growth of the
domestic debt.[338]

With intent to tackle these problems, the Tanzania Revenue Authority
was established as a statutory body corporate operating under an Act
of Parliament passed on 7th August 1995.[339] The TRA was inaugurated
in July 1996. Though a statutory body, the TRA is also a government
agency. Section 4 of the Tanzania Revenue Authority Act provides, in
part, as follows:

> (1) There is established an Authority to be known as the
> Tanzania Revenue Authority which shall consist of
> the Board and all operating Departments.
>
> (2) The Authority shall be a body corporate with perpetual
> succession and a common seal and, subject to this Act
>
> (a)   shall be capable of suing and being sued in its
>   corporate name;
>
> (b)   may borrow money, acquire and dispose of
>   property; and
>
> (c)   may do all other things which a body corporate
>   may lawfully do.
>
> (3) The Authority shall be an agency of the Government
> and shall be under the general supervision of the
> Minister.

Prior to the establishment of the TRA, the function of collecting taxes
was performed by three departments (the Income Tax Department,
the Customs Department, and the Sales Tax Department), operating
under the Ministry of Finance. Each tax department was headed by a
commissioner, each reporting separately to the Ministry.

Upon establishment of the TRA, all employment contracts with staff
working with the Income Tax Department, the Customs Department
and the Sales Tax Department were terminated. They could, if they
wished, apply for new positions in the TRA. Only 2,200 of the existing
3,300 tax staff were absorbed into the TRA. Of those absorbed, nearly
400 could not be confirmed after a probationary period. They were either
dismissed or allowed early retirement, mostly on account of integrity
considerations. Those who survived this transition were motivated by

---

338 USAID Paper, at 19.
339 Tanzania Revenue Authority Act No. 11 of 1995, Section 4 (1). All laws in Tanzania
were revised in 2006. The TRA Act is now Chapter 399 of the Laws of Tanzania.

very significant salary increases, sometimes ten times higher than is paid for a comparable civil service position.

The TRA, as an agency of the government, is responsible for collection and administration of all central government taxes, together with a few non-tax revenue items. Its functions are stipulated in Section 5 of the Act:

5. (1)　The Functions of the Authority are:

　(i)　to administer and give effect to the laws or the specified provisions of the laws set out in the First Schedule to this Act, and for this purpose, to assess, collect and account for all revenue to which those laws apply:

　(ii)　to monitor, oversee, coordinate activities and ensure the fair efficient and effective administration of revenue laws by revenue departments in the jurisdiction of the Union Government;

　(iii)　to monitor and ensure the collection of fees, levies, charges or any other tax collected by any Ministry, Department or Division of the Government as revenue for the Government;

　(iv)　to advise the Minister and other relevant organs on all matters pertaining to fiscal policy, the implementation of the policy and the constant improvement of policy regarding revenue laws and administration;

　(v)　to promote voluntary tax compliance to the highest degree possible;

　(vi)　to take such measures as may be necessary to improve the standard of service given to taxpayers, with a view to improving the effectiveness of the revenue department and maximizing revenue collection;

　(vii)　to determine the steps to be taken to counteract fraud and other forms of tax and other fiscal evasions;

(iii)   to produce trade statistics and publications on a quarterly basis; and

(iv)   subject to the laws specified under paragraph (a), to perform such other functions as the Minister may determine.

Looking at Section 5 (1), the primary function of the TRA is to administer and give effect to all tax laws which are levied by the central government. The taxes administered by the TRA are listed in the First Schedule[340] to the TRA Act. They are the following:

i. income tax, under the Income Tax Act No 11 of 2004;

ii. customs duties, under the East African Community Customs Management Act No 1 of 2005;

iii. excise duties, under the Excise (Management and Tariff Act) Chapter 147;

iv. stamp duty, under the Stamp Duty Act No 20 of 1972;

v. the hotel levy, under the Hotel Levy Act No 23 of 1972;

vi. estate duties under the Estate Duty Act;

vii. airport departure tax, under the Airport Service Charges Act 1962;

viii. motor vehicle registration tax, under the Motor Vehicle (Tax on Registration and Transfer) Act No 21 of 1972;

ix. training levy, under the Training Levy Act No 26 of 1972;

x. housing levy under the Housing Levy Act No 12 of 1985;

xi. land registration and transfer fees under the Land Act No 17 of 1997;

xii. any other taxes imposed by a law which may come into force and is enacted to mobilize and collect revenue.

In terms of Section 5 (1) (a) of the TRA Act, administering and giving effect to tax laws means to assess, collect and account for all revenue to which those tax laws apply.[341]

Section 5 is a significant section of the Act. It encapsulates the government policy objectives for creating the TRA. For example,

i. section 5 (1) (b) speaks of the need to ensure "fair, efficient and effective administration of tax";

---

340 The list of taxes under the First Schedule has changed over time as many taxes considered nuisance taxes were repealed following the establishment of the TRA as part of the tax modernization program. The original list had 25 different taxes.
341 Section 5 (1) (a).

ii. section 5 (1) (e) imposes on the TRA a duty to "promote voluntary tax compliance to the highest degree possible";

iii. section 5 (f) underscores the need to "improve the standard of service given to taxpayers"; and

iv. section 5 (1) (g) charges the TRA with the responsibility to take steps to "counteract fraud and tax evasion".

These objectives have come to form the core values of the TRA and, as it is shown later, they are the pillars of the TRA's three successive five-year Corporate Plans.[342]

The duties and responsibilities of the TRA are not clearly stipulated in the establishment statute. However, it is possible to formulate a clear set of duties and responsibilities from the statutory functions given to the TRA under Section 5 (1) and the powers of the TRA outlined in Section 5 (2). Section 5 (2) provides that:

(2) The Authority shall in the discharge of its functions, have power to

(a) study revenue laws and identify amendments or alternations which may be made to any law for the purposes of improving the administration of and compliance with revenue laws;

(b) study the administrative costs, compliance costs and the operational impact of all intended legislative changes and advise the Government accordingly;

(c) collect and process the statistics needed to provide forecasts of revenue receipt and the effect on yield of any proposals for changes in revenue laws and advise the Minister accordingly;

(d) negotiate and agree with the Treasury on the revenue collection targets for any given financial year;

(e) undertake work measurement exercises in order to determine the manpower needs for the functions of each revenue department in the Authority;

---

342 The first five year Corporate Plan was adopted in 1998, the second in 2003, and the third in 2008.

(f) set appropriate objectives and work targets in
each revenue department and monitor progress
in achieving them;

(g) take such other measures as it may deem
necessary or desirable for the achievement of the
purposes and provisions of this Act.

At the outset of this chapter, they were outlined as being: a duty to
ensure the fair, efficient and effective administration of revenue laws; a
duty to promote voluntary taxpayer compliance; and a duty to improve
the standard of service given to taxpayers with a view to improving the
effectiveness of tax collection. There are also additional instruments
such as the TRA Strategic Corporate Plan, which incorporates a Mission
Statement calling on the TRA "to be a Modern Tax Administration
rendering effective and efficient tax administration which promotes
voluntary tax compliance by providing high quality customer service
with fairness and integrity through competent and motivated staff."[343]
The Strategic Plan also charges the TRA employees with the following
core values:

   i. to be business oriented and professional in appearance and
approach;

   ii. to be fair and accountable for the decisions they make;

   iii. to be accessible and prompt in the delivery of service;

   iv. to treat taxpayers with dignity and respect; and

   v. to act with integrity and honesty.

These duties, as it will be recalled, are reiterated in the Taxpayer's
Charter, which was discussed in the previous chapter. There are
no sanctions against the TRA if it fails to discharge the duties and
obligations imposed on it, save for loss of standing in public perception
for a sound organisation.

Both from the TRA Statute and the Taxpayer's Charter, it does appear
that one of the core duties of the tax authority is to ensure a fair, efficient
and effective administration of taxes.[344] It is possible to measure the
efficient and effective collection of taxes from the effectiveness of the
tax system and also from the volume of tax revenues realised by the tax
administration.

---

343 TRA Third Five Year Corporate Plan 2008/09 to 2012/13 at (iii).
344 Section 5 (1) (b) of the TRA Act.

The TRA has since 1996 demonstrated an adequate capacity to meet tax revenue targets set by the Ministry of Finance. Tax collection figures for the years 2001 to 2010 (in Tables 3a and 3b below) show that, except for the initial years following its establishment, and for 2009/10 (because of the global economic crisis), the TRA has consistently met and exceeded revenue collection targets. However, a big challenge for the government remains the narrow tax base in Tanzania as discussed in Chapter Two. The tax collection targets are achieved from a relatively small pool of taxpayers.

TABLE 3A: REVENUE COLLECTION PERFORMANCE FOR 1996/97 TO 2002/03 (AMOUNTS ARE IN TRILLION TANZANIA SHILLINGS)

Year	1996/97	1997/98	1998/99	1999/00	2000/01	2001/02	2002/03
Revenue Target	0,632	0,672	0,667	0,770	0,815	1,102	1,102
Actual Collection	0,523	0,585	0,654	0,740	0,862	0,962	1,165
Performance	82%	87%	98%	96%	106%	87%	105%

* Sourse: The RA Directorate of Research and Policy

TABLE 3B: REVENUE COLLECTION PERFORMANCE FOR 2003/04 TO 2009/10 (AMOUNTS ARE IN TRILLION TANZANIA SHILLINGS)*

Year	2003/4	2004/05	2005/06	2006/07	2007/08	2008/09	2009/10
Revenue Target	1,310	1,631	2,026	2,448	3,457	3,847	4,855
Actual Collection	1,426	1,715	2,063	2,697	3,546	4,105	4,437
Performance	108%	105%	101%	110%	102%	106%	91%

* Sourse: The RA Directorate of Research and Policy

The steps taken by the TRA to ensure that taxes are efficiently and fairly administered,[345] and also in promoting voluntary tax compliance with the taxes administered by the TRA, are discussed in subsequent sections.

---

345 Section 5 (1) (b) of the Tax Revenue Authority Act.

For now, it is instructive to examine the tax reform scenario of
Tanzania's neighbouring countries: Uganda, Zambia, Kenya and Rwanda
have gone through and are continuing similar tax administration
reforms. These reforms are discussed below.

Tax Administration Reform in Uganda, Zambia, Kenya and Rwanda

Uganda

The Uganda Revenue Authority (URA) was established by statute in
1991.[346] It was set up as a semi-autonomous body charged with three
primary duties: to assess and collect specified taxes, to administer
and enforce the laws relating to those taxes, and to account for the
revenue collected. There is a fourth primary duty which is separately
stated in the establishment statute for the URA, namely that the URA
is required to advise the government of Uganda on matters of policy
relating to government revenue, whether or not they relate to the taxes
administered by the URA.

The URA was also established with another broad objective in mind,
namely, to provide the foundation for the development of Uganda
through revenue mobilization.[347] The taxes it collects are to finance
current and capital development activities of the government, increase
the standard of living of all Ugandans and reduce poverty and increase
the GDP/revenue ratio to a level at which the government of Uganda
can fund its own essential expenditure.

According to the URA, the role of the URA, as reflected in its
corporate plan,[348] is:

  i. to identify taxpayers and inform them of their tax obligations and
     rights, providing them with the necessary information to enable
     them to discharge those obligations;

  ii. to assess taxpayers fairly with regard to the taxes relevant to them;

  iii. to collect taxes in accordance with the laws, regulations and
       practice instructions; to enforce collection of taxes where default
       has occurred; and

  iv. to account to the government for the taxes collected.

The URA administers a wide range of taxes, including the income

---

346 Uganda Revenue Authority Act No. 6 of 1991.
347 *Ibid.*, Sections 3 and 4.
348 The URA Five Year Strategic Plan 1992-97.

tax,[349] stamp duty,[350] the road toll,[351] customs duties,[352] excise duty,[353] the value added tax,[354] and various fees, levies and license payments.[355]

There is some dispute regarding the autonomy of URA. The URA was the first modern tax administration to be established in the Eastern Africa region. The URA was expected to enjoy a much wider autonomy so as to have flexibility in decision-making, ability to implement incentives needed to improve performance and be protected from undue political interference. This lack of autonomy had been at the centre of the failure to perform by the former tax departments which operated as government units in the Ministry of Finance. However, it appears that autonomy has been difficult to achieve. The URA continues to be required to report to Treasury regularly on matters of day-to-day administration and to seek clearance from the Ministry of Finance on institutional management and policy issues. As a result, many people in Uganda still perceive the URA as a government department.

The URA also does not enjoy any autonomy in funding. Its operations are funded by government through the normal budget process. Shortfalls in funding requirement are made up by donor agencies, who invariably arrange their funding of the URA through the Ministry of Finance. An arrangement which would have enabled the URA to retain for its own use 15% percent of tax collections starting in 2001 had not been acted upon by the Minister for Finance by 2003.[356] This is still the case to date.

A study of the URA over a ten year period has shown that while its initial performance was impressive, it quickly stagnated amid accusations of corruption. Erosion of its autonomy and conflicts with the Ministry of Finance, as well as loss of taxpayer legitimacy are put

---

349 Uganda Laws, Income Tax Act of 1997.

350 Uganda Laws, Stamp Duty Act [Chapter 172].

351 The road toll was introduced in 1998 by Finance Act No. 4 of 1998 (Section 12 and the 7th Schedule), and is payable by road users as a road users tax.

352 Charged under both the Customs Tariff Act No. 17 of 1970 and the East African Customs Management Act 2004.

353 Uganda Laws, Excise Tariff Act [Chapter 174) and the East African Excise Management Act No. 1 of the East Africa Community Laws [Chapter 26].

354 The Value Added Tax Act of 1995.

355 For instance, under the Traffic and Road Safety Act No. 15 of 1998 and the Regulations made there under, the collection of license fees, or other fees, levies, and fines (other than those imposed by the Courts), are all administered by the URA.

356 O Therkildsen 'Revenue Authority Autonomy in Sub-Saharan Africa: The Case for Uganda' Danish Institute for International Studies, Paper prepared for the Workshop on 'Taxation, Accountability and Poverty' 23-24 October 2003, at 8.

forward as causes of the stagnation in performance.[357] Therkildsen,[358] Devas,[359] Glenday,[360] Fjeldstad,[361] and Clarke[362] have undertaken studies which show that this pattern of initial revenue increases, followed by stagnation or decreases, has characterised tax administration reforms in Ghana, Kenya and Tanzania. These authors suggest that the success, stagnation and decline syndrome may indeed affect much of Sub-Saharan Africa. Rakner and Gloppen warn that the plateau at which increases in tax revenue performance appear to go into stagnation is well below the level needed to achieve fiscal sustainability.[363]

Zambia

The Zambia Revenue Authority (ZRA) was established in 1994.[364] One would expect that the ZRA, coming into existence some three years after the establishment of the Uganda Revenue Authority, would be influenced by the URA in terms of its set up, its general objectives and its experience. This is not the case. There are key differences, not only between the ZRA and the URA, but also between the ZRA and the TRA and the Kenya Revenue Authority (KRA), these two having been set up only a year later in 1995.

The ZRA is a corporate body, similar to the semi-autonomous statutory government agencies such as the URA in Uganda, the TRA in Tanzania and the KRA in Kenya.

The ZRA Act charges the ZRA with the responsibility of collecting revenue on behalf of the Zambia government under the supervision of the Minister for Finance and National Planning.

---

357 *Ibid.* at 1.

358 *Supra* Note 294 at 3.

359 N Devas, S Delay and M Hubbard 'Revenue authorities: are they the right vehicle for improved tax administration?' (2001) 21 *Public Administration and Development* 211-222.

360 G Glenday 'Capacity Building in the Context of the Kenya Tax Modernisation Program' in M S Grindle (ed) *Getting good government: capacity building in the public sectors of developing countries* Harvard University Press, 1997.

361 O. H. Fjeldstad 2003 "Fighting fiscal corruption, Lessons from the Tanzania Revenue Authority".

362 J Clarke and D Wood 'New public management and development: the case of public service reform in Tanzania and Uganda' in W McCourt and M Minogue (eds) *The Internationalisation of Public Management: reinventing the Third World state* Edward Elgar, Cheltenham, 2001, 181-189.

363 L Rakner and S Gloppen 'Tax Reform and Democratic Accountability in Sub-Saharan Africa' in *Beyond Structural Adjustment: The Institutional Context of African Development*, Palgrave – Mcmillan, London, 2003.

364 This followed the enactment of the Zambia Revenue Authority Act of 1993 which provided for the establishment of the ZRA as a statutory corporate body.

The ZRA is overseen by the most inclusive of all the governing boards in Eastern Africa. The membership of this board includes the Secretary to the Treasury, the Permanent Secretary for the Ministry of Justice, the Governor of the Bank of Zambia, representatives from professional bodies such as the Law Society of Zambia, the Bankers' Association, the Zambia Institute of Certified Accountants, the Zambia Association of Chambers of Commerce and Industry, and two private persons nominated by the Minister of Finance and Economic Development. In contrast, the TRA Board of Directors, which has ten members, is made up almost entirely of government people. Of the ten members, five are ex-officio. Although the Minister of Finance has discretion to appoint four members, these appointments tend to go to members of Parliament and people within the government system. The current ten members of the Board of the TRA are the following: a public finance academician at the University of Dar es Salaam (Chairperson), two Permanent Secretaries (Finance/Planning), the Principal Secretary Finance (Zanzibar), the Governor of the Bank of Tanzania, two members of Parliament, the Commissioner General, the Commissioner of the Zanzibar Revenue Board (ZRB), and the Chief Legal Counsel of the TRA who is also the Board Secretary of the TRA. It is notable too that, in Zambia's case, the Board Members elect the Chairman of the Board. The Chief Executive of the Authority is the Commissioner General, who is appointed by the President. In contrast again, for Tanzania, both the Chairman and the Commissioner General of the TRA are appointed by the President. In Kenya, the Chairman of the KRA is appointed by the President, while the Commissioner General is appointed by the Minister of Finance.

The people-centred approach of the ZRA is reflected also in its perception of who its stakeholders are. The ZRA Strategic Plan and its customer care program recognize the following sections of society as important stakeholders: the Zambian people, as represented by the ZRA Governing Board and by the Government and its agencies; Parliament; the Zambian business community and those groups which represent their interests, together with their professional advisors; the banks and other financial institutions; the taxpayers in general; members of COMESA, SADC, WTO and other countries transacting business with Zambia, or transiting goods through Zambia; tourists, travellers and traders crossing Zambia's borders; the donor community and multilateral agencies, e.g. IMF, World Bank, DFID; staff and others within the ZRA; the mass media; NGOs and other interest groups.

As result of the marked break with the trend in the appointment of its board members and the commitment to wider involvement of sectors of society, the ZRA is described as an autonomous corporate body. The one thing the ZRA has in common with the rest of the revenue authorities in the region is that it is funded through the national budget. This funding system detracts from its otherwise apparent independence.

The ZRA administers several taxes: the value added tax, the customs and excise duty, surtax, income tax, property transfer tax and mineral royalty tax.

According to the statute establishing the ZRA,[365] the main responsibilities of the ZRA are:

i. to properly assess and collect taxes and duties timely;

ii. to ensure that all monies collected are properly accounted for and banked;

iii. to properly enforce all statutory provisions falling within the ZRA mandate;

iv. to provide statistical information on revenue to the Government;

v. to give advice to Ministers on aspects of tax policy; and

vi. to facilitate international trade.

Zambia has a taxpayer's charter[366] which is brief. It states that "the taxpayer is entitled to impartial and equitable treatment by the Zambia Revenue Authority in all dealings with it...."[367] It also states that the taxpayer is entitled,

i. to receive all the forms needed to comply with the legal obligations,

ii. to receive all the necessary information required to comply with the legal obligations under the Zambian tax laws,

iii. to provide fair treatment under the law,

iv. to provide prompt and courteous service from the ZRA at all times, and

v. to provide quality and efficient services at all times if the information received from the taxpayer is complete and accurate.

---

365 Zambia Revenue Authority Act No. 23 of 1993.
366 ZRA, Taxpayer's Charter, Zambia Revenue Authority, Lusaka, Internet source http://www.zra.org.zm/charter.php accessed 13/11/2007.
367 *Ibid.*

Finally, the ZRA Taxpayer's Charter says that "all personal and financial information provided to the ZRA is strictly confidential and is used only for the purposes allowed by law."[368]

These so called 'rights' in the Zambian Taxpayer's Charter are not really rights. They are, largely, performance standards espoused by the ZRA, but they are not quite as elaborate as those adopted in Uganda.

Kenya

The Kenya Revenue Authority (KRA) was established in 1995 by an Act of Parliament,[369] as a semi-autonomous government agency responsible for the administration of all taxes levied by the government of Kenya. The overall objective was to provide operational autonomy in tax administration and to enable the organization to evolve into a modern, flexible and integrated revenue collecting agency. The KRA's immediate purpose was to enhance the mobilization of government revenue, while providing effective tax administration and sustainability in revenue collection.

Consistent with its establishment objectives, the KRA was given the following functions:

i. to assess, collect and account for all revenues in accordance with the written laws and the specified provisions of the written laws;

ii. to advise on matters relating to the administration of, and collection of revenue under the written laws or the specified provisions of written laws; and

iii. to perform such other functions in relation to revenue as the Minister of Finance may direct.

The KRA has a Board of Directors consisting of members from both the public and private sectors. The Board is responsible only for making policy decisions to be implemented by the KRA management. It does not make policy relating to taxes. The Chairman of the Board is appointed by the President of the Republic of Kenya, while the Chief Executive of the Authority (the Commissioner General) is appointed by the Minister for Finance.

The KRA administers the following taxes:

i. the income tax[370]

ii. customs and excise duties[371]

---

368 *Ibid.*
369 Kenya Revenue Authority Act of 1995, Laws of Kenya [Chapter 469].
370 The Income Tax Act, Laws of Kenya [Chapter 470].
371 The Customs and Excise Tariff Act, Laws of Kenya [Chapter 472].

   iii. the value added tax[372]

   iv. road levies[373]

   v. the air passenger service charge[374]

   vi. the entertainment tax[375]

   vii. road licenses, transport licenses, traffic levies, and the second hand vehicle purchase levy[376]

   viii. Parliamentary pensions together with the widows and children pensions[377]

   ix. stamp duty[378]

   x. gaming levies[379] and

   xi. levies under the civil aviation law.[380]

However, in addition to assessment and collection of taxes, the KRA has a much wider role[381] to play in the Kenyan economy. A large part of this wider role relates to tax compliance, as well as compliance with import/export restrictions. Below is a broad list of the wider functions given to the KRA:

   i. to administer and to enforce both tax and non-tax laws as specified in the Kenya Revenue Authority Act as regards assessment, collection and accounting for government revenues;

   ii. to advise on matters relating to the administration and the collection of government revenue;

   iii. to enhance efficiency and effectiveness of tax administration by eliminating bureaucracy, promoting efficient procurement and promoting training and discipline of staff;

   iv. to eliminate tax evasion by simplifying and streamlining procedures, and by improving taxpayer service and education thereby increasing the rate of compliance with taxes;

---

372 The Value Added Tax Act, Laws of Kenya [Chapter 476].
373 The Road Maintenance Levy Fund Act No. 9 of 1993.
374 The Air Passenger Service Charge Act, Laws of Kenya [Chapter 475].
375 The Entertainment Tax Act, Laws of Kenya [Chapter 479].
376 Levied under the Traffic Act, Laws of Kenya [Chapter 403]; the Transport Licensing Act, Laws of Kenya [Chapter 404]; and the Second Hand Motor Vehicle Purchase Tax Act, Laws of Kenya [Chapter 484].
377 The Parliamentary Pensions Act, Laws of Kenya [Chapter 196]; the Widows and Children's Pensions Act, Laws of Kenya [Chapter 195].
378 The Stamp Duty Act, Laws of Kenya [Chapter 480].
379 The Betting, Lotteries and Gaming Act, Laws of Kenya [Chapter 131].
380 The Directorate of Civil Aviation Act, Laws of Kenya [Chapter 394].
381 The Kenya Revenue Authority Act of 1995, Laws of Kenya [Chapter 469].

v. to promote professionalism and eradicate corruption amongst KRA employees by paying adequate salaries that enable the institution to attract and retain competent professionals of integrity and sound ethical morals;

vi. to restore economic independence and the sovereign pride of Kenya by eventually eliminating the perennial budget deficits by creating organizational structures that maximize revenue collection;

vii. to ensure protection of local industries and facilitate economic growth through effective administration of tax laws relating to trade;

viii. to ensure effective allocation of scarce resources in the economy by effectively enforcing tax policies thereby sending the desired incentives and shift signals throughout the country;

ix. to facilitate distribution of income in socially acceptable ways by effectively enforcing tax laws affecting income in various ways;

x. to facilitate economic stability and moderate cyclic fluctuations in the economy by providing effective tax administration as an implementation instrument of the fiscal and stabilization policies; and

xi. to be a 'watchdog' for the government agencies (such as Ministries of Health, Finance, and Agriculture) by controlling exit and entry points for Kenya to ensure that prohibited and illegal goods do not pass through Kenyan borders.

There are serious questions concerning the autonomy of the KRA. There have been repeated calls for the strengthening of the KRA and tax administration in general.[382] The focus of administrative reform has not shifted sufficiently to such areas as the implementation of the provisions of the KRA Act which provide the KRA with both operational and financial independence. Security of tenure for the tax commissioners is paramount so that they are able to make tax decisions without ministerial/political interference. Financial independence is also desirable so that the KRA can develop a performance based culture founded on its ability to raise and retain for its operations a specified percentage of tax collections.

---

382 H Waruhiu 'An Economic and Public Policy Agenda for Kenya' in W Gatheru and R Shaw (eds) *Our Problems, Our Solutions* 1998, Kenya, at 6-7, internet source http//www. iea.or.ke/ourpoblems.asp accessed 1/5/2001.

However, if financial independence is the measure of autonomy, none of the Eastern African tax administrations surveyed have been able to achieve such independence, nor have they been given the freedom to retain for their own use a percentage of taxes collected. Provisions in the KRA Act of 1995 relating to percentage retention remain largely ignored. This situation is also the case for the TRA in Tanzania, where initial proposals to fund the TRA by percentage retention and guarantee its independence, were shelved at the last minute when establishing that organization.

Rwanda

The Rwanda Revenue Authority (RRA) was established as part of the reform program by the Government of Rwanda, designed to restore and strengthen the main economic institutions of the country. These reform programs were instituted following the total collapse of government institutions during Rwanda's genocide of 1994 in which more than 800,000 people were killed. The law establishing the RRA was part of a package of measures aimed at restoring government institutions in Rwanda. The government sought to use this tax administration modernization program to improve its resource mobilization capacity, while at the same time, providing the public with quality customer service.

Like the TRA, the KRA and the URA in East Africa, the RRA is a quasi-autonomous revenue collection agency of the government. It was established in 1998 under a law enacted in November 1997.[383] The RRA is charged with the function of assessing, collecting and accounting for government revenue. In addition, the RRA is also responsible for the collection of some non-tax revenues of the government in accordance with a Ministerial Order issued in May 2003.[384]

The RRA has two other broader functions. It is responsible for providing advice to the government on tax policy matters relating to revenue collections. It is also required to assist taxpayers in understanding and meeting their tax obligations. These broader functions are reflected both in the Vision and Mission Statement of the RRA Corporate Plan. Through an organization's Corporate Plan, one is able to see its strategies and appreciate its immediate and future objectives. The 'vision' and 'mission' encapsulate the objectives of the organization. The vision represents a desired view of the organisation; it is a statement

---

383 Law No. 15 of 1997, Laws of Rwanda.
384 Ministerial Order No. 006/03/10/Min of May 2003.

of its future. On the other hand, the mission is a statement of purpose, the *raison d'être*. It shows why the organization exists. According to the RRA 6th Corporate Plan adopted in 2006, the RRA Vision is "To become a highly efficient and modern revenue collection agency enhancing national growth and development and instilling equity, transparency, and professional values among RRA staff." Its Mission Statement is "To contribute to the national development of Rwanda by maximizing revenue collection at minimum cost and providing quality input to tax policy development, while ensuring a high quality and equitable service."[385]

The taxes administered by RRA include the income tax,[386] customs duties and excise,[387] the value added tax,[388] the property tax and the tax on licenses for carrying out trade and professional activities. The value added tax was introduced in 2001 to replace the sales tax/turnover tax in place since 1991.

The revenue performance of the RRA has been reasonably good. In 2005, the RRA exceeded the revenue collection target by 15.4%, realizing Rwf 173.49 billion against a target of Rwf 150.33 billion. The RRA's revenue performance from 1998 to 2005[389] is reflected in Table 4 below and shows that revenue targets have consistently been surpassed during these eight years, except for the financial year 1999.

TABLE 4 RWANDA REVENUE AUTHORITY PERFORMANCE 1998-2005[390]*

Year	1998	1999	2000	2001	2002	2003	2004	2005
Target	62,8	63,2	62,3	76,8	93,9	112,4	126,3	150,3
Actual	68,2	60,7	65,3	79,5	94,6	118,1	136,2	173,4

* Source: RRA Annual Report 2005

** All Values in Rwandan Francs[390]

Tax Administration Reform and Compliance

It has been said before that taxation generally serves one main objective, to raise revenue to finance government operations. However, a good

385 Rwanda Revenue Authority 6th Corporate Plan 2006, the RRA, Kigali.

386 Levied under the Law on Direct Taxes on Income, Law No 16 of 2005 as complimented by Law No. 25 of 2005 on Tax Procedure, Laws of Rwanda.

387 The Customs Law - Law No. 21 of 2006 and the Import Duty Law - Law No 27 of 2004, Laws of Rwanda.

388 The VAT is levied under the Code of Value Added Tax - Law No 06 of 2001, Laws of Rwanda.

389 Data for later years could not be obtained.

390 RRA Annual Report 2005. All values are in Rwandan Francs (520.45 Rwandan francs is equal to 1 USD$.).

tax system also stimulates economic activity by rejuvenating the productive sectors and generating employment. Tax system reform in Africa has aimed at achieving both revenue adequacy, as well as wider economic objectives. There is a belief that the existence of efficient tax administrations enables governments to formulate effective tax policies and to maximize revenue collections to sufficiently fund government operations.

Looking at the tax modernization programs undertaken in Tanzania, Kenya, Uganda, Rwanda and Zambia, a key purpose in creating new and efficient tax administrations has been to enhance the capacity of the tax administrations in collecting taxes. Therefore, the focus of tax reform has been increased taxation. Rejuvenation of the productive sectors has not been central to the reforms, although tax measures have been taken which aim in this direction.

With optimization of tax revenues in mind, all the statutes setting up the modern tax administrations have included, as a core function of the tax administration, the need to promote optimum compliance with taxes. Ironically, however, while the laws establishing new tax administrations in Kenya, Tanzania, Uganda, Zambia and Rwanda charge the tax authorities with the duty to promote tax compliance through enforcement as well as voluntary compliance, the tax authorities have devoted themselves almost entirely to having in place effective tax enforcement measures. The promotion of voluntary tax compliance has received, at best, token mention in the form of taxpayer charters, as is the case in Tanzania[391] and Zambia,[392] or in the form of adoption of customer service standards, as is the case in Uganda.[393]

Strategies for promoting taxpayer compliance have not varied much among the new tax administrations in Kenya, Tanzania, Uganda, Rwanda and Zambia. At the centre of the measures taken is the desire to adopt the service-culture of market driven private enterprise. Tax administrations in the region are all concerned with the service given to taxpayers. Phrases such as "prompt and courteous", "quality and

---

391 Relevant parts of the Tanzania Taxpayer's Charter are discussed in Chapter 3.

392 ZRA, Taxpayer's Charter, Zambia Revenue Authority, Lusaka, Internet source http://www.zra.org.zm/charter.php accessed 13/11/2007.

393 Uganda has a very elaborate document stipulating the service standards to be adhered to by the URA staff. As is the case for large parts of the TRA Taxpayer's Charter, the URA document sets down performance standards only. The lofty pronouncements contained in this document are not rights that are enforceable in a court of law. They range from the manner of taking telephone calls to such things as dress code for the URA staff.

efficiency", "impartial and fair" constantly recur in taxpayer leaflets issued by the tax administrations in connection with their customer care programs.

In incorporating these customer service concepts into their administration culture, the tax authorities aim to change the mindsets of tax officers so as to enhance procedural justice in the tax administration's interaction with taxpayers.

Taxpayer treatment is an important factor of procedural justice. It impacts significantly on voluntary taxpayer compliance. In dealing with the psychology of the tax compliant mind, particular attention must be given to those things said and done which drive a person to comply with the obligation to pay tax.

Previously, the point has been made that the notion of voluntary taxpayer compliance, as an ideal, assumes the unquestioning acceptance of the noble civic duty to pay taxes. With acceptance of this civic duty, taxpayers voluntarily come forward to disclose their taxable activities accurately and honestly.

This ideal form of voluntary taxpayer compliance is something that was taken for granted in the 1950s and 1960s, when it was generally thought that taxes were the price paid for public services. In developed societies, ideas of 'good citizenship' led citizens to believe that the tax system belonged to the people and that everyone would suffer if some people in the society defaulted on their tax payment obligations or engaged in tax avoidance practices.

However, in today's context, voluntary taxpayer compliance in its ideal form is no longer a reality. Firstly, there is no quid pro quo between taxes paid and government services provided. For developing countries in particular, poor governance invariably leads to an eschewed co-relation between revenue collection and revenue expenditure, such that persistent irresponsible spending by governments bears no relationship to the expectations of the taxpayer. Secondly, in today's world and more so in developing countries, tax regimes have substantially changed. Marginal rates of tax have increased significantly since the 1970s. The high tax rates make it difficult for taxation to gain easy acceptance. In addition, tax laws have grown in complexity and are less understandable. This complexity has led to taxpayers disowning the tax system.

Side by side with the growing alienation of taxpayers from the tax system, has emerged the growing size of tax administrations and the growing extent of their powers, ranking in many countries as the single most feared instrument of the government.

Along with the increased powers of the tax administrations, has been the increased arbitrariness in the use of taxing power and the use of taxes to service interests, which are at times inimical to those of the society at large.

The lack of rules which entrench procedural justice has also made taxing decisions difficult to challenge. In general, there is a growing disquiet reflective of the fact that fairness is fading in tax systems. In this setting, the lofty pronouncements on fairness, equity and courtesy, contained in the emerging taxpayer's charters and tax service standard manuals of the reformed tax administrations, seemed to herald a new beginning. But a decade of living with these reforms, without a significant shift in the service culture and without substantive improvement in procedural justice, has made the sound of these pronouncements ring hollow.

Moreover, as wealth disparities continue to grow in these countries, an apprehension that the tax system is inequitable and favours a few, also grows steadily, leading to an increase in tax avoidance and tax evasion activities. Increased tax evasion and avoidance jeopardises tax collection and the revenue efficiency of the tax system.

It seems that the present day notion of voluntary compliance must shift from that of yester years. It must focus on those factors which influence taxpayer behaviour. If tax laws could be more transparent and understandable,[394] the challenge of guiding taxpayers back into the fold may not be so difficult. While taxpayer education may play a role in tax acceptance, it can only be a limited one. Much effort must be directed at making the tax system relevant and making it more taxpayer friendly. Both the administration of taxes and the use of tax revenues must be directed to the common good of the society. This is the context within which voluntary taxpayer compliance becomes an integral part of the drive for good governance. It is also from this perspective of responsible governance, that taxpayer resistance can be properly understood and effectively combated.

---

394 In one UK case, an exasperated judge had this to say to a taxpayer contesting a tax claim by the Inland Revenue: "Your appeal must be dismissed. I will pass you back your documents. If I may add a word to you, it is that I hope you will not trouble your head further with tax matters, because you seem to have spent a lot of time in going through these various Acts, and if you go on spending your time on Finance Acts and the like, it will drive you silly" (Singleton J in *Briggenshaw v Crabb* (1948) 30 TC 331). In line with the desire for simplicity in tax laws, the Rwanda Revenue Authority claims that, while implementing the tax modernization process, it has revised its tax laws to make them 'modern', 'simple', and 'clear' (Address by the Rwanda Revenue Authority Commissioner General, Mary Baine, Kigali, 2006, internet source http://www.rra.gov.rw/en/ accessed 13/11/2007).

In the context of tax administration, voluntary taxpayer compliance does not merely address taxpayer willingness to pay taxes. The realities of the past years have compelled a shift from the 'ideal based' understanding of voluntary taxpayer compliance underpinned on responsible citizenship alone. The challenge now is to pursue and attain voluntary taxpayer compliance as an objective of tax strategy and tax reform.[395]

The quest for attaining high levels of voluntary taxpayer compliance has proved to be a tortuous one, particularly in developing countries. In developed countries, the current focus is on making tax laws more acceptable and respectable by ensuring that taxpayers' rights are enshrined and observed. In these countries a perception has grown that public trust in tax administration is a prerequisite for fostering voluntary taxpayer compliance. Where people perceive the tax system to be unjust, they remonstrate through non-compliance and other forms of tax resistance.

On the other hand, tax reforms in developing countries appear to focus on prescriptive measures. Since the mid-1990s, many developing countries have embarked upon tax reforms aimed at aligning their tax systems with the shift from centrally planned economies to market economies. In these countries, tax reform often strives to sustain the needs of a nascent market economy, especially the expanding private sector. Initially, it was envisioned that as governments relinquish the centre-stage in the economic playing field, the tax system will be less stringent, both in terms of levels of taxation and the manner of taxation. This shift would lead to the emergence of a more taxpayer-friendly tax system, both in regard to the burden of tax borne by the taxpayer and the manner of extracting that tax. The reform would make the tax administration less intrusive and less coercive. Tanzania proceeded on these assumptions when it embarked on the tax reforms implemented from the mid 1990s.

For Tanzania, the tax reform which was embarked on aimed at the expansion of the tax base, the repeal of taxes which were seen as outmoded or those fringe taxes seen merely as a nuisance to business and to private sector growth, the enhancement of private savings and the improvement of the tax administration to make it more

---

395 This is the pursuit in many developed countries and resulted in emphasis being placed on balancing revenue needs and observance of taxpayers' rights. See K. C. Messere, 'Tax Policy in OECD Countries: Choices and Conflicts' in IBDF Publications BV, Amsterdam, 1993, at 1-16.

compliant with the requirements of due process.[396] Additionally, the tax reforms implemented also sought to achieve technical and revenue efficiency. Thus the reforms adopted were under the banner of revenue maximization from an efficient tax administration. Indeed, successive studies carried out to inform the tax reform process in Tanzania have all focused on this approach.[397]

The assumption by tax policy makers was that once a proper and efficient tax administration is in place, then taxpayer compliance can be achieved. In large measure, this thinking which informs tax administration reform in developing countries, hinges on the notion that voluntary taxpayer compliance must be compelled. This notion of unwilling compliance, relying almost entirely on the design of the tax system, assumes that once captured in an efficient tax net, the taxpayer will comply without having to make a conscious choice as to compliance. Expressed this way, tax compliance becomes dependent on the creation of a tax administration which is well equipped, well staffed and well positioned to administer the taxes levied and to overcome taxpayer resistance. All forms of unwillingness, ignorance, or selfish un-civic tendencies are cast aside. Looking at the trends in taxpayer compliance reform strategies which flow from the TRA, evidence of this thinking clearly abounds.[398]

Tanzania started implementing tax reform strategies in 1995,[399] when the government took seriously the decision to reform its tax laws. What has emerged from this tax reform is that the laws have become more compulsive and in many ways more oppressive as well. Numerous provisions of law have been enacted, giving much wider discretionary powers to tax officers and empowering them to enforce tax collection with the least resistance from taxpayers. The tax laws give the TRA extra-judicial powers such as the power to access taxpayer monies from bank

---

396 Report of the Presidential Commission of Enquiry into Public Revenues, Taxation and Expenditure. Government Printers, Dar es Salaam, 1991.
397 'Tanzania: Proposals for Tax Reform in 1995/96 and Beyond' Ministry of Finance, FAD-IMF, Dar es Salaam, 1997; 'Tanzania: Strengthening the Tax System' Ministry of Finance, FAD-IMF, 1997; and 'Manual of Fiscal Transparency' Washington DC., International Monetary Fund 1999.
398 The TRA Tax Revenue Report for August 2001' 1, Dar es Salaam, 2001;   ' T a x Administration and Structure in Tanzania' The TRA Taxpayer Education Department, 1999; The TRA Annual Report for 1998/1999, Dar es Salaam, 2000, 1-57; 'Proposals for the Review of the Tax Structure in 2001/2002' Report by the Tanzania Revenue Authority, 2001, 1-120.
399 'Amendments made to Tax Laws from 1996 to 2001' Tanzania Revenue Authority, Dar es Salaam, March 2002.

accounts without the need for a court order (even if the tax is disputed and under appeal), the power to attach and sell assets to recover taxes (even where there are ongoing proceedings with respect to the disputed tax), the power to collect taxes from third parties by issuance of agency notices (which can mean the transfer of a taxpayer's liability to the third party) and many more powers. Simultaneously, much wider information gathering powers have been given to tax officers in carrying out audits and verification exercises.[400]

While the tax measures implemented so far have succeeded in increasing revenue collections substantially, this has not been on account of any demonstrated expansion of the tax base, or a demonstrated increase in 'voluntary taxpayer compliance'. Many attribute the increased revenue collection to the unfettered use of taxing power and the use of extra-judicial powers by the TRA in meeting revenue collection targets. There has been no corresponding increase in the taxpayer base.

Tanzania implements 'revenue collection targets', whereby the TRA is assigned by Treasury an annual tax collection amount arising from the Government Budget. This omnibus figure is broken down into monthly revenue collection targets for the TRA. In turn, the TRA assigns sectional targets to the TRA Regional Managers and Section Heads. All have to strive to meet the set targets in a timely manner or risk their employment (which is performance based) being terminated. Such a system is prone to marginalizing the importance of taxpayer rights and the need to foster voluntary taxpayer compliance.

What is also acknowledged is the persisting inability of the tax system to capture a large number of the fast growing economic activities within the informal sector. A number of explanations are put forward for this phenomenon. One is that little effort has been directed to the development of a suitable social infrastructure to support the tax system. Items of social infrastructure which are not yet in place include all those things which enable tracing and verification of taxable persons and taxable entities. Among them are a formal system of personal identification on a national level (the national identity card), a voters' register, an efficient form of business licensing and registration, the surveying and registering of land and many other forms of tracking economic activities. The negative effect which this lack of social infrastructure has on tax compliance is demonstrated by empirical evidence, especially having

---

400 The Income Tax Act 2004, the VAT Act 1997 (as amended), the East African Community Customs Tax Management Act 2005, and the Stamp Duty Act 1977 (as amended).

regard to the reaction of taxpayers to attempts to implement some of the above measures.

In 2004, a pilot scheme was undertaken for the registration of citizens in the Voters Register in the southern regions of Mtwara and Lindi in Tanzania. This exercise is ongoing for the rest of the country. The scheme has encountered strong resistance. Media reports show that people in those two regions were reluctant to be entered in the voters' register because they believe the purported voters' register is only a ploy to identify their existence and whereabouts for the purpose of taxation.[401] People are similarly apprehensive about the initiative of the Government to implement a project which seeks to ensure that all land is registered and owners issued with ownership licenses (a lesser form of certificates of title).[402] While the stated objective of the project is firstly to secure people's ownership of land and enable them to access credit financing, many refuse to accept this explanation at face value. They suspect there is a tax motive and are reluctant to cooperate. The TRA's Taxpayer Education Department repeatedly faces similar resistance in its various campaigns to enhance taxpayer awareness and inculcate the culture of voluntary taxpayer compliance.[403]

Preliminary inquiries on what appears to be the perplexing challenge of achieving voluntary taxpayer compliance in developing countries suggest that tax reform strategists are pursuing an incorrect approach. Research carried out in Tanzania has ascertained that people are not averse to taxation. They understand the role and importance of taxation in society.[404] What has been lacking is the necessary effort to put in place the social and economic conditions which enhance the desire to comply with taxes.

It seems that efforts aimed at achieving voluntary taxpayer compliance have not been as successful because voluntary taxpayer compliance is not properly contextualized. While it is correct to take voluntary taxpayer compliance as a tax administration challenge, it is wrong to confine

401 President Benjamin Mkapa was reported to have condemned politicians who were bringing up tax to scare people. See, Daily Newspaper of 13/10/2004.

402 The President has invited Professor Hernando De Soto (the re-knowned Peruvian economist) to Tanzania to implement the sort of economic rights reforms suggested in his book *Why Capitalism Triumphs in the West and Fails Everywhere Else*, (2000) Basic Books.

403 This was revealed by the Taxpayer Education Director, Mr. Mmanda in reply to a question asked at a workshop held in Dar es Salaam at Bahari Beach Hotel on 14th February 2005.

404 O. H. Fjeldstad and J. J. Semboja "Why People Pay Taxes: The Case of the Development Levy in Tanzania" 2001: p.21-29.

it to an exclusively tax administration issue. Such a narrow approach leads to emphasis being placed upon the behaviour of taxpayers, rather than the manner of governance which underpins the tax administration and to a large extent determines taxpayer attitude to government and to taxation. The significance of good governance and that of the tax authority/taxpayer relationship is not sufficiently appreciated. Properly contextualised, this trio relationship places taxation within the context of governance. In this broad context of governance, it is possible to develop compliance principles which enhance voluntary taxpayer compliance. It is for this reason that the objective of voluntary taxpayer compliance and the understanding of it is being re-examined in this study.

As it is, the responses to tax resistance by tax authorities and governments over the years have been varied. In their bid to combat taxpayer resistance, governments have succeeded only in making tax laws more complex and tax administrations more oppressive. There are recorded instances of heavy reliance on stringent and indiscriminate sanctions in dealing with taxpayer resistance,[405] which trend has produced more non-compliance. Professor Shavell once stated that, "it is impossible to deter a person with no assets by the threat of monetary sanctions."[406] The taxpayer will indulge in avoidance or evasion if such conduct produces more benefit than the total punishment provided for violation, multiplied by the likelihood of punishment.[407]

In examining the impact of procedural justice and customer care on taxpayer attitudes towards payment of tax, the question posed is whether a fair/courteous treatment of taxpayers will boost taxpayer disposition towards voluntary tax payment. What role does effectiveness of service delivery play in shaping taxpayer attitudes towards the tax administration and towards the tax system in general? An attempt is made here to contrast effectiveness of service with the 'detection and punishment' approach to see whether the two approaches contradict or compliment each other. In doing this, an attempt is made to show how taxpayer attitudes and tax compliance are affected differently by certain tax regimes.

---

405 S Kramer 'An Economic Analysis of Criminal Attempt: Marginal Deterrence and the Optimal Structure of Sanctions' (1990) 81 *Journal of Criminal Law and Criminology* 398.

406 S Shavell 'Criminal Law and the Optimal Use of Non-monetary Sanctions as a Deterrent' (1985) 85 *Columbia Law review* 1232-1262.

407 A Blumstein *in* P Sawicki (ed) *Income Tax Compliance: A Report of the ABA Section of Taxation* International Conference on Income Tax Compliance, American Bar Association, Chicago, Ill., 1983.

In this discourse, the mind-set of both the tax officer as well as the taxpayer is addressed, so as to assess whether the tax modernization programs that have been embarked on are correctly premised.

It is human nature to expect to be treated with courtesy and respect. Nobody wants to suffer indignity, more so where the indignity results from the taking by another person of what one believes to be rightfully owned. Personal endeavour, economic enterprise and employment toil are intrinsically individualistic. If a person's gain from endeavour, enterprise and toil must be shared with the government, as taxes aim to do, then the appeal for sharing has to be directed to the psychology of the producer/taxpayer.

In most cases however, the method traditionally used or preferred in collecting tax revenues is enforcement. Enforcement, to a large measure, entails the actual use of force or the threat of use of force. Enforcement relies on the detection and punishment of non-compliant persons. The use of tax audits and inspections, criminal prosecutions, fines and jail terms, all seek to induce submission by intimidation.[408]

However, enforcement presupposes the existence of sufficient capacity to police non-compliance. This ability to undertake audits and inspections extensively must exist at a level sufficient enough to reach all the non-compliant taxpayers. No tax authority has that unlimited ability, or possesses such ability to the ideal levels desired. The inability to provide unlimited funding to tax administrations makes it impossible to achieve enforcement levels which would make it unnecessary to rely on other compliance strategies.

It is notable that the modernized tax administrations of Kenya, Tanzania, Uganda, Rwanda and Zambia, all made it a priority to set up tax audit and tax investigation departments. A close look at these audit departments shows that they have spent the best part of ten years of existence putting in place systems and procedures that will improve the tax administrations' ability to detect and counteract tax non-compliance. It is possible to argue on behalf of these young tax administrations that, given the short period that the TRA, the URA, the ZRA, the KRA and the RRA have been in existence, it is too early to judge whether their enforcement strategies are effective. However, a ten year period is by no means a brief one. If the effectiveness of the enforcement program of the audit and tax investigation departments has not borne significant positive results, there may be a need to rethink this enforcement compliance strategy. In Chapter Seven, the effectiveness of the enforcement program of the TRA is assessed.

---

408 C Rossoti, 'Modernizing America's Tax Agency' (1999) 83 *Tax Notes* 1191 at 1195.

There is also another drawback with enforcement, namely that it triggers a negative chain reaction. It produces more tax resistance because of its intrusiveness. Tax planning and avoidance activity become more intricate, aiming to beat the increased detection ability.

On the other hand too, the inadequate record keeping of tax administrations such as the TRA and the poor state of records kept by many taxpayers in countries such as Tanzania, make it unrealistic to rely only on detection and punishment for effective tax compliance.[409] As noted before, fear of detection and punishment becomes an effective tool of compliance only when there is a real likelihood of being caught. When that likelihood recedes, either because of a perceived lack of capacity, or because of the sheer enormity of the task, then detection and punishment cease to be an effective deterrent against non-compliance.

In the past chapters, it was noted that the tax base in Tanzania is still very narrow. Taxpayer registration is proceeding at a very slow pace with only 686,980 taxpayers registered and assigned a Tax Identification Number (TIN) for income tax purposes.[410] The reported population of Tanzania by 2006 was 37.5 million people.[411] One may safely assume that at least one third of these (12 million) are of adult age, and therefore productive and liable to payment of tax. If one adds to this number the companies and other forms of business entities also given TIN registration, then clearly a very small number of taxpayers are captured, demonstrating that tax registration has been quite ineffective.

The position is said to be the same in Kenya,[412] leading to calls for extending the type of transactions which should require a Personal Identification Number (PIN)[413] to complete, so that such information can build up a good pool of data on taxable activities and the scales

---

409 The study by Professor Maliyamkono referred to in Chapter One shows that most individuals in Tanzania do not keep a record of their income earning activities. Likewise, many small companies do not maintain proper financial records, or engage auditors to examine their transactions and prepare audited accounts for submission to tax or other regulatory authorities.

410 A large part of those having a TIN registration are corporate entities, which shows that there is very little success in bringing more individual taxpayers into the tax net.

411 The Economic Survey 2006, Ministry of Planning, Economy and Empowerment, Dar es Salaam, June 2007, Table A – Basic Economic Statistics, xv.

412 E Maina 'Reduction and Payment of domestic debt' in W Gatheru and R Shaw (eds) *Our Problems, Our Solutions* 1998, Kenya, at 6, internet source http//www.iea.or.ke/ourpoblems.asp accessed 1/5/2001.

413 While taxpayers in Tanzania are assigned a TIN, in Kenya they are assigned a PIN (personal identification number). In both cases the TIN or PIN is a unique computer generated number used by the tax authority for the identification of a taxpayer.

of revenues by various people and entities within the economy.[414] This extension has not happened in Kenya.

The TRA estimates that the underground economy in Tanzania constitutes about two thirds of the official GDP.[415] A report issued by DANIDA[416] in October 2003 seems to agree. The report notes that Tanzania's tax base is very narrow with 28% of GDP being generated by non-market production and an estimated 15% by the informal sector. The non-government formal sector accounts for only 47% of GDP.[417] More recent data published by Professor Maliyamkono in 2009 (already discussed) shows the trend to have worsened since the DANIDA report was issued.

If taxpayer identification and registration remains at a very low level, enforcement cannot work effectively. Alternative strategies must be pursued rigorously.

Given the above limitations for enforcement as a compliance strategy, persuasion (otherwise referred to as the cooperative approach) is now emerging as a serious alternative to enforcement in the quest for developing effective taxpayer-compliance strategies. Using the cooperative approach, taxpayers are encouraged to pay their taxes voluntarily, without the need to invoke sanctions. Rossoti[418] has argued that the use of this strategy in tax revenue collection bolsters taxpayer's willingness to pay their taxes voluntarily.[419] He is supported in this by Torgler,[420] who believes that rather than resort to high-handed directives and the issuance of threatening notices, tax administration efforts must now be focused on taxpayer education, the provision of free tax compliance information, the giving of taxpayer compliance kits and the application of reward and incentives.[421] Torgler believes that these efforts show greater promise in increasing taxpayer compliance than intimidation does.

---

414 E Maina, 'Reduction and Payment of domestic debt' in W Gatheru and R Shaw (eds) *Our Problems, Our Solutions* 1998, Kenya, at 6, internet source http//www.iea.or.ke/ourpoblems.asp accessed 1/5/2001.

415 The TRA *A Decade of TRA Transformation 1996-2006*, Tanzania Revenue Authority, October 2006, Chapter 8 at 87.

416 DANIDA, Project Document, 'Danish Support to the Tanzania Revenue Authority, Phase II 2003/04 – 2007/08' October 2003, Danida File 104.Tanzania.213

417 *Ibid.* 7.

418 C Rossoti 'Modernizing America's Tax Agency' (1999) 83 *Tax Notes* 1191 at 1195.

419 *Ibid.*

420 B Torgler *Tax Compliance and Tax Morale: a Theoretical and Empirical Analysis* Cheltenham UK 2007; also B Torgler *Tax Morale: Theory and Empirical Analysis of Tax Compliance*, PhD Dissertation, University of Basel, 2003, at 123.

421 *Ibid.*

The cooperative approach has also come to be favoured in tax collection because research has shown that tax enforcement does not explain entirely the patterns of taxpayer compliance.[422] In many jurisdictions, it is known that very few tax evaders are detected and prosecuted. Yet compliance levels even in these countries of low enforcement remain relatively high.[423] This seems to be the case in Tanzania as well. In these circumstances, to argue that direct enforcement provides a complete answer to tax non-compliance is not logical. Other factors are at play in influencing tax compliance. Factors such as the trust people have in the government, the reasonable level at which social services are provided by the government, the transparency with which the government operates, the fairness of the tax system, the accountability of the tax administration and the accountability of the government generally, all have a significant impact on tax compliance. These factors combine well to produce a public desire to assume tax obligations voluntarily and to own the tax system.

The tax collecting authority has a big role to play when it comes to influencing the taxpayer's behaviour towards voluntary tax payment. Its treatment of taxpayers will largely determine their behaviour and response to taxation.

So what role should be played by tax administrations such as the TRA in shaping taxpayer behaviour and moving the taxpaying public towards higher levels of voluntary tax payment?

The available data shows a compelling case for a cooperative approach, rather than an antagonistic one as represented by enforcement. In the survey carried out by the National Bureau of Statistics referred to previously, the report indicated that only two in every ten taxpayers have confidence in the tax regime.[424] The report also noted a widespread perception that the TRA officers demand or accept bribes in the discharge of official duties.[425] Of the 2,399 taxpayers surveyed, 10.5% had offered bribes to get services. This number may not reflect fully the seriousness of the problem as many other persons interviewed declined to answer the survey question on bribes within the TRA for fear of prosecution.[426]

---

422 There are scholars who argue that the level of compliance is higher where the threat of sanction is not the only driving force behind tax compliance. See J Andreon, B Erard and J Feistein 'Tax Compliance' (1998) 36 *Journal of Economic Literature* 818-860.

423 One needs to caution that this is true only in the context of the limited tax base within which taxes are regularly collected from the known taxpayers. In taking this view, no consideration is given to the big number of individuals and entities which operate in the informal sector and are largely untaxed.

424 National Bureau of Statistics 2003: p.14.

425 *Ibid.*

426 *Ibid.*

The reasons given for this serious integrity problem in the TRA are worth noting. According to this survey report, one third of those who gave bribes to the TRA officers said that their motive was to speed up the process in receiving the services they wanted.[427] However, another group, making up 41.7% of those interviewed, said they gave bribes so as to get assistance from the tax officers to pay reduced taxes.[428] A third group, making up 14.2%, gave bribes to create a conducive relationship with the officers in relation to future tax transactions.[429] Whatever the reasons for seeking and/or accepting bribes, the lack of integrity on the part of tax officers and the officers' failure to discharge their tax functions impartially, greatly undermines the public respect and confidence for the TRA and prevents acceptance by the public of the tax system.

It is no surprise, therefore, that the same report shows that 28.4% of taxpayers surveyed believe that the tax administration is not good. That is to say, it does not meet taxpayer needs. Only a meagre 3.2% of those interviewed responded that the services of the tax authority were excellent. At the other extreme, 6.3% responded that the services offered were poor or very poor.

The survey results documented by the National Bureau of Statistics, as shown above, demonstrate the degree to which taxpayer thinking is influenced by the treatment received from those who administer taxes. Taxpayers wish to be served with dignity. The customer care concept which has come to be applied to tax administration and now shapes the thinking of tax administrators, has found favour because there is significant taxpayer dissatisfaction with the tax authorities.

The TRA has declared as one of its strategic objectives the desire to provide high quality and responsive customer service.[430] The TRA identifies two ways for achieving this. The first is to enhance the level of tax knowledge among taxpayers. The second is to improve the quality of customer service provided to taxpayers.[431]

---

427 The ploy used by tax officers is to delay the services so that the statutory time limit may expire. The threat of time bar, the burden of interest and penalties for late payment, leave the taxpayer vulnerable to bribe extraction.

428 *Supra,* note 355 at 15.

429 *Ibid.*

430 The TRA second Five Year Corporate Plan 2003/04 – 2007/08.

431 The TRA First Five Year Corporate Plan 1998/99-2002/2003 and the TRA Second Five Year Corporate Plan 2003/2004-2007/2008. The same thrust is being carried into the Draft TRA Third Five Year Corporate Plan 2008/2009-2012/2013 to be adopted some time in 2008.

Deliberate steps have been taken to change the institutional orientation of the TRA from a government department/parastatal, to a more corporate entity. There is an improved telephone inquiry system in place with toll free numbers for taxpayers to use to access information on any tax issue or compliance requirement. The TRA has also made its front desk operations more responsive to quality customer care, ensuring that front desk officers are sufficiently knowledgeable about the organization and about the various taxes administered, or at least know where to direct an inquirer for appropriate answers.

The TRA seems to be vindicated in its recognition of premier customer care as an imperative in the drive to better taxpayer compliance. In the survey report by the National Bureau of Statistics, referred to above, a majority of 69% of taxpayers interviewed believed that better customer relations would encourage taxpayers to be compliant.

The more recent survey report by PricewaterhouseCoopers[432] recommended *inter alia* that the taxpayer education program of the TRA be expanded to reach more taxpayers. It also recommended that a help line be set-up to assist in dealing with taxpayer inquiries, giving taxpayers information which improves their ability to comply with taxation. The view shared here is that taxpayers who receive sufficient guiding information on taxation are likely to comply better with tax filings and tax payment requirements. The availability of tax information will reduce the amount of errors in filling tax returns and claiming tax relief. This reduction in errors will, in turn, reduce the workload of tax officers who process tax returns and claims.

In improving the quality of its service to taxpayers, the TRA has adopted a wide range of measures. These measures now comprise the TRA tax compliance program,[433] and include the following measures:

   i. Taxpayer education;

   ii. Taxation teaching in schools;

   iii. Improved access to tax services;

   iv. Simplification of procedures for tax payment;

   v. Improved data keeping;

   vi. Simplifying tax filings;

   vii. Front desk improvement;

---

432 PricewaterhouseCoopers 2006.

433 R. M. Bird, 2004: p.134-150 at 136, makes the point that "facilitating compliance involves such elements as improving services to taxpayers by providing them clear instructions, understandable forms, and assistance and information as necessary."

viii. Taxpayer satisfaction surveys and

ix. Taxpayer registration;

According to the TRA Act, the TRA has a duty to take all necessary measures to ensure that the revenue laws are complied with.[434] In doing so, the TRA is required to educate taxpayers on their tax responsibilities with regard to all taxes administered by the TRA. It is also the duty of the TRA to educate taxpayers on taxpayer rights. With this responsibility in mind, taxpayer education was one of the initial tax measures embarked upon by the TRA when established in 1996. It was seen as a key component in promoting taxpayer compliance.

A department known as the Taxpayers' Public Education Department, with the mandate to educate the public on tax matters, was created within the TRA. The functions of this department are mainly to disseminate knowledge to the public on the importance of paying taxes voluntarily, and the role of taxpayers in meeting their civic responsibility with regard to taxes.

The program for taxpayer education includes a weekly radio program, regular radio announcements, live radio talk back programs, television programs explaining various taxes, seminars and workshops which target various types of taxpayers, advertisements/commercials on radio, television programs, infomercials, print media advertisements, press releases/statements, booklets, tax guides, leaflets, pamphlets, public announcements done by mobile units in residential areas, distribution/sale of souvenir articles such as calendars, T-shirts, bags, pens, (which carry a tax message), and music performances or drama pieces involving taxation.

However, an examination of the taxpayer education program undertaken by the TRA shows that it focuses almost entirely on tax compliance. There is very little effort to educate taxpayers on taxpayer rights. The Taxpayer's Charter, which was adopted at the end of 2006, stands out as a lone effort in this direction. But, as noted above, the TRA has taken seriously the duty to impart knowledge of taxes and tax payment procedures as a civic obligation.

It is arguable that the funding of the Taxpayer Education Department has not sufficiently reflected the importance that the TRA claims to attach to this compliance measure. Money provided to fund taxpayer education since 1996 is shown in Table 5.

---

434 Section 5 (2) (g).

TABLE 5: BUDGET ALLOCATION FOR THE TRA TAXPAYER EDUCATION
ACTIVITIES* (VALUES ARE BILLION TANZANIA SHILLINGS)

1996/97	1998/99	2002/03	2003/04	2004/05	2005/06	2006/07	2007/08
0,210	0,240	0,287	0,491	0,382	0,671	1,175	1,232

* Source: The TRA Annual Reports (amounts given for some of the years could not be obtained)

** Values are billion Tanzania Shillings

Although Table 5 shows that there has been a consistent growth in annual budget allocations for taxpayer education activities, the allocation as a percentage of total TRA expenditure has been negligible at around 1% only. This level of funding does not seem to reflect the seriousness that both the TRA and government claim to attach to promoting taxpayer education as an important component in voluntary taxpayer compliance.

The taxpayer education program of the TRA has not been directed only to those already at the tax-paying age. The TRA recognizes that the culture of tax compliance needs to be nurtured from an early age if young people are to grow into adulthood as law abiding citizens and tax compliant individuals. Given this recognition, the TRA has introduced tax education in primary schools as part of its civic education program to promote tax awareness. The TRA also carries out school visits to secondary schools, explaining to youngsters the various taxes levied in the country, but also explaining to them the importance of payment of tax as a civic duty.

The other customer service improvement measure undertaken by the TRA is to restructure itself as an institution in order to improve accessibility to its offices and to its officers. Traditionally, the TRA offices have been set up on a tax-type basis, namely, VAT Office, Income Tax Office and Customs Office. The TRA is now moving away from this tax-type arrangement and promoting office integration, whereby one office of the TRA undertakes all tax functions. Such integrated tax offices have been set up at the regional and district levels. Officers for the three major taxes share the same building, even though their operations and reporting lines continue to be distinct. A further move to actually merge the administration of some taxes commenced with the creation in 2002 of the Large Taxpayers Department, which made it possible for large taxpayers to deal with one office only in respect of all taxes (excluding customs). This reorganisation was followed in 2005 by the merging of VAT and Income Tax into what is now known as the

Domestic Revenue Department. These administrative reforms were also carried out at the district level, then at the regional level and have been finally implemented at the zone level.[435]

Another customer service improvement measure undertaken by the TRA to improve tax compliance is the simplification of tax payment procedures. In 2001, the TRA invited one of the commercial banks to locate a bank branch at the TRA headquarters dedicated to receiving tax payments on the TRA account. With time, more commercial banks have become involved in the project. Direct payment into banks has now been extended to all regional centres. The banking facilities are located within the TRA premises in all places where this service is available. With time too, it is intended to remove the burden of paying tax by cash so that taxpayers are able to use bank cards for all tax payment transactions. Direct payment into banks has also improved cash management, reducing theft incidents and cheque frauds.

Improvement of the payments procedure also aimed to interface the TRA electronically with commercial banks. Currently, the TRA is interfaced with the CRDB Bank, NBC Ltd and National Microfinance Bank. Arrangements are underway to interface the TRA with three more banks: namely, Standard Chartered Bank, Citibank and Stanbic Bank. The TRA provided these commercial banks with specifications of the TRA requirements. By June 2007, NMB and CRDB completed the development of the interface between the TRA and their systems, and NBC Ltd did so soon thereafter using the ITAX.[436]

The initiative for electronic interfacing with banks had to be supported by an amendment of the Evidence Act,[437] to allow electronic records obtained in the course of investigations to be used as evidence. Since the introduction of the system of payment through banks, 97% of payments made through banks are collected free from fraudulent acts. The remaining 3% of revenue is collected from district offices and other revenue sources such as stamp duty, driving license and road license fees, for which payment is made by cash transaction.

Another customer service improvement measure undertaken by the TRA is in relation to data keeping. Improved data keeping is the key

---

435 There are 127 Administrative Districts, falling into 26 Regions. The Regions are grouped into 5 Zones.

436 ITAX stands for Integrated Tax Administration System.

437 Written Laws Miscellaneous Amendment Act No 2007 (enacted by Parliament in February 2007). This is an amendment to the rules of evidence to enable the use of electronic evidence in courts of law. Previously, the only evidence allowed with regard to written material was printed matter in original form. The amendment became effective in March 2007.

component of the computerization program of the TRA and aims at improving access to taxpayer data by tax officers. The TRA believes that if, at the press of a button and through the TIN, a tax officer is able to access all the information relating to a taxpayer's activities for all tax purposes (income tax, stamp duty, VAT), then the tax officer is able to serve the taxpayer better, attend to inquiries faster and also provide more precise answers to taxpayer queries.

The computerization of the TRA systems also aims at doing away with manual systems and providing officers with electronic systems in relation to the collection of income tax, VAT and customs, which improves the functionality of the TRA as a tax collection agency. Electronic storage of taxpayer data makes information retrieval easy, enabling the tax officer to access and work with the available information all the time. This reduces substantially the guess work or arbitrary estimates which have characterized tax collection practice in Tanzania for a long time. With accurate tax assessments, there are fewer tax disputes and the tax system gains easy acceptance.

In its desire to ensure that it provides high quality services to its customers, the TRA commenced the implementation of a Quality Management System (QMS) in 2004/05 with the aim of being ISO 9001:2000 certified by the International Organization for Standardization (ISO). A Working Group for the implementation of the QMS was appointed in July 2005. The group comprised the Quality Coordinator, Quality Auditor and Quality Manager for Large Taxpayers Department (LTD). Fourteen Internal Quality Management System Auditors (QMSA) were appointed in March 2006 to oversee the Quality Management System audit throughout the organization. The Quality Policy and Quality Manual were prepared and approved by the Quality Management System Steering Committee in June 2006.

Awareness training was conducted for all heads of department at the LTD, attended by LTD staff (as this was the pilot site), the QMSA and representatives from all other departments. The QMSA attended further intensive Quality Management System Audit training. As a result, the QMSA was able to carry out two audits at LTD in June and October 2006.

An External Auditor, M/S BVQI Company Limited of the United Kingdom, was appointed to carry out a certification audit in November 2006. The auditor recommended LTD for ISO 9001:2000 certification. LTD was ISO certified on 18th December 2006.

Following this achievement, a commitment was made by the TRA Management to ensure that the entire organization implements the

Quality Management System and for it to be ISO 9001:200- certified during the 2007/08 financial year. This was achieved in 2008/09.

Another customer service improvement measure implemented by the TRA is simplification of information filing by taxpayers. Income tax returns and import declarations have been re-designed, making them simpler to complete and also streamlining the information required. For instance, previous customs import forms comprised nine separate documents, but now the customs declaration required is only the Single Bill of Entry (SBE), which caters for all purposes for clearing goods from customs. This move cuts out much of the bureaucracy normally attending the clearing of goods, and assists importers and their clearing agents to go through the customs process more quickly.

Front desk improvement is another customer service improvement measure being undertaken by the tax administration in Tanzania. The TRA has set up front desks as the first contact point at every office of the TRA. In doing so, it has endeavoured to ensure that the front desk becomes an efficient enquiry point for taxpayers. The front desks are designed to project a friendly image, enhancing the customer care program of the TRA.

The TRA professes to take seriously any feedback or suggestions it gets from taxpayers, encouraging them to make suggestions and to express views about the service they receive from the TRA through suggestion boxes installed at its offices. All suggestions and views collected from the suggestion boxes are referred to the Public Relations Manager for follow-up action.

Taxpayer registration is also an important part of the TRA program for customer service improvement. Taxpayer registration promotes compliance by ensuring that each taxpayer is unique and that there is no duplication of identities. The TIN was introduced as a sole identifier for all taxpayers in 2004/05.

In an effort to enhance the TIN system and improve efficiency in the registration process, ten regions, namely Arusha, Mwanza, Kilimanjaro, Shinyanga, Dodoma, Morogoro, Mbeya, Tanga, Zanzibar and Dar es Salaam, were linked to the Central Server. This link enabled these regions to print and issue certificates, update taxpayer information, query and search in the TIN central database from local workstations.

After centralization, an average of one hour is taken to process the certificates, compared to three weeks prior to centralization. As previously noted, by June 2010 a total of 686,980 taxpayers were registered on the system. The system has been incorporated and operates as the registration module for the ITAX system.

However, as noted in Chapter One, taxpayer registration has proceeded quite sluggishly with only a total of 686,980 taxpayers registered by June 2010 in a country whose adult population is at least 18 million.[438] These TIN registrations include companies and other business entities. So it is baffling that the number is so low,[439] especially taking into account the wide range of activities which the TIN rules say cannot be completed without a TIN registration.

In speaking of an adult population of 18 million, who in one way or another must be income earners, only marginal allowance needs to be made for unemployment.[440] There is very little unemployment in Tanzania because Tanzania has a very small urban population. Most people of productive age live in the rural areas, engaged in primary agriculture. Therefore unemployment is not a significant factor in defining the tax base.

However, the real consideration in bringing the rural population and informal sector operators into the tax net would be the structure of the income tax rates. As noted in Chapter Two, the taxpayer surveys carried out in Tanzania show that there are already complaints that income tax rates are too high. It was also noted that the tax rates peak at a much lower level of income because of generally low incomes in Tanzania, as compared to other countries, where the higher tax bands apply only to truly high incomes. Given this consideration, income tax thresholds will need to be lowered, as well as the income tax rates, to ensure that expansion of the tax base to include the rural population and the informal sector does not distort the equity of taxation.

One needs to refer to the desire to vastly expand the TIN registration program, especially with the enactment of the Income Tax Act 2004. In

---

438 According to the census statistics issued by the government, Tanzania had a population of 33.6 million people by 2002 (the last census). At least 54% of these are above the age of 15 years. Internet source http://www.tanzania.go.tz/census See also *The Economic Survey 2006*, issued by the Ministry of Planning, Economy and Empowerment, Dar es Salaam, June 2007 which estimates the current population in 2007 to be 37.5 million people (Table A at xv).

439 One would expect an aggressive taxpayer registration program to reach at least half the adult population in a period of ten years from 1997, but information from the TRA Modernisation Program Manager indicates that the TIN registrations shown in the Table relate mostly to corporate taxpayers, as very few individuals have been captured.

440 The Economic Survey 2006, Ministry of Planning, Economy and Empowerment, Dar es Salaam, June 2007, where it is noted on page 88 that in 2005/06, out of the 18.3 million people in employment, 76.5% were in agriculture, 9.3% were in the informal sector, 8% in the private formal sector, 3.5% were domestic workers, and 2.8% were in the public sector; only those in the private and public sector make up the tax base (for direct taxes).

terms of this Act, a TIN registration became a mandatory requirement for a wide range of transactions, including the registration or transfer of vehicles, registration of land title, application for business license, or other licenses such as fishing, logging, hunting, mining, industrial licenses, VAT registration, incorporation of new company or registration of patent or mark, clearing of goods through customs and contracts for supply of goods or services to public sector institutions. Given this wide ranging requirement for the TIN, the low number of TIN registrations can only be attributed to failure to enforce the requirement.

On a completely different point, considering the broad requirement for a TIN, a real concern is the use to which the information fed against a taxpayer's TIN will be put when it is fully computerized and bar-coded. This concern arises from what was said earlier when discussing the right to privacy and confidentiality of information: that it is quite easy for the tax information gathered or provided to the TRA to be shared between tax departments, as well as with other government departments.

5

The Tax Framework in Tanzania

Introduction

Building on the theme that tax laws ought to be designed to encourage voluntary tax compliance, this chapter examines the tax framework in Tanzania. It analyses the Income Tax Act, the VAT Act and Customs Act. These three statutes regulate the payment of income tax, VAT and customs duties, which are the three major taxes in Tanzania. The objective is to examine the content and show how these laws are administered and to assess the extent to which provisions in these statutes encourage or discourage voluntary taxpayer compliance. The question to be answered is whether the content of the laws creates an environment that is conducive to voluntary taxpayer compliance.

Income Taxation and Payment

In Tanzania, income tax is levied under the Income Tax Act (ITA).[441] For residents, it is an annual charge on total income on a world-wide

---

441 The Income Tax Act No. 11 of 2004.

basis.[442] A resident taxpayer's total income from all sources world-wide is computed for the year and subjected to income tax. Non-residents are liable to income tax only on income derived from Tanzania. Income tax is mostly on a calendar year basis (January to December), but a taxpayer may seek approval to report income on a different year basis to coincide with the financial year of his/her business.

There are three methods of paying income tax. Tax may be withheld at source,[443] or may be paid by the taxpayer in quarterly instalments,[444] or may be paid at the end of the year after an assessment is issued by the TRA.[445]

Looking fairly at the scheme of the Income Tax Act, it appears that the legislature tried to strike a balance for competing considerations and addressed the varying positions of different taxpayers with regard to the manner of payment of tax and the timing for such payments. The three payment methods, namely, withholding tax arrangement, instalment payment and payment by assessment, all serve different objectives.

Payment by withholding tax applies to three categories of income. Firstly, it applies to income from employment and is collected by employers through the *pay as you earn* (PAYE) arrangement.[446] Employers deduct and remit the tax to the TRA. The withholding tax arrangement also applies to income in the form of dividends, interest, natural resource payments, rents, royalties and retirement payments. All persons making such payments are required to deduct income tax at the time of making the payment, whether to a resident or a non-resident.[447] Finally, the withholding tax payment applies to payment of fees for technical services in mining operations and to payment of insurance premiums from Tanzania to a non-resident person.[448] The obligation to withhold tax is on the resident person who makes a payment to which the withholding tax arrangement applies.

The withholding tax arrangement is intended to maximise tax collection by trapping the tax at the source of payment, be it a salary, a dividend, a royalty, rent, or other. In collecting tax at source before the

---

442 Sections 4, 5, and 6 (ITA). Under section 20 (2) it is possible to pay income tax on a basis other than the calendar year provided approval by the Commissioner for Domestic Revenue is obtained.
443 Section 81 of the Income Tax Act.
444 Section 88 of the Income Tax Act.
445 Section 91of the Income Tax Act.
446 Section 81 (1) of the Income Tax Act.
447 Section 82 (1) (a), (b) of the Income Tax Act.
448 Section 83 (1) (a), (b) of the Income Tax Act.

payment reaches the recipient, the possibility of tax evasion is minimised. There is also a psychological advantage to both the tax authority, as well as the taxpayer. For the taxpayer, there is an advantage in avoiding the agony of receiving money and then having to surrender it to the tax authority, which experience when in financial need can be quite disconcerting. For the tax authority, there is a significant psychological advantage in avoiding the aggravation that comes with dealing directly with the taxpayer when demanding tax.

There is also cost saving for the tax authority when the expenditure associated with collecting tax on salaries, rents, royalties, dividends and fees (i.e. the cost of the paperwork, the accounting, the record keeping and the bank payments) is all passed-on to third parties.

There are complaints from entities upon which the duty to withhold tax is imposed, complaints that the cost of tax withholding ought not to be borne by them without allowing a tax deduction for the cost or some other form of compensation. The explanation that this is a civic duty or service to the nation is inadequate to answer this complaint. If the ITA was to provide a tax deduction for the withholding costs incurred by the third parties in withholding tax for the TRA, this would go a long way in bringing fairness to the system.

Taxpayers, who derive income from business, an investment, or from employment, where the employer is not under the obligation to withhold tax, are required to pay income tax using the instalment payment arrangement.[449] There are four quarterly instalments falling due on 31st March, 30th June, 30th September and 31st December. A taxpayer who pays income tax by instalment must work out an estimate of the income tax payable for the year of income during the first quarter of the year and make the four payments on the due dates.[450]

The payment of tax by instalment serves a dual purpose. It spreads the burden of payment, thus easing the strain on cash flow. It also accelerates tax payment and evens the flow of tax revenue into government coffers. In addition, the instalment payment mechanism is intended to increase the trust levels between the tax authority and the taxpayers. It reinforces the trust in the authority by taxpayers, which is important in increasing the levels of voluntary taxpayer compliance. By allowing taxpayers to assess themselves and pay taxes accordingly, this mechanism internalises a civic responsibility owed by every citizen to discharge tax obligations without being forced to do so by the state's coercive instruments.

---

449 Section 88 (1) (a), (b) of the Income Tax Act 2004.
450 Section 89 (1) (b) of the Income Tax Act 2004.

All taxpayers (who are not covered by the withholding tax arrangement) are required to file income tax returns with the Commissioner for Domestic Revenue not later than six months following the end of the income year.[451] They include persons deriving income from business or the self employed. The ITA provides for three types of assessments, namely: self assessments,[452] best judgement assessments,[453] and jeopardy assessments.[454] However, all assessments are subject to adjustment if it transpires that the original assessment did not truly reflect the full extent of the taxpayer's tax position.[455] Employees subject to the PAYE system do not have to file income tax returns unless they have income from other sources. Where this is the case, the employee's total income, including salaries, is recomputed upon filing a return and tax is assessed at the appropriate scale, taking into account the total income.

A self assessment is one made by the taxpayer upon filing the income tax return. In essence it is the estimated amount of the tax payable for that year of income as shown in the taxpayer's return.[456] The assessment is taken to be made on the date of filing the income tax return and, where no return is filed, the assessment is deemed to be made on the date the income tax return ought to have been filed.[457] Even with self assessment income returns, the Commissioner for Domestic revenue is given power to examine the return for accuracy and make any necessary adjustment to taxable income as well as the tax payable on the adjusted income.[458]

Where the Commissioner receives an income tax return which he/she has reason to believe is not a true reflection of the taxpayer's tax position, he may, to the best of his judgement, estimate an income amount which accurately reflects the tax position of the taxpayer and assess tax on it. Such assessments are referred to in the ITA as best judgment assessments, or simply, estimated assessments,[459] because the Commissioner bases his assessment on an estimation of taxable income.

Estimated or best judgment assessments are also made where a taxpayer has not filed an income tax return, but the Commissioner

---

451 Section 91 (1) Income Tax Act 2004.
452 Section 94 (1) (a) (b) Income Tax Act 2004.
453 Section 94 (4) Income Tax Act 2004.
454 Section 95 ITA.
455 Section 96 ITA.
456 Section 94 (1) ITA.
457 Section 94 (2) ITA.
458 Section 96 ITA.
459 Section 94 (4) ITA.

considers that such person has income chargeable to tax.[460]

While tax payment is usually required following year end and only upon filing the tax return, it is possible for a jeopardy assessment to be made and payment to be required at any time. This requirement may happen when a taxpayer has become bankrupt, or whose business is completed, or goes into liquidation, or is about to leave the country with an apparent intention not to return, or is about to cease doing business in Tanzania. In such scenarios the Commissioner for Domestic Revenue may require such persons to file an income tax return at any time and pay tax.[461] If a return required is not filed, or the Commissioner has not required a return to be filed, the Commissioner may issue a jeopardy assessment.[462] A jeopardy assessment is a protective assessment and is issued to protect the revenue against the events which make it unlikely for the proper tax to be paid if the Commissioner waits for the normal due dates for payment of tax. However, any income tax paid on a jeopardy assessment is available as a tax credit against the tax payable on assessment made for the full year of income,[463] if such taxpayer is still available for payment of tax.

The power of the Commissioner to adjust the amount of tax on a return is predicated on reliability or otherwise of the tax return. Where a person files a tax return under self assessment provisions,[464] and the Commissioner has reason, or information, showing that the return filed is unreliable, he may adjust the tax shown on the return. An assessment, following the adjustment of taxable income, is referred to by the ITA as an adjusted assessment.[465] Under the ITA 1973, the assessment used to be known as an amended or an additional assessment,[466] and is still referred to as such under the Tax Revenue Appeals Act.[467]

Where an assessment is actually made by the Commissioner for Domestic Revenue, he must issue a notice of assessment[468] to the taxpayer notifying the taxpayer of the assessed tax and the time limit for paying the tax assessed. Where the taxpayer does not agree with the tax assessment made, he/she may file a notice of objection with

---

460 Section 94 (5) ITA.
461 Section 91 (3) (d) ITA.
462 Section 95 (2) (a) and (b) ITA.
463 Section 95 (4) ITA.
464 Section 94 and 95 ITA.
465 Section 96 ITA.
466 Section 83 Income Tax Act 1973.
467 Section 13(1)(a) Tax Revenue Appeals Act, [CAP 408 R.E.2002].
468 Section 97 ITA.

the Commissioner[469] within thirty days of being served with the notice of assessment. Upon the objection being made, the Commissioner is required to: issue an Amended Assessment in the light of the objections raised; amend the assessment in light of new information, which was not before him at the time of making the assessment; or refuse to amend the assessment and thus confirm the original assessment.

One can say that the income tax assessment and payment method is more of an enforcement measure, unlike the self-assessment which is clearly a voluntary tax payment mechanism. Payment following assessment involves examination of the taxpayer's accounts and other financial information. It is the final step in processing income tax returns. As shown above, the failure to submit an income tax return, or the failure to make truthful declarations in the income tax return, will not prevent tax officers from making an assessment on an estimated basis.

As payment following assessment captures even those who have not filed tax returns, and those who have filed untruthful tax returns, such a payment system is characterized by enforcement, rather than voluntary compliance.

The Value Added Tax

The value added tax (VAT) in Tanzania is levied under the authority of the Value Added Tax Act.[470] It is an indirect tax levied on the supply of goods or services by a business which is registered for VAT. A taxable supply is a transaction made in the course of business or in the exercise of a profession or trade.[471] Taxable supply in relation to goods[472] includes:

    i. the sale or delivery of taxable goods (including imports) to another person;

    ii. the appropriation of taxable goods for personal use;

    iii. the making of gifts or loans in the course of business;

    iv. letting, hiring, or leasing of goods; and

    v. barter trading or exchanges of goods.

VAT in relation to the supply of services covers things such as:

    i. the supply of professional or commercial services by accountants, engineers, architects, lawyers, secretaries, plumbers, builders,

---

469 Section 12 (1) of the Tax Revenue Appeals Act.
470 The Value Added Tax Act [Cap 148] of the Laws of Tanzania (originally enacted as Value Added Tax Act No. 24 of 1997).
471 *Ibid.* sections 4 and 5 of the VAT Act.
472 *Ibid.* sections 5 (1) (a) – (d).

motor vehicle repairers, employment agencies, advertising agencies, transport service operators and the like;

ii. registrations for intellectual property rights (patents, trademarks and copyrights); and

iii. any other supply which is not money or goods.

VAT also applies to the importation of goods or services.[473]

Sections 18 and 19 of the VAT Act as originally enacted in 1997 required every person with a business whose annual turnover exceeded Tanzania shillings 20 million to register for VAT. By 2004, it had become obvious that this threshold was too low because many of those registered ended up in a credit position. In July 2005, the annual turnover threshold was raised to Tanzania shillings 40 million. This change of threshold resulted in a 50% drop in VAT registrations. All persons registered for VAT must file monthly VAT returns[474] to the TRA, reflecting all the transactions carried out during the previous month together with the VAT payable on each of those transactions. The standard VAT rate was reduced to 18% in July 2010. The rate had been 20% since VAT was introduced in 1997. However, certain items liable to VAT are zero-rated.[475] There are also categories of goods and services which are exempt from VAT.[476] Additionally, certain persons and organisations are also relieved from liability for VAT.[477]

A VAT registered person is issued with a VAT registration certificate bearing his/her registration number. Upon being registered, every supply transaction by a VAT registered person must be evidenced by a tax invoice. Output VAT is accounted for on a monthly basis.[478] VAT collected during the previous month must be remitted to the Commissioner for VAT. Late lodgement of a VAT return carries a 1% penalty on the total VAT payable for that period.[479] Any VAT or penalty remaining unpaid beyond the due date attracts interest at the commercial bank lending rate.[480]

---

473 Sections 4 and 5 of the VAT Act.
474 Section 26 of the VAT Act.
475 Sections 8 and 9 read together with the First Schedule.
476 Section 10 VAT Act read together with the Second Schedule.
477 Section 11 VAT Act read together with the Third Schedule (Diplomats and diplomatic missions, bilateral and multilateral organizations, aid agencies, certain charitable organizations, religious and educational institutions, medical practitioners and veterinary personnel).
478 Section 26 VAT Act.
479 Section 27 VAT Act.
480 Section 28 VAT Act.

Customs and Excise Duties

Since July 2004, the importation and exportation of goods in Tanzania is governed by a harmonised customs tariff arrangement under the East African Community (EAC) Protocol on the EAC Customs Union[481] which binds Tanzania, Kenya and Uganda. The EAC customs protocol creates a trading block with harmonised tariffs and common classification of goods. The protocol also provides for either free movement of goods between member states, or preferential customs tariffs compared to those used in respect of non-EAC countries.

The payment of customs and excise duties in Tanzania is one area of taxation which has lengthy compliance requirements. These compliance requirements emanate mostly from departmental manuals and technical instructions used by customs officers.[482] They are not listed in the customs statute.

The Customs Department within the TRA is responsible for enforcing all compliance procedures associated with the movement of goods in and out of the country. Entry or exit has to be through authorized points and routes. Goods crossing the borders should pass through Customs clearance formalities. Clearing and forwarding processes involve the facilitation of other institutions such as clearing and forwarding agents, the Tanzania Ports Authority (TPA), a customs inspection company and other shipping agencies.

In addition to the enforcement of compliance with customs requirements, the Customs Department does enforce other government laws such as certification, verification and testing of quality or standard of imported goods, which are administered by other government institutions with respect to imports and exports. These institutions include the Tanzania Food and Drugs Authority (TFDA), the Tanzania Bureau of Standards (TBS), the Tanzania Radiation Commission, the Ministry of Agriculture (for importation of plants and animals) and the Tanzania Pesticides Research Institute (TPRI).

Prior to 1st July 2004, goods entering the country were subjected to Pre-shipment Inspection (PI) in the country of export. However, with effect from July 2004, Tanzania moved away from pre-shipment inspection and adopted Destination Inspection (DI).

---

481 Protocol on the Establishment of the East African Customs Union adopted on 2nd March 2004, issued by the East African Community Secretariat, Arusha, Tanzania.

482 J J Mbunda Customs and Excise Department: Practical Experience on Processing of Customs Data in Tanzania, presented as a Paper by the Tanzania Revenue Authority at a Workshop on the Compilation of International Merchandise Trade Statistics held in Addis Ababa, Ethiopia, 8-11 November 2004, under the auspices of the UN Department of Economic and Social Affairs, Statistics Division.

Under DI, all imports are inspected[483] upon arrival in Tanzania by a government-contracted company called TISCAN.[484] Inspection is either physical inspection, or X-ray scanning for Full Loaded Containers (FLC). All imports are also now risk-profiled. Each import is assigned a profile according to the perceived risk associated with it. Three profiles are in use. Low Risk (Green Channel) goods are often released without physical inspection. These are goods belonging to an importer who, as a business entity, has a good customs compliance history and the goods are themselves low risk (e.g. normal consumer items or machinery) and the clearance is being done using a reputable clearing agent. Medium Risk (Yellow Channel) Full Container Load (FCL) goods are subjected to x-ray scanning. These are goods which fall short of low risk, yet are not high risk. High Risk (Red Channel) goods are subjected to physical inspection to verify compliance with importation restrictions. These are goods which are susceptible to contraband or contamination. They include: arms and munitions, edible products, drugs and medications.

DI involves the following procedures:

- Submission of an Import Declaration Form (IDF) to a bank and payment by the importer of 1.2% of the FOB value to a TRA bank account;
- Review of the IDF by TISCAN and verification of the import information by a TISCAN affiliate in the country of origin of the goods;
- Classification and valuation of the goods on the basis of the Final Invoice and the freight/shipping document;
- Price verification by a TISCAN affiliate overseas and indication of the appropriate tariff code(s) and the value for duty;
- Preparation of a Clean Report of Findings (CRF) by TISCAN and submission by the importer of the Single Bill of Entry (SBE) along with the Provisional Classification and Valuation Report (PCVR), a copy of the IDF, original or certified true copies of the Final Invoice, Airway Bill/Bill of Lading and originals or certified true copies of supporting documents if the importer applies for a particular tax relief or duty exemption; and

---

483 The following imports are exempted from DI: commercial samples and goods returning after repair, supplies to diplomatic missions and international organizations, transit goods to other countries in the region, postal/courier goods with a value less than USD 5,000, airlifted emergency supplies as are approved by the TRA, goods for use by educational institutions, charitable and religious organizations, and approved non-profit NGOs.

484 The Tanzania Inspection Service Company (TISCAN) is a subsidiary of the COTECNA SA Group.

- Issuance by TISCAN of a Final Classification and Valuation Report (FCVR) together with the SBE signed by the importer followed by payment of the duty and other taxes (e.g. VAT on imports) at a TRA bank account;

The TRA requires that the importer or the importer's customs clearing and forwarding agent is required to lodge the SBE attaching the following original documents: the bill of lading or airway bill; the commercial invoice; the Import Declaration Form (IDF); a permit in the case of restricted goods; a packing list; the Certificate of Origin; and any other certificates if they exist and if relevant to the clearance of the goods. The SBE is signed and stamped by an authorized customs officer.

The documents are first subjected to a completeness check and, if there is a required document missing, the SBE is rejected and returned to the importer or agent. If complete, the SBE is forwarded to the Data Input Section. At this stage, no further documents are envisaged and the documentation process is deemed to be complete. All declarations are keyed into the computer through the Automated System for Customs Data (ASYCUDA). This computer program is now used in most developing countries. In its initial form, it was simply ASYCUDA; then it was upgraded to ASYCUDA+. The generation now in use in East Africa is ASYCUDA++, which has advanced on-line features that enable clearing and forwarding agents to input shipping data on line.

All declarations have to pass through HDO electronically for risk profiling so that an appropriate risk category is assigned ('Low Risk', 'Medium Risk' and 'High Risk'). The combined implementation of CRMS and X-ray scanning allows the Customs Department to focus physical inspection on high risk shipments, while creating a fast clearance channel for the majority of compliant importers.

The valuation stage is one area of customs clearance procedure which generates many disputes. Valuation of goods for customs purposes involves two considerations which can impact significantly on the import duty to be paid by the importer. The first consideration is classification of the goods. Goods are rated according to classification. A wrong classification can result in higher or lower duties. Tanzania uses the Harmonised Commodity Description and Coding System (HS Code 1996), which falls under the Agreement on Customs Valuation adopted by the WTO and GATT. Often though, zealous officers misclassify goods so that they fall into a higher duty rate category. Even when the goods are properly classified, when they come to the second consideration which is determination of value, some controversy still arises. The EAC

Customs Management Act[485] in Tanzania requires that customs officers use the transaction value. This is the invoiced price paid for the goods. But customs officers are allowed to use an alternative value where the invoiced price is unreliable. In doing so, consideration must be given to the market value for identical or similar goods. Instead of performing the valuation process judiciously, there have been repeated cases of arbitrary uplifting of value to maximize customs duty collections.[486]

Compliance with Taxes

Globally, tax authorities use a combination of voluntary tax payment and enforced tax collection in trying to ensure that every person pays tax. The prevalence of one type of method over the other is indicative of the dominant tax collection strategy used in that country. In Tanzania there appears to be a dominance of enforced collection to realise tax. While there is repeated mention of voluntary tax payment in TRA working documents, TRA practice and the tax laws do not demonstrate that voluntary tax payment is a strategy of equal importance.

In the following section, the tax collection measures used by the TRA are examined so as to ascertain whether these measures are in line with the overall objective of "promoting voluntary compliance to the highest degree possible" as stipulated in the TRA Act and boldly proclaimed in the Taxpayer's Charter issued by the TRA.

Of the three tax statutes examined here (income tax, VAT and customs), the Income Tax Act[487] incorporates more voluntary tax payment provisions.[488] As stated earlier, it requires all persons who derive or expect to derive income chargeable to tax either from business or from investment to make payment of tax in four quarterly instalments.[489] The tax instalment payments must be made on the last day of March, June, September and December.[490] Taxpayers required to pay tax by instalment must file a statement declaring the amount of income they

---

485 Section 122 read together with the Fourth Schedule. This provision has reproduced Section 108 of the East African Customs Transfer Management Act (Cap 27), which applied to Tanzania until 2005 when the new EAC law was adopted.
486 A good example is the case of *Samuel John Ezekiel v Commissioner General TRA* Tax Appeal No. 11 of 2004, where the taxpayer successfully challenged the Customs Department over its action, disputing the invoiced price and uplifting the value of an imported vehicle belonging to the taxpayer by nearly 100%. An appeal by the TRA was not successful (*Commissioner General v Samuel John Ezekiel* Tax Appeal No. 13 of 2005).
487 Income Tax Act No. 11 of 2004.
488 Sections 78 and 79.
489 Section 88 (1).
490 Section 88 (2).

expect to derive for the following year, at least three months prior to the end of the preceding year.[491] The estimated amount they declare is the basis on which they pay the four instalments.

Other tax statutes such as the Stamp Duty Act,[492] the Land Act[493] and the Companies Act,[494] also have provisions for voluntary payment of tax. Under the Stamp Duty Act, no instrument for which stamp duty is chargeable can be registered, or used in evidence if no proof of payment of stamp duty is produced. Stamp duty must be paid at the time of the transaction. A similar provision exists in the Land Act, which requires all taxes payable in a land transaction to be made at the time of the transaction or else the transfer of title, or assignment or mortgage will not be registered. In addition, under the Companies Act, no sale of shares or other change occurring in the company will be registered if the taxes payable have not been made.

In the discussion of the customs duty payment arrangements in use under the East Africa Community Customs Management Act,[495] several voluntary payment methods were outlined by which customs duty is paid in Tanzania. These include the pre-payment of 1.2% of expected duty through the bank on lodgement of import documents and the payment of duty following final classification and assessment where value for duty and tariff classification is not disputed. There is also the payment of a bond for duty in respect of goods imported into the country for a temporary period.

In order to reinforce voluntary tax payment, the TRA uses both persuasion and punishment. The taxpayer education program is used by the TRA to persuade taxpayers to meet their tax obligations voluntarily. Radio and television broadcasts, seminars and workshops, are held all over the country, trying to win the hearts and minds of taxpayers.

In addition, the tax laws provide for a wide range of penalties for non-compliance with the tax payment requirements described above. These will be discussed in the succeeding section.

The withholding tax arrangement applying to a wide range of payments

---

491 Section 89 ITA 2004.
492 Stamp Duty Act 1972 (Cap 198).
493 The Land Act No. 4 of 1997.
494 The Companies Act No. 12 of 2002.
495 The EAC Customs Management Act No. 1 of 2005.

such as employment income,[496] dividends, interest, rent, royalties,[497] management/professional fees and/or technical fees, is an example of enforced tax payment. There is no requirement for the taxpayer to declare the payment; instead, a duty is cast on the person making the payment to deduct tax. Heavy penalties attend non-compliance.

The value added tax operates in nearly the same manner. It is not the buyer of goods or services who must declare and account for the VAT to the TRA; it is the supplier of goods or services who has that duty.[498]

As pointed out earlier, the withholding tax payment mechanism is an effective tax collection arrangement, not only in its ability to reduce tax evasion, but also in easing the taxpayer's psychological burden related to cash or direct payment which affects the pocket immediately. By capturing the tax before the payment gets to the recipient, the trauma of receiving a payment only to see a significant amount of it disappear in taxes is avoided and so is the aggravation associated with that trauma.

Dealing with Non-payment of Tax

Both voluntary tax payment and enforced tax payment are backed up by a number of measures which aim at enforcing compliance by the taxpayer.

The powers of access to information already discussed and which are the basis on which tax audits and tax investigations are undertaken, seek to uncover non-compliance with tax. Whenever discovered, non-compliance is dealt with by prosecuting the offenders, or imposing fiscal penalties for the tax breach.

The Customs Management Act[499] has the most sweeping powers of prosecution. All offences alleged to have been committed may be prosecuted in subordinate courts regardless of the enormity of the

---

496 Under Section 81 ITA 2004, an employer must withhold and remit to the TRA the income tax on salaries, wages, allowances and other emoluments paid in connection with an employment.

497 Section 82 ITA 2004 indicates that a company must withhold tax on dividends; banks and financial institutions must withhold tax on interest earned; a landlord must withhold tax on the rent received; and all persons making payments of royalties are subject to the withholding tax requirement.

498 Value Added Tax Act No. 148 of 1997 (Sections 3, 5 and 17).

499 EAC Customs Management Act No. 1 of 2005.

offence or the monetary quantum involved.[500] In this regard, the Customs Management Act overrides the civil procedural laws, which allocate the jurisdiction of courts by setting tiered pecuniary limits and the nature of subject matter. The Customs Management Act also overrides normal rules of evidence in criminal matters, which require proof beyond reasonable doubt by the accuser. Section 112 of the Evidence Act [Cap 6] provides that the burden of proof as to any particular fact lies on that person who alleges its existence. In terms of Section 3 (2) of the Evidence Act, a fact is said to be proved in criminal matters when it is established beyond reasonable doubt that it exists. Admittedly, tax laws are not alone in setting a lower threshold for the standard of proof. Other examples in Tanzania include: Sections 26 and 49 of the Drugs and Prevention of Illicit Traffic in Drugs Act 9/2002; Section 30 of the Immigration Act; Section 28 of the Pools and Lotteries Act; and Section 34 of the Sugar Industry Act. For most customs offences, the standard of proof required is only a *prima facie* case.[501] In cases involving smuggling or possession of smuggled goods, the burden of proof is shifted to the person accused.[502] There is a good case for arguing that, as customs offences are criminal offences, the procedure for prosecution ought to conform to criminal procedural laws.

Criminal prosecutions are also provided for under the Income Tax Act, the Value Added Tax Act and the Stamp Duty Act and, in the majority of cases, the burden of proof is shifted to the accused, but the standard of proof is on a balance of probability.[503]

In nearly all the tax statutes, moreover, the Commissioner for Domestic Revenue, the Commissioner for Customs and the Commissioner for Large Taxpayers have been given power to compound offences.[504] This wide penal power enables the Commissioners to seek and obtain admission of offence and to proceed summarily to impose fiscal penalties which can be quite substantial. For instance, for interfering

---

500 Section 220. Notably too, there is a wide range of offences provided under Part XVII of the Customs Management Act (Sections 193 to 217). They include offences against vessels and crafts used by customs officers, possession of un-customed or prohibited goods, interfering with customs seals or signs, conspiracy to commit offence, impersonation of an officer, smuggling, false documents and aiding and abetting the commission of an offence.

501 Sections 209 and 223 Customs Management Act.

502 Section 223 Customs Management Act.

503 For instance, Section 77 of the Stamp Duty Act relating to whether an instrument is subject to stamp duty, or that it is properly stamped, or that it was stamped at the time it was required to be stamped.

504 See for instance Section 119 (3) ITA and Section 49 VAT Act [CAP 148 R.E.2002].

with a customs seal, or warning an offender against arrest, the fine is USD 2,500.[505] The fine for offences relating to importation of prohibited, or un-customed goods, is half the duty payable on those goods.[506] Use of false documents, which is a commonplace offence, carries a fine of USD 10,000.[507] An order of the Commissioner compounding an offence is final and conclusive. It cannot be challenged in any court of law,[508] and is also enforceable as if it were a court order.

However, the powers which are most regularly used by the TRA are: the power to attach and sell assets, the power to issue agency notices and attach bank accounts, and the power to prosecute for tax breaches. The use of these powers has diverse impact on tax compliance attitudes and patterns.

The power to attach a taxpayer's bank account(s) is widely used. The TRA can seize or freeze the bank account of any person to recover taxes claimed. All tax laws in Tanzania have provisions which empower the Commissioners to issue an Agency Notice declaring the manager of a bank holding an account for the taxpayer to be an agent of that taxpayer and compel the manager to pay over to the TRA the taxes claimed.[509] A bank manager's failure to comply with an agency notice will result in prosecution and a fine, and make the bank directly liable for the taxes claimed.

The power to attach and sell assets is also regularly used by the TRA to recover unpaid taxes. In doing this, the TRA can undertake to sell attached assets itself, or it can appoint any person to be a receiver and compel such receiver to sell the property or assets of the person against whom the unpaid tax is claimed.

As said before, the TRA is required to administer taxes fairly. Therefore one needs to assess the fairness of the above compliance measures. However, it is not easy to measure the fairness of tax collection, or the general fairness in the exercise of tax powers, because fairness is largely a matter of perception. Tax commentators tend to look at certain

---

505 Section 195 and 197 EAC Customs Management Act 2005. The fiscal penalties under the Customs Management Act are expressed in US dollars because the Act applies to all three EAC countries. Although Tanzania, Kenya and Uganda are a customs union and common market, they are yet to adopt a common currency.

506 Section 200 EAC Customs Management Act 2004.

507 Section 2003 EAC Customs Management Act.

508 It is doubtful if this exclusion removes the power of the High Courts to inquire into the validity of actions taken by the Commissioners, given the court's inherent power for judicial review.

509 For instance Sections 117 and 118 of the ITA 2004, and Section 32 of the VAT Act (Cap 148).

elements which are essential in forming a perception of fairness. These elements include: transparency in the application of tax laws; consistency and impartiality in the decisions made or actions taken; allowing for sufficient taxpayer input in reaching tax decisions; respect for the right to challenge decisions or actions taken, both administratively and through external impartial bodies; and respect for the decisions of adjudication bodies. The presence of these elements in large measure denotes the existence of fairness in the tax administration.

One way to ensure that there is transparency in the application of tax laws is for the government and the tax administration to ensure that everyone who ought to pay tax is paying tax. As indicated previously, one problem with the tax system in Tanzania is the narrow tax base. The 2003 DANIDA report,[510] previously referred to, noted that Tanzania's tax base is very narrow with 28% of GDP being generated by non-market production and an estimated further 15% by the informal sector. This amount shows that taxes are collected from a very small section of society. Although the government is aware of this problem, there appears to be a reluctance, or lack of political will, to attack the rural sector in order to bring rural farmers into the tax net. Additionally, not enough is being done to expand the taxpayer registration program to people deriving incomes from the informal sector. A narrow tax base results in selective taxation and undermines transparency in the application of tax laws.

The small size of tax revenue and selective taxation is also caused by substantial tax exemptions allowed by the government. Maliyamkono[511] says that for 2005/2006, tax exemptions amounted to 38.6% of total revenue. An earlier DANIDA report notes that in 2001/2002 exemptions from indirect taxes resulted in revenue losses estimated at approximately 250 billion Tanzania shillings (3.1% of GDP). A majority of these were exemptions on import duties amounting to 183 billion Tanzania shillings (2.2% of GDP). VAT exemptions amounted to 67 billion Tanzania shillings. The DANIDA report recommended that these exemptions be removed in order to broaden the tax base.

The two taxpayer survey reports already referred to have shown that taxpayers do not think there is sufficient consistency and impartiality in the decisions made or actions taken by the TRA. Often too, the decisions or actions taken defy the common notion of justice. Coupled with a robotic application of tax laws even when it leads to absurd

---

510 DANIDA, Project Document, Danish Support to Tanzania Revenue Authority, Phase II 2003/04-2007/08, Danida File:104.Tanzania.213, October 2003, at 7.
511 Op cit. at p20.

results, the verdict on consistency and impartiality is a negative one. Justice Marshall wrote that,

> The jurist concerned with public confidence in and acceptance of the judicial system might well consider that, however admirable its resolute adherence to the law as it was, a decision contrary to the public sense of justice as it is, operates, so far as it is known, to diminish respect for the courts and for law itself.[512]

The TRA ought to heed this warning.

In fairness to the TRA, there is, visibly, respect for the right to challenge decisions or actions taken by the TRA. This respect is seen in the administrative arrangement put in place to enable taxpayers to complain to a superior officer against the actions of a tax officer. The respect for the right to challenge tax decisions is also visible in the TRA's respect for the tax objection and tax appeals procedures already discussed.

> The objection procedure being the first tier of tax dispute resolution aims to give the TRA an opportunity to review the assessment or action they have taken when disputed, before the dispute goes on appeal to an adjudicative body. However, as the TRA does not have a system which ensures that the objection is received and reviewed by someone other than the officer who first made the assessment, the benefit of the objection system is many times lost. There is an obvious bias and self interest, which often prevents an objective review being undertaken by the tax officer who made the assessment or took the decision contested. Nonetheless, there are many instances where this first tier of objection/ review has helped resolve tax disputes which would otherwise end up on appeal.

There is a real impediment, though, to the success of the objection/ review process because of the requirement that an objection will only be entertained upon payment of one third of the disputed tax. Section 12 (6) of the Tax Revenue Appeals Act[513] requires that a person who objects (disputes) to a tax assessment and wishes the assessment to be reviewed must first pay the amount of tax not in dispute or one third of the assessed tax if the whole tax is disputed. The prepayment condition in Section 12 (6) puts revenue efficiency ahead of the taxpayer's right to appeal to judicial bodies.

Section 12 (6) flies in the face of accepted good governance principles, such as observance of the rule of law and the age-old presumption of

---

512 Justice Marshall in *Flood v Kuhn* 1972.
513 Act No. 15 of 2000.

innocence, because it condemns the taxpayer to a fiscal burden before the legal validity of that tax burden is established by an impartial body. The provision breaches this fundamental principle of rule of law and good governance, which is stipulated in the Constitution of Tanzania under Article 13 (6) (b). Similarly, the provision contradicts Article 13 (6) (a) of the Constitution of Tanzania, which provides for an unhindered right of appeal. Every person has this right, regardless of any circumstances in which he finds himself/herself. While this provision in the Tax Revenue Appeals Act does not explicitly take away the right to dispute a tax assessment and even appeal against it, the condition precedent put in place for the exercise of the right of objection and appeal make it difficult for some taxpayers to exercise this fundamental right.

Provisions which impose some pre-payment of disputed taxes have been justified on the reasoning that, while allowing for the right to dispute tax assessments, there is higher interest in ensuring that the flow of government revenue is not jeopardized by litigation. Additionally, it is argued that the risk must be reduced for the appeal process to be used to delay payment of taxes which are properly due. It is difficult to argue against the merits of both cases, but a balance needs to be struck in favour of protecting the right to contest a tax assessment. If need be, there must be a system in place which enables evaluation of pre-payment claims in every case. There must also be discretion built into the system to waive the pre-payment requirement in meritorious cases.

Quite apart from the constitutionality or otherwise of provisions like Section 12 cited above, such provisions are likely to increase resistance to taxation because they undermine the trust that must exist between the taxpayers and the tax administrators. Rather than build confidence, prepayment provisions, which operate unfairly, or are used badly by tax officers, breed and nurture hostility towards the tax authority and the tax system.

Notwithstanding, it is fair to acknowledge that the TRA maintains high regard for the decisions of the courts and the judicial tribunals charged with the responsibility of adjudication upon tax disputes.

Another area of concern is tax refunds. Tax statutes provide for refunds of overpaid tax, or wrongly paid tax. This provision is in line with the principle that the subject should pay no more than the law requires.

The VAT administration is an area where immense difficulties are being experienced with the processing and payment of refunds. The VAT procedure in Tanzania is that input tax is deducted from output tax and any credit resulting is claimed as a cash refund by the VAT registered person.[514] The VAT Act requires the TRA to refund VAT credits within 30 days of lodging the refund claim.[515] When first introduced in 1997, the VAT refund procedure worked well. Within a short while, the turn around period stretched to three months. As the years have gone by, it has become quite common for VAT refunds to remain unpaid for periods stretching to a year or two.

The figures in Table 6 below, presented by the TRA in September 2009 at a Tax Forum meeting, give a misleading impression of the delays experienced with VAT refunds. The percentages in the Table refer to the total VAT refund claims paid as against those received. They do not show the percentage of what has been paid against what is owing to taxpayers, i.e. the total VAT claim amounts still outstanding. In other words, the percentages are not for the amount of money paid, but rather for the number of claims paid. As there is a tendency for the TRA to sit on big claims, such as those made by mining companies[516] and big manufacturers, significant amounts of money have become tied up in delayed VAT and fuel levy refunds. For example, by June 2010, the TRA owed VAT refunds to Geita Gold Mine Ltd amounting to 57 million USD; Africa Barrick Gold, 62.7 million USD; Resolute Tanzania, 11.3 million; and DTP Terrassement, 8.6 million USD. The TRA also owed significant fuel levy refunds to these companies: Geita Gold Mine Ltd, 48.4 million USD; Africa Barrick Gold, 65.2 million USD; and Resolute Tanzania, 12.9 million USD. These unpaid refunds have become a source of aggravation to taxpayers attempting compliance with VAT and customs payments.

TABLE 6: PERCENTAGE OF VAT REFUNDS MADE WITHIN 30 DAYS*

2002/03	2003/04	2004/05	2005/06	2006/07	2007/08	2008/09
36%	80%	92%	62%	75%	63%	55%

* Source: The TRA Modernisation Program Section

The fairness of the tax system also means that the tax rates used are fair. Taxpayer compliance is improved by the realisation that the tax laws are fair and equitable, easy to comply with and difficult to evade.[517] In Tanzania, these principles are not heeded. Many taxes are levied at rates which are higher than those prevailing in other countries within

---

514 Section 16 of the VAT Act.
515 Section 17 (2) of the VAT Act.
516 The TRA VAT Refunds Section.
517 R K Gordon 'Law of Tax Administration and Procedure', in V Thuronyi (ed.) *Tax Law Design and Drafting*, Vol 1, IMF, Washington, 1996, at 17.

the region, to the extent that, rather than improve compliance, the high rates exacerbate tax resistance.[518] Many taxpayers cry that tax rates are too high, thus making the paying of taxes too burdensome.

Comparing the tax rates in East Africa, Tanzania has higher rates for income tax and VAT. While Kenya and Uganda have 17% and 18% respectively for VAT, the VAT rate in Tanzania has been 20% (reduced to 18% only in July 2010 to comply with the requirement to harmonise taxes within the EAC framework). The corporate tax rate is 30% for both resident and non-resident companies, which rate is higher than the 25% rate applying in Kenya and Uganda. Individual marginal rates are also quite high as they stand at about 30% for higher income earners. The 30% percent rate may be comparable to tax rates used in developed countries, but the wages in Tanzania are quite low. Therefore, the tax on individuals peaks at a much lower level in Tanzania than it does in countries where wages are relatively high. The government appears to recognise the problem of high tax rates and is beginning to bring them down. In the 2007/08 budget, the income tax rates were reduced by 3% for each income bracket,[519] and in 2010/11 the thresholds for each income bracket were increased.

The high tax rates act as a significant disincentive with regard to voluntary taxpayer compliance. In fact, high tax rates may encourage taxpayers to evade taxes. When the tax burden is perceived to be unfair, many find it justifiable to devise ways of evading the tax, rather than complying with it. The only way to achieve higher tax collections and lower rates of tax is to widen the tax base. A wider tax base enables government to lower tax rates without affecting the ability of government to meet tax revenue targets.

Conclusion

Tax compliance is a vast and complex issue. Voluntary tax compliance is even more complex. There is no single approach to achieving voluntary tax compliance. Tax compliance requires multiple strategies. Since non compliance (tax resistance) has multiple causes and spans as well, different taxes and different taxpayers, an effective response must be equally multifaceted.

---

518 It is notable as well that in Tanzania, partnership firms cannot opt to be taxed as companies, as is the case in some countries, so as to avoid the application of the high personal rates to partnership income.

519 Budget Speech to Parliament by the Minister for Finance Zakhia Meghji on 14 June 2007; see also Finance Act of 2007.

The question to be asked is whether tax enforcement alone can provide an effective answer to the compliance paradigm. Quite apart from the cost element, which is a significant limitation to enforcement, there are psychological factors against enforced tax compliance. For emerging economies, as in Tanzania, the more immediate problem is the limited capacity to undertake wide ranging enforcement that is effective.

Witte and Woodbury[520] present an economic model of compliance which indicates a negative relationship between the probability of being caught and the severity of punishment. An increase in either the probability or severity of punishment can alter the non-compliance from positive to negative, thereby deterring the "would be tax evaders". The correlation between increased enforcement and compliance appears to be stronger when the probability of punishment is increased, more so than when the punishment is more severe.[521] In either case, however, enforcement policies relying on punitive strategies with severe punishment do not always alleviate the problem of non-compliance and, at times, might even worsen the situation.[522]

Cheng[523] also suggests that enforced compliance increases where the detection risks are higher.[524] In terms of the punishment parameter, fines and other types of penalties also generally improve compliance. Some studies indicate, however, that when it comes to real life behaviour, small changes in penalties are easily overlooked and are unlikely to affect compliance.[525]

However, Becker[526] argues that despite the increased deterrent effect achieved through detection and punishment, the desire to keep tax administration costs low may lead policy makers to favour raising penalties over increasing costly detection in order to improve compliance.[527] Also, in the effort to maximize deterrence and raise the most revenue at minimal cost, consideration may be given to extreme, but rare punishments.

---

520 A D Witte and D F Woodbury 'The Effect of Tax Laws and Tax Administration on Tax Compliance: The Case of the U.S. Individual Income Tax' (1985) (1) 38 *National Tax Journal*, 1.
521 *Ibid.*
522 *Ibid.*
523 *Ibid.*
524 E K Cheng 'Structural Laws and the Puzzle of Regulating Behaviour' (2006) 100 *Northwestern University Law Review* 655, at 659.
525 *Ibid.*
526 *Ibid.*
527 G. S. Becker 1968: "Crime and Punishment: An economic approach" (1968) 76 Journal of Political Economy p.169.

Braithwaite[528] arrives at the inevitable conclusion that, given the conflicting scenarios above, enforcement efforts which rely exclusively on punitive measures and the severity and probability of punishment are likely to be short sighted at best, and counterproductive at worst. They are authoritarian attempts at shaping behaviour, and they often lead to a never ending process, as each piece of new legislation or amendment brings new opportunities for evasion.[529]

It seems, therefore, that there is a real case for recognizing the complimentary relationship that must exist between cooperative strategies and enforcement strategies. The question as to which of these strategies best drives tax compliance largely remains moot.

---

528 V Braithwaite 'Dancing with tax authorities: Motivational postures and non-compliant actions', in V Braithwaite (ed) *Taxing Democracy: Understanding Tax Avoidance and Evasion*. Ashgate, Aldershot. 15-39.
529 *Ibid.*

6

Tax Policy Formulation and
Tax Compliance

Introduction

In discussing governance and the legitimacy of government, it was observed that an important attribute of good governance is the ability of government to formulate policies, to deliver services and generally put in place a sound framework for economic and social participation. This chapter examines the role of taxation policy and seeks to make the point that when the government is able to formulate sound tax policies, it is possible for the public to identify with the tax system and accept the various taxes levied by the government, all leading to higher tax compliance levels.

Tax Policy

It is easier to speak of what tax policy entails, rather than to provide a definition of it. Tanzi and Zee[530] state that tax policy involves both

---

530 V Tanzi and H Zee *Tax Policy for Developing Countries* (March 2001) International Monetary Fund.

macroeconomic (the level and composition of tax revenue) and microeconomic (the design of specific taxes) considerations. It deals with determining the level of tax revenue appropriate to the spending requirements of the country. It also addresses the composition of revenue (taxation of income vs. taxation of consumption).

Tax policy formulation and the design of the tax structure seek to achieve the following main objectives:

    i. to raise revenues to finance government operations and development activities;

    ii. to stimulate economic growth and employment generation;

    iii. to encourage investment (and discourage consumption);

    iv. to promote investments;

    v. to protect domestic industries;

    vi. to promote exports;

    vii. to redistribute wealth; and

    viii. to stabilise the economy and combat inflation.

It has been stressed in this study that taxation is the key source of government revenue. As a result, the tax policies of many developing countries show that tax generation is central to the tax policy pursued. Tax administrations pride themselves in meeting and exceeding tax revenue collection targets. Tax administrations are also keen to increase the performance of taxation in funding the government budget, as well as increasing the ratio of taxation to GDP.

At a Taxpayers' Day event in November 2007 (an annual event to commend and reward compliant taxpayers), the then Tanzania Minister for Finance, Zakhia Meghji spoke glowingly of the ability of the TRA to surpass repeatedly its revenue collection targets.[531]

Tables 3a and 3b above show that tax revenue collection statistics for the past six years from 2002 to 2009 have exceeded the tax revenue collection targets set by the Ministry of Finance (except for 2010 largely due to the global economic crisis).

Figures for the period 2001 to 2007 published by the Bank of Tanzania confirm that tax collections have remained consistent with the government budget and have often surpassed projections. Table 7 below shows total government revenue in relation to tax revenue and provides a breakdown of the performance of specific taxes.

---

531 Minister's speech at the Taxpayers' Day 20th November 2007 as reported in the *Daily News* and the *Guardian* of 21st November 2007.

TABLE 7: TAX REVENUE COLLECTION PERFORMANCE FOR
THE YEARS 2001/02 TO 2006/07[532]
(VALUES ARE IN BILLION TANZANIA SHILLINGS)

	2001/02	2002/03	2003/04	2004/05	2005/06	2006/07	2006/07 to April
Total Revenue	1,042	2,217	1,459	1,773	2,124	2,460	2,218
Tax Revenue	9396.8	1,105	1,342	1,615	1,946	2,269	2,046
Customs	402	458	575	679	819	979	845
VAT/ Excise	216	259	325	402	478	566	505
Refunds	33	36	-48	-64	-69	-133	-88
Income Taxes	220	276	366	465	581	657	604
Other Taxes	100	111	123	132	136	198	179
Non-tax Revenue	103	111	158	158	178	191	172

* Source: Bank of Tanzania, Monetary Policy Statement, June 2007[532]

** Values are in billion Tanzania Shillings

Another trend, which is notable in the tax collection statistics of Tanzania (and which is also the case for Kenya, Uganda, Zambia and Rwanda), is the dependence on indirect and consumption taxes. Customs duties and value added tax are bigger contributors than income tax. This disparity is evidence of either a lack of productive activities to a sufficient degree, or a failure to efficiently enforce income tax collection in respect of income generating activities. A tax study carried out in Kenya concluded that the poor performance of direct taxes, which is mainly the income tax, results from the narrow tax base upon which income tax collections rely.[533] In the previous chapter, it was shown how

---

532 Bank of Tanzania, Monetary Policy Statement, June 2007, 41.

533 H Waruhiu 'Taxing the People; An Economic and Public Policy Agenda for Kenya, AGENDA Publication Series, May 2001, at 6-7, internet source http://www.iea.or.ke/ourproblems.asp? This publication holds the view that reliance on indirect taxation has a sound philosophical basis, because income adds to the national wealth and should not be overtaxed, whereas consumption reduces national income. Greater taxation on consumption will lead to greater retention of incomes and greater national savings and investment. This view is not shared by many, especially in developed economies, where more reliance is placed on revenue from income tax because of the wide tax base created by favourable economic policies.

income generating activities in the agricultural and informal sectors are not captured for income tax purposes. This situation is true for Kenya as well. The failure to effectively capture the informal sector in the tax base undermines the performance of direct taxes. Governments desperate for revenue are forced to rely on indirect taxes. Table 8 below shows the extent to which import taxes and value added tax are major contributors to domestic tax revenue in Tanzania. Table 8 also shows that generally taxation in Tanzania is unable to fund government expenditure, and that a significant budget deficit persists, despite the good performance in tax collections. It is notable that the tax collection figures in Tables 7 and 8, taken from different sources within the government, are not identical. However, the discrepancy is not significant and may be from failure by one source to capture all types of taxes, especially the fringe taxes.

TABLE 8: TRENDS IN GOVERNMENT FINANCE*[534]

(VALUES ARE IN BILLION TANZANIA SHILLINGS)

		2001/02	2002/03	2003/04	2004/05	2005/06	2006/07
		Actual	Actual	Actual	Actual	Actual	Actual
A	DOMESTIC REVENUE	1042945	1217517	1459303	1773710	1929625	2066752
1	Tax Revenue	938478	1105746	1342798	1615248	1738209	1895967
	Import Duty and Excise Duty	266322	293695	352320	350532	180587	419260
	Value Added Tax (VAT)	351894	424338	548572	731597	834767	837912
	Imports	208675	249854	315958	439796	430891	496361
	Domestic	143219	174484	232614	291801	403876	341551
	Income Tax	219852	276050	366651	465455	657763	549074
	Other Taxes	100410	111663	123500	132040	198576	157555
	Refunds Accounts			-48245	-64376	-133484	-67834
2	Non-Tax Revenue	104467	111771	116505	158462	191416	170785
B	TOTAL EXPENDITURE	1462767	1989538	2516943	3248352	4788497	4035114
1	Recurrent Expenditure	1118156	148864	1780115	2017490	3054030	2649931
2	Development Expenditure	344611	500897	736828	1230862	1734467	1385183
	Local Funds	50236	95662	133041	239651	641766	370038
	Foreign Funds	294375	405235	603787	991211	1092701	1015145
C	DEFICIT/ SURPLUS	-419822	-772021	-1057640	-1474642	-888650	-1968362

* Source: Ministry of Planning, Economy and Empowerment, Annual Economic Survey 2007[538]

** Values are in billion Tanzania shillings

Taxation is also used to stimulate economic growth and redistribute wealth. Despite the clear dominance of revenue generation as the driving objective for taxation in developing countries, promotion of economic growth and redistribution of wealth continue to form part of the fiscal policies of these countries.

All Eastern African countries have adopted tax policies aimed at promoting economic growth by encouraging foreign investment. There is recognition in these countries that the lack of domestic capital must be

534 Ministry of Planning, Economy and Empowerment, The Economic Survey 2007, 73.

supplemented by foreign capital, which will only flow into the country if there is a favourable investment climate.

Tanzania has set the pace in creating what is billed as a well-balanced and competitive package of fiscal incentives[535] in comparison with other African countries. In the mid-eighties, Tanzania abandoned twenty years of socialist economic policies and embraced open market reforms. After fifteen years of major political and economic reforms starting in 1986, by 2000/2001 Tanzania was ranked the number one investment destination in benchmarking macro economic and investment climate success factors.[536] Tanzania's fiscal policy incorporates fiscal measures for promotion of foreign investments, protection of local industries, encouragement of export trade and protection of the domestic market from dumping. These economic measures find the most expression in taxation in the form of tax incentives, although non-tax measures, such as the streamlining of compliance requirements for doing business, have an important effect too.

The Tanzania Investment Centre (TIC)[537] was formed as a one stop centre for promoting investments. It performs the following main functions: to create and maintain a positive private sector investment climate; to stimulate investments in the private sector; to attract foreign investments; and to provide assistance to all investors. TIC issues investment certificates to all approved investments. When issued with a Certificate of Incentives and Protection, the approved enterprise is entitled to enjoy tax and non-tax benefits provided under Part III of the Tanzania Investment Act of 1997.

Taxation benefits given to holders of TIC certificates relate to income tax, customs and value added tax. For income tax, TIC certificate holders enjoy the following tax relief: a 100% capital allowance for expenditure on capital assets for the approved enterprise, allowed at 50% in the first year the machinery is put to use and 37.5% per annum for subsequent years; 5 year tax holiday on profits from the

---

535 Bank of Tanzania Publication, Creating Optimal Conditions for Foreign Investment, Occasional Publication, December 2005, 14. Tanzania also secured top spot in Africa's Improvement Index 2000, a ranking carried out by the World Bank and the International Monetary Fund.

536 The Africa Competitiveness Report 2000/2001, Centre for International Development, Harvard University. The Report ranked Tanzania first, followed by Morocco, Mozambique, Nigeria and Uganda.

537 The Tanzania Investment Centre (TIC) was established under the Tanzania Investment Act of 1997 [Tanzania Laws, Chapter 38], which replaced the National Investment (Promotion and Protection) Act (NIPPA) of 1990.

day the approved enterprise commences operations; and an indefinite carry forward of losses until they are exhausted. In respect of VAT, approved enterprises enjoy deferment of VAT on start-up supplies until commencement of production and they also enjoy zero rating of VAT on manufactured exports. Regarding customs, certificate holders are entitled to: reduced import tariffs at 5% on project capital items for use in priority underdeveloped areas;[538] zero rating for capital items for use in lead sectors (these are agriculture, road infrastructure, mining and investment in export processing zones); and import duty drawback for duty paid on imported raw materials used in the manufacture of goods.

Apart from taxation relief, the TIC also offers several non-tax investment incentives. A company issued with a certificate of incentives is entitled to the following investment guarantees:

- an unrestricted right to repatriate profits and dividends attributable to the investment;
- the right to make payments in respect of foreign loan servicing;
- the right to transfer funds for payment of royalties' fees and charges;
- the right to remit proceeds in the event of sale or liquidation of the investment;
- the right to remit payments of emoluments or other benefits to foreign personnel;
- protection against nationalisation or expropriation by the Government; and
- protection against being compelled by law to cede any interest in the capital to some other person.

The TIC believes that Tanzania's fiscal policy offers a well-balanced and competitive package in comparison with other African countries, and these fiscal measures are responsible for the recent significant growth of the Tanzania economy. The view of the TIC is vindicated by the recent trend in Tanzania's GDP growth as shown in Chart 1.

---

538 The normal customs duty rate is 25%.

CHART 1: TANZANIA'S GDP GROWTH 1996 TO 2006*

Real GDP Growth - At 1992 Constant Prices

* Source: The Economic Survey 2006, Ministry of Planning, Economic and Empowerment, June 2007

Tanzania's GDP growth figures for 2000 to 2007 are better than many countries in the SADC[539] region, exceeded only by Angola, Botswana and Mozambique. Table 9 below shows the GDP growth figures for the SADC countries.

---

539 SADC (Southern African Development Community) is a trading block south of the equator and consists of 15 member countries.

TABLE 9: PERCENTAGE GROWTH OF REAL GDP FOR SADC COUNTRIES
FROM 2000 – 2007*

Country	2000	2001	2002	2003	2004	2005	2006	2007
Angola	3.6	5.2	15.5	3.4	11.7	20.6	19.5	19.8
Botswana	7.3	9.1	1.6	9.5	3.4	9.2	-0.6	6.2
DRC	-6.9	-2.1	3.5	5.8	6.6	6.5	5.6	6.3
Lesotho	1.3	3.2	3.5	3.3	3.2	4	7.2	5.1
Madagascar	N/A	6.0	-12.7	9.0	5.3	4.6	5.0	6.3
Malawi	0.8	-4.1	2.1	3.9	5.1	2.3	8.2	7.9
Mauritius	9.5	5.4	2.1	4.4	4.7	2.3	5.4	8.7
Mozambique	1.9	13.1	8.2	7.9	7.5	6.2	8.5	7.3
Namibia	3.5	2.4	2.5	3.7	4.4	4.8	4.1	4.8
Seychelles	4.2	-2.2	1.3	-6.3	-2.0	1.2	4.5	5.0
South Africa	4.2	2.7	3.7	3.0	4.5	4.9	5.4	5.1
Swaziland	2.0	1.8	2.8	2.4	2.1	2.3	2.8	2.8
Tanzania	4.9	5.7	6.2	5.7	6.7	6.8	6.7	7.1
Zambia	4.0	5.0	3.3	4.0	5.0	5.1	6.2	5.7
Zimbabwe	-7.9	-2.8	-5.7	-8.3	-2.5	-4.0	-4.8	-5.7
SADC Average	2.3	2.9	2.5	3.4	4.3	4.9	5.4	6.2

* Source: Bank of Tanzania[540]

The GDP growth figures for Tanzania are supported by the data on growth of investment flows into Tanzania for the years 1996 to 2006 as Chart 2 shows.

---

540 Bank of Tanzania, Annual Report 2007/08, at 62.

CHART 3: RECORD OF INVESTMENT INFLOWS 1996 TO 2006

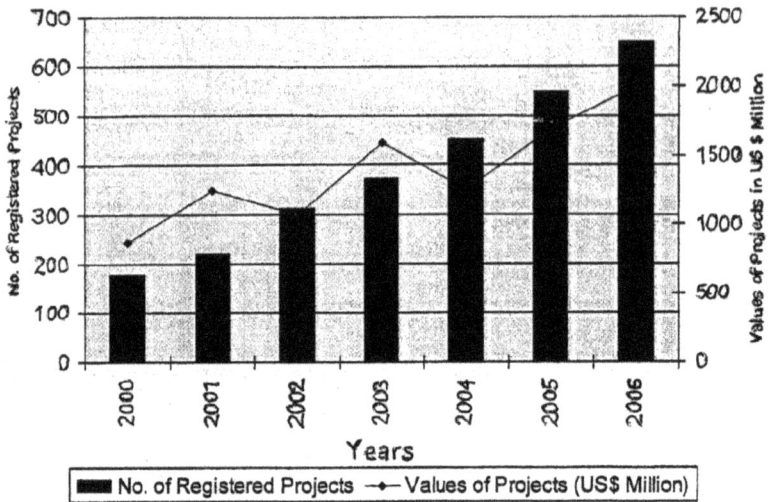

The TIC is also able to point to the significant growth of the mining sector as evidence that fiscal and non-fiscal incentives to investors are working in Tanzania. Tanzania is now said to be among the countries which host the most vibrant exploration and mining scene in Africa.[541] Investments made in mineral development and exploration exceeded US$ 2.5 billion by 2006. Mining is the fastest growing sector in Tanzania[542] in terms of its contribution to GDP and its share of export earnings. The value of mineral exports has increased from US$ 54.10 million in 1996 to over US$650 million in 2004. In 2006, total mineral exports were US$ 823.9 million, which was about 42.4% of Tanzania's total export earnings.[543] Tanzania is now Africa's third largest producer of gold, behind South Africa and Ghana, with a production capacity of 50 metric tons of gold per annum from six mines. The Geita Gold Mine (owned by South Africa's Anglo Gold Ashanti) is the largest project, with annual output of 650,000 ounces. Other gold mines include: Bulyanhulu Gold Mine, owned by Canadian company Barrick Gold with an annual output of 400,000 ounces; Golden Pride Mine owned by Resolute of Australia, producing 240,000 ounces per annum. The

541 Investment Opportunities in Tanzania, TIC Publication, 2006, 6.
542 In 2006 the mining sector grew by 16.4% compared to 15.7% in 2005. The Economic Survey 2006, Ministry of Planning, Economy and Empowerment, June 2007, 149.
543 In 2005, mineral exports were valued at US$ 711.3 million, The Economic Survey 2006, op. cit., 149.

remaining three gold mines (North Mara acquired by Barrick from Placerdome, Tulawaka also of Barrick, and the Meremeta Mine being mined by a joint venture company involving the Chinese and a local company) are much smaller in size with a life span of around 10 years only. The TIC believes that these mining developments have proceeded and appear to be succeeding largely because of Tanzania's favourable fiscal incentives.

Even with these economic initiatives, the balance of trade figures for Tanzania are still negative. To redress this loss, fiscal policies aimed at promoting exports have been put in place. The economy is responding to these measures as evident from the improving balance of trade figures shown in Table 10 below.

TABLE 10: BALANCE OF TRADE BETWEEN TANZANIA AND REGIONAL ECONOMIC GROUPINGS* (VALUES IN MILLION US $)

Region/ Year	1998	1999	2000	2001	2002	2003	2004	2005	2006
EU	-254.0	-177.4	-31.3	-52.8	-52.8	-210.5	-176.7	-3.9	-77.8
SADC	-164.7	-182.5	-176.0	-200.6	-143.6	-233.7	-213.4	-64.0	-56.7
EAC	-75.5	-75.4	-58.3	-63.9	-57.1	-35.6	-42.3	64.0	-56.7

* Source: Ministry of Planning, Econoy and Empowerment[544]

** Value in Million US$

The Dichotomy between Tax Policy and Tax Practice in Tanzania

From the above analysis, it is fair to state that all three objectives of taxation, namely, generation of revenue for government expenditure, stimulation of economic growth and redistribution of wealth, are all incorporated into the tax policies of Tanzania. However, it is also fair to state that taxation measures which seek to stimulate economic growth and to redistribute wealth have not been the driving force behind taxation policy. Research has shown that, both promoting economic growth and redistributing wealth, as objectives of taxation, tend to be overshadowed by the pursuit of revenue to fund government expenditure. As a result, even where these two objectives are incorporated into fiscal policy, or written into the tax statutes (as is the case for tax relief and tax incentives), tax administrators tend to find ways not to give full effect to these objectives.

---

544 Ministry of Planning, Economy and Empowerment, The Economic Survey 2006, June 2007, 49.

Glossy as the picture on tax incentives in Tanzania may appear on paper, the reality on the ground is different. The TRA pursuit for tax collections seems to sit uneasily with government effort to offer tax incentives for promoting economic growth in key sectors. Tax officers are reluctant to give full effect to the whole range of taxation incentives provided for in the tax statutes. The following examples demonstrate the extent of this uneasiness.

Example 1:

The TRA has been reluctant to let enterprises approved by the Tanzania Investment Centre (TIC) enjoy the full benefit of the five year tax holiday given to new enterprises in the initial years. When the Tanzania Cigarette Company (TCC), formerly a public enterprise, was sold to R. J. Reynolds, the investor applied in respect of its capital investment in the TCC for the company to be accorded the status of an approved enterprise. A certificate of incentives (No 041575) was issued to the TCC on 17th May 1996, stating the project implementation period to be March 1996 to September 1997. The approved five year tax holiday period was to run from October 1997 to September 2002.

Owing to some delay in the rehabilitation and expansion works at the TCC, an application was made to extend the implementation period and to put forward the commencement date for the tax holiday period. This change was approved by the TIC, which had succeeded the Investment Promotion Centre (IPC). An amended certificate (No 040050) was issued on 5th November 1997, showing the implementation period to be March 1996 to December 1997, with the tax holiday period running from January 1998. This certificate was promptly withdrawn because it failed to capture the implementation period and the tax holiday periods correctly. A fresh amended certificate (No 041575) was issued on 25th June 1998 stating the implementation period to be March 1996 to July 1998. The operative date stated on that certificate was August 1998, which meant that the tax holiday period would run from August 1998 to August 2003; Instead, the tax holiday period was stated as ending 10th September 2002.

> The TRA issued a corporation tax assessment for the years 2002 and 2003 on the basis that the amendment to the TCC certificate was invalid and that the period of holiday ended September 2002.

The TCC had to fight the assessment made and deal with the two issues raised by the TRA, namely, whether the amendment to the TCC certificate(s) embodying the new dates were validly made and whether, given that the tax holiday period provided under Section 21 of the **National Investment (Promotion and Protection) Act** of 1990 (NIPPA) is five years, the TRA could be right in stating that the tax holiday period was from August 1998 to 10th September 2002.

Regarding the validity of the amended certificate, the TRA's position was that the amendment was made when the TIC had no statutory power to make the amendment. The TRA's stand was incorrect when one examines the sequence and effect of the changes that were made to the investments law. NIPPA was repealed and replaced by the Tanzania Investment Act of 1997. According to Government Notice No 691 of 1997, the new Act came into force on 10th September 1997 and, when it did, NIPPA lost its force of law. However, if one examines the objectives of the new investment Act, one notes that it aimed simply to,

> re-write afresh the legislation on investment in Tanzania in order to restructure the organization of the center for the purpose of ensuring efficient discharge of the functions of the center.

The functions of the new Tanzania Investment Centre (TIC) remained very much the same as that of the IPC.

While NIPPA itself ceased to be law, the validity of all certificates of approval issued under NIPPA was preserved by a transitional provision contained in Section 31 of the Tanzania Investment Act. It reads:

> 31 (1) Notwithstanding the repeal of the National Investment (Promotion and Protection) Act, 1990, on the coming into operation of this Act, a certificate of approval issued by the Investment Promotion Centre and which immediately before the commencement of this Act is still in force, shall on the commencement of this Act, continue to be valid on the terms and conditions on which it was issued, as if it were a certificate of incentives issued under this Act and shall be so valid –

> (a) until the expiration of the term under which its holder was entitled to enjoy any benefit, incentives or protection; or

> (b) up to five years from the date of commencement of this Act, if on the coming into operation of this Act, the holder has not utilized any benefit, incentive or protection.

> (c) And on expiration of the period specified in paragraphs (a) and (b), the provisions of this Act shall commence to apply to the business of the enterprise.

Like all saving clauses, the objective of Section 31 (1) was to ensure that the change in the law of investments did not prejudice benefits given to existing holders of certificates of approval in order that the confidence of investors as to the stability of Tanzania's investment laws is maintained. Ordinarily, the repeal of an act does not apply retrospectively, unless expressly stated. Saving clauses, such as is contained in Section 31 (1), seek not to undo what has been validly done under the repealed law.

The TCC argued that one needs to examine the saving clause carefully to understand what is preserved. The pertinent words under Section 31 (1) are the following "a certificate of approval issued by the Investment Promotion Centre … and which is still in force…(1) shall continue to be valid (2) on the terms and conditions on which it was issued (3) as if it were a certificate of incentives issued under this Act" (emphasis added).

The TCC maintained that from the wording of the saving clause, two distinct things are saved as far as existing certificates are concerned. Firstly, the validity of the existing certificates is saved, and, secondly, the terms and conditions on which the certificates were issued are also saved. The other thing that the saving clause did is to carry the existing certificates from the repealed NIPPA into the new Act, thereby locking-in the previous regime until the period of the certificate expires.

The other point for the TCC was that, under NIPPA there existed a power vested in the IPC to amend the certificates it issued. This power was contained in Section 16 and the circumstances under which an amendment would be required and allowed to be made, included the case where an approved business is transferred to another person, or where the name of the enterprise is changed, or where the investment period is extended, or such other appropriate reason. Therefore, where a need for amendment arose, the holder of a certificate under NIPPA was entitled to apply for and obtain the sort of amendment that was necessary in the new circumstances of the holder, and so that the amendment enabled the holder of the certificate to enjoy the incentives granted. For the TCC, these were "the terms and conditions on which those existing certificates were issued," and if the validity of these certificates was preserved on the "same terms and conditions", it must have included "the right to seek and obtain amendment" to a certificate held (emphasis added). With this TCC view, the amendment of the TCC certificate, coming as it did after the repeal of NIPPA, was still valid because of the saving clause under Section 31 (1).

The TRA perspective on the repeal of NIPPA was untenable, because if an enterprise holding a certificate issued under NIPPA were to change name or were to be transferred to another entity through a merger or an acquisition and taking the view that the power to effect a name change on the certificate was already lost as alleged by the TRA, the certificate would become valueless to the enterprise, even though it has not expired and the holder would not be able to use the incentives given. This view completely defeats the whole purpose of the saving clause and is untenable.

As to the question of the proper dates for the TCC tax holiday period, the TCC contended that the certificate documents spoke for themselves. In terms of certificate No 041575 issued on 25th June 1998, the implementation period is March 1996 to July 1998. The operative date is August 1998, but the tax holiday period is stated to be August 1998 to 10th September 2002. One would think that, as a matter of arithmetic, a five year period counting from August 1998 runs to August 2003. To allege that it terminates in September 2002 makes the tax holiday less than the five-year period stipulated under NIPPA.

The TCC argued that there can only be one reason why this date was inserted in the certificate. There must have been some reliance on Section 31 (1) (b) of the new Act which restricted the tax holiday period to five years "from the date of commencement of this Act, if on the coming into operation of this Act, the holder has not utilized any benefit, incentives or protection" (emphasis added). As the new law came into force on 10th September 1997, five years from that date ended on 10th September 2002. That would explain why September 2002 was used as the cut-off date, when the TCC certificate was re-issued.

However, for one to invoke paragraph (b) and take the TCC out of the arithmetical five years, there is a critical statutory test to pass. If, at the time the new law came into force, the TCC had not used any of the incentives granted under its certificate, the new cut off date would apply. The TCC produced proof that this was not the case. The TCC had already used the customs duty remissions and the sales tax exemptions in connection with the capital works undertaken at the TCC during the implementation period.

It is possible for one to think that if the holder of a certificate had not used the tax holiday period when the new Act came into force, then paragraph (b) applies. This view would be wrong at law because paragraph (b) is collective. It covers not only the tax holiday, but all "incentives, benefits or protection". In addition to customs and sales tax incentives used, the TCC would have used other benefits such as the foreign staff quota. Section 31 (1) paragraph (b) cannot apply to the TCC.

If paragraph (b) does not apply to the TCC, then the only other paragraph relevant to determining the TCC's tax holiday period is paragraph (a), which states that the issued certificate shall be valid "until the expiration of the term under which its holder was entitled to enjoy any benefit, incentives or protection." Such term for the TCC is the full five years as from the operative date.

Clearly, the attempt by the TRA to make a corporation tax claim within the TCC's tax holiday period was contrary to law and was driven only by a desire to collect tax. No regard was given to the fiscal policy that aims at assisting new and/or expanded enterprises a period to recoup some of their capital investment before they are obliged to pay tax.

Example 2:
This second example shows how the TRA is too willing to curtail tax relief or advantages and to jump to new provisions, if they are less favourable to taxpayers.

When 60% of the shares of Tanzania Breweries Limited (TBL) were sold to the South African Breweries Corporation (SABC), the investor applied in respect of its capital investment in the TBL for an 'approved enterprise' certificate. Certificate number 041195 was issued to the TBL by the IPC (predecessor to TIC), on the 17th September 2001. This certificate was in addition to certificate number 041196, which was issued on the same date as a joint certificate with the view of consolidating all the TBL branches in Dar es Salaam, Arusha, Moshi and Mwanza. The certificate was issued under Section 21 of NIPPA, giving the TBL a five-year tax holiday from 1996 to 2001.

A tax dispute with the TRA emerged when the TRA attempted to apply Section 16 (2) (w) of the Income Tax Act 1973 (enacted as an amendment in 1998) to deny the TBL the wear and tear deductions the TBL had claimed under the Second Schedule to the Act. The TBL's position was that, although NIPPA was repealed in 1997, the incentives to which the TBL was entitled as holder of a Certificate of Incentives issued under NIPPA survived in a way that a change in law cannot water them down or remove them. The TRA, on the other hand, took the view that NIPPA was no longer law and, in any case, Section 16 (2) (w), being a more generous provision, cannot be overridden by the saving clause which affects only provisions which are detrimental to the holder of a NIPPA Certificate.

The TRA's position was that the introduction of Section 16 (2) (w) by the Finance Act of 1999 brought something new, whereby capital expenditure incurred is allowed in full in the year it is incurred, inclusive of work in progress and that there is no provision of law which allows either the deferment of the expenditure or the granting of wear and tear on work in progress. However, the TCC argued that the TRA was wrong in insisting it must apply Section 16 (2) (w) with respect to the capital deductions claimed by TBL. Section 16 (2) (w) has a less favourable tax result in comparison to the tax result under the Second Schedule. Because of that, the provisions of Section 20 (2) of NIPPA come into play to prevent the watering down of benefits given to TBL under the certificate of incentives it held.

Sections 20 (2) of NIPPA provided:

(2) The benefits conferred upon an approved enterprise shall apply in relation to that enterprise notwithstanding the provisions of any other law save that where there is any change in any law, such that the benefits conferred under this Act would be less favourable, the Minister shall adjust such benefits accordingly.

TBL was certainly right in saying Section 16 (2) (w), as introduced, was less favourable than Schedule Two. Subsection 16 (2) (w) provides that:

(w) where a person holding a certificate of incentives granted by Tanzania Investment Centre under the Tanzania Investment Act 1997, carries on business and has incurred expenditure in any year of income, there shall be made, in computing his gains or profits for that year of income, a deduction equal to the amount of that expenditure.

The intention of this amendment to the Income Tax Act was to enable approved companies holding TIC certificates to make an outright deduction of all expenditure in that year of income. The effect is to prevent the carry-forward of losses from the initial years (when the enterprise is unlikely to be in a profit situation capable of fully absorbing the capital expenditure incurred). For this reason, Section 16 (2) (w) was less favourable than Schedule Two.

Subsequently, the government thought it was desirable to expand the outright deduction provision to all companies, instead of restricting the application of the subsection to holders of TIC certificates. Subsection 16 (2) (w) was amended by the Finance Act 1999 to read as follows:

(w) without prejudice to the provisions of the Second Schedule where any corporation carries on business and has incurred expenditure in any year of income, there shall be made in computing his gains or profits for that year of income deduction equal to the amount of that expenditure.

Provided that:

> (i)   the provisions of this subsection shall not apply to capital expenditure on buildings.
>
> (ii)   For the purposes of ascertaining the total income of any corporation for any year of income no deduction shall be allowed in respect of any interest on any money borrowed and employed on the capital expenditure expensed in full under this subsection.

While the 1999 amendment expanded the application of Section 16 (2) (w) beyond holders of certificates of incentives, provisos were introduced to limit and exclude its application to buildings and interest on capital loans. These further restrictions made Section 16 (2) (w) more unfavourable.

In addition, Finance Act 2002 removed sub-clause (ii) of Section 16 (2) (w) and replaced it with the following provision:

> (iii)   The provisions of this subsection shall apply to a corporation holding a certificate of incentives granted by the TIC not later than 30th June 2002.

This small amendment may have been an afterthought. On the one hand, it stems from the saving clause in Section 31 (1) of the Tanzania Investment Act 1997. As noted above Section 31 of TIA saved the validity of incentive certificates issued under NIPPA in terms of subsection (1) (a). But Section 31 also enacted a sunset clause in subsection (1) (b), so that surviving incentive certificates in all cases would cease to apply by September 2002. The amendment in 2002 of Section 16 (2) (w) sought to bring the Income Tax Act in line with the sunset clause in the Tanzania Investment Act. So an attempt was being made through the amendment in 2002 to make Section 16 (2) (w) apply to holders of certificates of incentives.

The fact that the TRA seized on these new provisions to deny expenditure deduction claims for TBL on industrial buildings and machinery in clear violation of the protections given to investment certificate holders demonstrates how overbearing the drive for tax revenue has become.

One needs to look at the provisions of Section 19 (2) of the Tanzania Investment Act, 1997, which provided that for the purposes of creating a predictable investment climate, the benefits referred to under Section

19 (1) of the Tanzania Investment Act 1997 shall not be modified or amended to the detriment of such an investor. In essence therefore, Section 19 of TIA does the same thing that Section 20 of NIPPA did. Their combined effect is to protect certificate holders against legislative changes which would otherwise water down the benefits given at the time of investing. In applying Section 16 (2) (w) against TBL instead of Schedule Two, the TRA was not acting in accordance with law. The tax assessment made in respect of 2001 based on the erroneous view of the TRA was subsequently withdrawn.[545]

Example 3:
A third example of the TRA's ambivalence with tax relief is demonstrated in the TRA's tax dispute with DTP Terrassement, a French mining contracting company operating at the Geita Gold Mine.

DTP Terrassement recently won an appeal to the Tax Appeals Board [546] against the TRA for the imposition of income tax of Tzs 8,595,720,396 on the amount paid for the roll-over of assets back to Geita Gold Mine Ltd (GGM) upon the premature termination of its contract with GGM. The assessment was based on the contention that the sale value to be used in computing liability to corporation tax is the written down value calculated under Section 144 (1) (a) which assumes that wear and tear was available to the taxpayer.

The taxpayer disputed this assessment on the ground that depreciation and wear and tear were not available to DTP by reason of Section 17 (2) (j), which, when read together with Section 33 (3B) of ITA 1973, prevented DTP as a provider of technical services to a person carrying on mining operations from claiming the wear and tear deduction. DTP argued that the cost of DTP assets for which no depreciation was available must be the market value in terms of Section 144 (1) (b). DTP objected to the computation of asset value based on Section 144 (1) (a) as the TRA was intent on doing. DTP maintained that it was wrong to impute wear and tear values which had not been given to the assets being disposed of. The correct value to use was the economic cost/market value, especially because the parties were un-related and were dealing at arms length [Section 144 (1) (b), (c) and (d)].[547]

---

545 Information supplied by law firm FK Law Chambers which was retained by the TBL for this case.
546 DTP v Commissioner General TRA, Appeal No. 5 of 2006 decided in favour of DTP Terrassement by the Tax Revenue Appeals Board on 14th September 2007. The TRA has appealed this case. A decision by the Tax Revenue Appeals Tribunal is still pending.
547 *Ibid* (submissions of legal counsel on pages 12, 13, 16 and 18 of the proceedings).

The second ground on which DTP protested the assessment was that the TRA had used the wrong tax rate of 30% as the DTP project at Geita was a single purpose project and the activities undertaken by the taxpayer were only as provider of technical services to a person carrying on mining operations. The 30% tax rate applies to a taxpayer engaged in activity other than mining operations. The tax rate applicable to DTP as provider of technical services to a person carrying on mining operations is 3%, and this had been the tax rate used by the TRA throughout the contract period.

The TRA initially had wanted to apply the 5% rate brought in by the Income Tax Act 2004. But DTP argued that the fiscal stability clause in the Development Agreement with the Government (Article 10) provides that the tax rate of 3% must continue to apply, notwithstanding the change in the law.

DTP also successfully argued that, under the terms of the Agreement between Geita Gold Mine and DTP Terrassement, the roll over of assets to GGM was not a commercial transaction at profit. It was a simple transfer of mining equipment at residual book value. GGM needed to take-over the equipment so that it could move to an owner-operated mine consistent with Schedule 5 paragraph 2.2 of the Agreement with DTP Terrassement.

In this case, DTP was able to prevent an attempt at enforcing the tax claim of Tzs 8,595,720,396 based on a view of the law which is driven more by the need to collect tax, rather than being driven by the justice of the case.

Example 4:

A fourth example relates to fuel levy exemption. The remission order for road toll and fuel levy was promulgated on 1st July 1999 under Government Notice No 99. It applied to holders of mining licenses who have signed a Mining Development Agreement (MDA) with the Government of Tanzania and was intended to exempt mining companies which consume significant fuel in areas not serviced by power from the national grid. Fuel consumption in excess USD 200,000 was exempted from fuel levy. There was a similar remission arrangement for excise duty on fuel under Government Notice 480, effective from 1st July 2002. In both cases, the tax relief would be lost if the relieved fuel was sold or transferred to a person not entitled to enjoy similar privileges.

Fully aware that industry practice in the mining sector is to use contractors and subcontractors to carry out mining activities for the mine owner, the TRA rejected remission claims where the fuel was used by a contractor, notwithstanding that the contractor carried out mining activities exclusively for the mining license holder and had no other activities to which the contractor could have diverted the exempt fuel.

The TRA also imposed compliance and stationery requirements which are impossible to comply with, well outside the compliance requirements prescribed by the Government Notices referred above. The TRA also claimed the existence of a time-bar of twelve months, not present in the statutory instruments which govern tax relief. As a result, as of June 2010, mining companies have accumulated substantial unpaid fuel levy refunds amounting: in the case of Geita Gold Mine Ltd to 48.4 million USD; Africa Barrick Gold, 65.2 million USD; and Resolute Tanzania, 12.9 million USD.

Faced with continuing TRA reluctance/refusal to pay, Resolute has issued notice of international arbitration against the Government of Tanzania, protesting the breach of law and breach of the MDA. Barrick and Geita Gold are contemplating similar action.

The Cause of Conflict between Policy and Practice

The reluctance of the tax administration to apply tax provisions which result in foregoing tax revenue is, at least on face of it, reflective of a desire to collect more tax and meet or exceed revenue targets. The TRA sees tax relief as a loss of revenue and does not see the wider economic benefits which are the reason for the tax incentives. On this point, the TRA seems quite short sighted, as some loss of revenue today will lead to more tax revenue tomorrow, and the economic growth arising from tax incentives brings other benefits such as increased employment.

However, the TRA's apprehension against tax exemptions is not entirely without reason. In Tanzania, it is currently estimated that tax exemptions add up to 22.8% of the total tax revenue. This percentage translates to about Tzs 560 billion of tax revenue which was foregone for the year 2006/2007.[548] Figures from the TRA show that, in relation to customs, the cost of exemptions has gone down in recent years, compared to 1997/98 when exemptions were 82% of the total customs duties collected during that year. Although the scale of exemptions appears to have fallen to around 23% for 2002/2003, even at this level, the TRA believes the cost to revenue is still too high.

The TRA's ambivalence with tax exemptions stems from a belief that tax exemptions are mostly abused, despite the good intentions in having

---

548 Editorial, *The Citizen*, Thursday, March 22, 2007, page 8.

them.[549] For instance, the TRA says the customs duty relief on imports given to mining companies are used by these companies to import large quantities of goods which have very little to do with mining activities. Mining companies are also accused of passing on to third parties (contractors) their VAT relief on supplies of goods.

As a result, one of the objectives, which the TRA has given prime importance to in the Third Corporate Plan launched in 2008, is the need to streamline and reduce the extent of tax relief.

In the last three years, public opinion in Tanzania has shown signs of clear opposition to government policy on tax exemptions, especially for the mining sector. In August 2007, a Member of Parliament for Kigoma North, Mr. Zitto Kabwe, was suspended from Parliament for three months for what was alleged by the Speaker to be unfounded criticism of the minister responsible for mining. His suspension was roundly criticized by the media and the public held rallies and marches on the street to support Zitto. His suspension was seen by the public and the media as an attempt by the government to muzzle comment on the "plundering of our mining resources being carried on by foreign mining companies." Zitto Kabwe became an overnight celebrity[550] applauded by many and invited to be lead speaker at various forums and radio and television talk shows.

Such has been the persistence of public criticism that the President had to form a Special Mining Committee to review all the Mining Development Agreements, the mining laws and the taxation provisions, which erode the ability of the country to realize a fair return from its mineral resources. The Bomani Report from this inquiry made wide ranging recommendations aimed to improve the government's benefits from mines.

Tax Policy and Fairness of Taxation

Responsible tax policy formulation requires that tax policies be rational and have wider benefits in mind. Any suggestion of arbitrariness or favouritism in the tax policy and in the taxation system undermines public confidence in government and generates resistance to the taxes imposed by government. On the contrary, where there is public confidence in the fairness of taxation, the cooperation between the tax

---

549 *Ibid.*
550 Zitto Kabwe's suspension was announced on 14th August 2007 on the floor of Parliament, Hansard of 14/8/2007; and reported on the front pages of *The Guardian* of 15/8/2007, *Majira* and *Nipashe* of 15/8/2007 (both Swahili dailies). The media criticism, street marches and protests, lasted for a month following the suspension.

administration and the taxpayers is enhanced and, with heightened confidence, the level of voluntary tax compliance also rises.

The point has been made throughout this study that taxes must be fairly imposed and the public must see that fairness exhibited both in the content of the tax laws and in the administration of the tax laws.

The two taxpayer surveys discussed in Chapter Two indicate that there is now a widely held feeling among taxpayers in Tanzania that the tax exemptions which are contained in the tax system are *ad hoc*, too numerous and widely abused. Public opinion equates tax exemptions with tax injustice. The argument made is that many exemptions are provided without justification and those which are justified are not effectively monitored. In consequence, there is believed to be wide abuse of tax exemptions.

The tax-paying public in Tanzania also has issues with the distribution of the tax burden. The burden of taxation is not cast wide enough, such that those paying tax feel unfairly singled out. This widespread public dissatisfaction with taxation belies the official accolades coming from government officials (TIC and Treasury), which, it has been shown, describe the fiscal policies of Tanzania and its taxation system as well-balanced and effective.

These contradictory perspectives of the government and the public underline a basic problem of understanding and perception. The point was made in Chapter One that the assumption that tax laws (and policies) are understood is not borne out, given the survey findings examined. The public is largely excluded from participation in the formulation of tax policy. There is also no wider involvement in discussing taxation bills before they are passed into law. A lot of secrecy characterises the tax legislative process.

On the other hand, there are insufficient guarantees against unfair taxation of the public. There is no provision in the Constitution of the United Republic of Tanzania sufficiently constraining the powers of taxation. The only provision existing is Article 138 (1). But, Article 138 (1) declares simply that "no tax of any kind shall be imposed save in accordance with a law enacted by Parliament or pursuant to a procedure lawfully prescribed and having a force of law by virtue of a law enacted by a Parliament." This provision addresses itself only to the manner of bringing a tax into existence; it does not deal with the content of the tax or the involvement of the public in its introduction.

The taxing power granted to the Parliament without any real restraint has enabled Parliament to cede to the Finance Minister wide discretionary powers for either giving tax exemptions, or withdrawing them.[551] The only condition imposed on the exercise of this discretion is a procedural one. The Minister must gazette any exemption, amendment, variation, or replacement of exemption made.[552]

It has been suggested by Holmes[553] that the most reliable restraint against possible abuse of the power to tax is the inclusion of restraining provisions in a constitutional clause which stipulates the nature of taxes to be imposed and the procedure of taxation.[554] It is argued that this mechanism has the ability to restrain, not only the taxing authority, but even the legislature of the day, as no amendment can be easily made to such a clause.[555] As a result, some scholars propose that the best policy option is to make the powers of taxation a constitutional issue so that it gets the mandate of the majority in the state, thus building consensus.[556]

Where taxation is a constitutional issue, the taxpayers participate directly in determining how they want to be taxed. The degree of discretion, both for the framers of tax policy and for the tax authority, is diminished. Taxpayer-participation in the formulation of tax policy, in the making of tax laws and in the administration of the tax system, makes them part and parcel of the taxation process. It destroys the justification for resisting taxation, because it creates understanding and acceptance of taxation.

Looking at Tanzania, the extent of public participation in tax formulation is severely limited. The only forum for public input into tax policy and tax administration issues is the Stakeholders Tax Forum. The Tax Forum was conceived by the TRA principally to collect views from stakeholders and then use those views in formulating the TRA's advice to the Minister for Finance on matters of tax policy and tax administration. The Tax Forum is made up of wide representation, drawing together professional bodies such as the association for accountants and auditors, the bar association, the medical association, the engineers and contractors association, the chamber of commerce, the chamber of mines, the chamber of industries, the oil dealers association and the shipping association.

The Forum is chaired by the Commissioner General of the TRA and its secretariat is headed by the Director for Taxpayer Education of the

---

551 See for example Section 10 ITA 2004 and Section 9 and Schedule 1 of VAT Act 1997.
552 Section 10 (1) (a).
553 J Holmes 'The Taxing Power' (1986) 134 *Arizona Law Review* 32.
554 *Ibid.* 37.
555 *Ibid.*
556 B G Peters *The Politics of Taxation: A Comparative Study*, Blackwell, 1991, at 67.

TRA. All the revenue commissioners for VAT, Customs and Domestic Revenue attend in their official capacities.

The Forum largely serves the purpose of deliberating on taxation proposals from various sectors, thus insulating the TRA from succumbing to individual lobbies and pressure groups. It meets once every three months.

The Forum is fairly limited in its ability to influence tax changes in Tanzania. It cannot engage the Minister directly as all its proposals are screened by and must rely on the support of the TRA.

A more powerful body in terms of influencing taxation policy is the Task Force on Tax Reform. This group has no public participation. It is made up exclusively of representatives from government departments (the Treasury, the TRA, the Bank of Tanzania and the Ministry of Economic Planning and Empowerment). Anyone wishing to make a representation before this group must file an application. The application is evaluated on merit, before a hearing is allowed. At every session, verbal and visual representations are limited to a maximum of an hour, followed by a question and answer session. No decision is made on the spot. Deliberations are carried out in camera following the presentations. Applicants are informed only of the rejection or acceptance of their submission. There is no requirement to give reasons for acceptance or rejection of a taxation proposal.

Apart from these two forums, the only other way for the public to participate in tax policy formulation is through the suggestion boxes used by the TRA. These are largely ignored by both the public and the TRA and, in any case, the bulk of items that find their way to suggestion boxes are nuisance complaints against tax officers. Contributions from the public through media publications or radio talk shows are also largely ineffective.

This scenario underlines the lack of inclusiveness in tax policy formulation. The public is largely left out such that it is difficult to speak of taxpayers owning the tax system and identifying with its objectives.

It has been argued by Rakner and Gloppen[557] that, while taxation issues rank high on the agenda of political parties, parliaments and governments of developed countries, taxation issues are far less prominent public issues in developing countries. It is said that taxpayers in developing countries rarely mobilise politically. Two reasons are put

557 L Rakner and S Gloppen (2002) "Tax Reform and Democratic Accountability in Sub-Saharan Africa' internet source http://www.ids.ac.uk/gdr/cfs/activities/rakner-gloppen.pdf .

forward for this political state. The first is that in developing countries only a small number of people form the tax base, especially for direct taxes. The second reason is that there is not enough direct taxation, as governments in developing countries tend to rely mostly on indirect taxes.[558] This view could be overstated. The revolt which occurred in Uganda against the introduction of the value added tax in 1996 is one example that shows taxation is an equally emotive issue in Africa. A more recent example in Tanzania is the way the opposition parties were able to mobilize the public to hold rallies and public marches between October and November 2007, which forced the Tanzanian government to form a commission to review tax concessions given to mining companies.

The substantive and procedural aspects of tax equity, tax fairness, and justice of taxation have been examined. Both Chapters One and Three make the point that the governmental power to tax is legitimised by both the rationality of the objectives of taxation and the equitable imposition and collection of taxes. Where the government has played its role as an investor and has provided the public services in the form of security, education, health and welfare, its claim to taxation is legitimised. In the absence of these benefits the government will find itself, at least in public perception, in a position similar to a street robber whose claim over stolen property is based only on might.

The justice of taxation in this regard refers to the way the government legitimises its claim to taxation. Trust is an important factor; when taxpayers have trust in their government, tax compliance is bolstered. A government which does not command the trust of the public will need to rely on tax enforcement, as many taxpayers will rightly question the legitimacy of the government to tax them.

Institutional accountability is also a factor, for both the government and its institutions (e.g. the TRA). They must show that they are accountable to the people. Accountability to the public plays a key role in influencing taxpayers to be tax compliant. A government which is not accountable to its people is alienated from them and has no right to expect cooperation. Taxpayers want the assurance that their taxes will serve the purposes they are intended to serve and those purposes must resonate with public expectation over the use of taxpayer money.

Fairness, trust and accountability form the core part of substantive justice. They are indicators of the government's attempt to justify its right over taxes in society. They give the government of the day the legitimacy

---

558 *Ibid.* at 7.

to demand tax payment from society. A government which fails to meet these conditions loses the justification to levy taxes. In the absence of public acceptance, such government will resort to enforcement to realize taxation. It has no right to expect voluntary tax payment.

The other factor promoting equity in taxation is procedural justice. This is embodied in the principle of fair play between the taxpayers and the tax authority. It requires that the tax administration observes the due process of law. An adherence to the due process of law enables the tax administration to gain acceptance with taxpayers.

Procedural justice requires that the tax authority should not be allowed an unfair advantage in its dealings with taxpayers.[559] This is reflected in a number of administrative requirements. One of these is the requirement that the tax authority must notify the taxpayer of any action the authority proposes to take against the taxpayer in connection with taxes. The other is that during the dispute resolution process, the taxpayer and the tax authority must be afforded equal treatment. The third requirement is consistency in decision making. The tax authority must be bound to the positions it has taken in respect of the taxpayer unless those positions are adjudged incorrect by a judicial body.[560] The tax authority must also make the same decision in respect of taxpayers who are in the same tax position. This creates desirable predictability in taxation. In all its decisions, the tax administration must observe the principles of justice.[561]

It is appropriate to refer to an incident where the courts in Tanzania found fault with the manner of exercise of power rendering a taxpayer taxable in disregard of a lawful exemption given to them. This relates to the case of *Karibu Textile Mills Limited v The Minister for Finance and the Honourable Attorney General,*[562] where the taxpayer had to seek orders of *certiorari* to quash the decision of the Minister for Finance purporting to revoke the tax concession which the Minister had granted to the taxpayers by Government Notice No. 162 of 2005. The taxpayer challenged the decision of the Minister as unreasonable, unfair, illegally made with improper motives and in disregard of the principles of natural justice.

---

559 V Thuronyi (ed) *Tax Law Design and Drafting,* Kluwer Law International, Netherlands, Vol 1, 2000, at 7.
560 *Ibid.*
561 Such as the presumption of innocence, the right to be heard, the right of appeal, the duty to give reasons for a decision, and others.
562 Misc. Commercial Case No. 43 of 2005.

The Finance Minister revoked the concession which he had granted pursuant to the signing of the Memorandum of Understanding with the taxpayers, followed by the publication of the Government Notice. The Minister revoked the said concession by a mere letter without giving any prior notice to the taxpayers, after the taxpayer had incurred substantial costs amounting to more that Tzs 15 billion, in reliance on the Memorandum of Understanding.

The High Court agreed with the taxpayers that the decision of the Minister was wrong in principle. The High Court reiterated the need for the state agencies to act judicially in these words:

> An administrative body exercising functions that impinge directly on any legally recognised interest has the duty to act judicially in accordance with the rules of natural justice…the party adversely affected…has the right to be given a reasonable and fair deal.[563]

The Court also agreed with the taxpayers that the decision of the Minister having been reached without due regard for the fundamental procedure was a nullity and could not stand.[564] The Court further observed that the decision was unfair because it was reached without considering that the Applicant had incurred substantial costs to implement the conditions of the Memorandum of Understanding, which led to the grant of the tax concessions. It held that the decision was made in error of law, because the decision to revoke the concession was made by a mere letter; it ought to have been gazetted in the same way as the granting was made by way of a Government Notice. On these grounds, the High Court quashed the decision of the Minister.

The idea that there is a relationship between the perceived injustice of certain laws and a diminished general compliance with those laws is aptly documented. The possibility that law breaking can flow from perceived injustice is assumed on the ground that individuals have different reasons and motives for both compliance and non compliance with laws. This understanding applies to taxation laws as well.

The diminished respect for the legal system that follows can cause resistance where previously there was law abiding behaviour.[565] Others have noted that the power of law can backfire when a law inadvertently generates disrespect.[566] Kahan[567] has observed that a well publicized

---

563 *Ibid.* at 17.
564 *Ibid.* at 19.
565 J. Nadler "Flouting the Law"(2005) 83 *Texas Law Review*, 1399, § p.1401.
566 H. R. McAdams 'The Origin, Development, and Regulation of Norms' (1997) 96 *Michigan Law Review* 338 at 355.
567 D. M. Kahan "Trust, Collective Action and Law" 2001: p.342.

government crackdown on tax cheating can implicitly send the message that everyone cheats, thereby generating more cheating than would occur without the crackdown.

In a scathing article against brutalism in law, Arthur[568] argues that when a law is perceived as failing to accurately reflect popular notions of justice, then citizens will be less likely to view the law as a moral standard that should guide their behaviour. Consequently the public will view that law as not commanding their deference.

Robinson and Darley argue that when the criminal law gains a reputation for assigning liability and punishment in ways that correspond to the intuition of the community as a whole, it is more likely to be viewed as morally authoritative.[569] As a result, people are more likely to defer to the commands arising from such law. Robinson and Darley add that most people obey the law, not so much because they are deterred by the possibility of being caught and punished, but because they either fear disapproval from their peer group, or they want to do the morally correct thing or both.[570] Criminal law theorists, who support the notion that liability and punishment track commonsense justice, are joined by others, who are concerned with the fairness of specific laws. They cite a report of the commission of police officers, academics and politicians appointed to study Britain's drug problem, which concludes that Britain's tough marijuana laws produce more harm than they prevent.[571]

A renowned jurist said that perceived injustice and the ill-feeling it causes have serious repercussions on compliance with law. He wrote:

If a person sees unfairness or illegitimacy or unworthiness of trust in one instance, how far does his disillusionment extend? How much of his attitude spills over into his actual behaviour? The hypocrisy and unfairness of Prohibition, it is said, brought the whole legal system into disrepute. Legal scholars claim that marijuana laws "hasten the erosion of respect for the law." But how much "erosion of respect"? And where? And what are the consequences?[572]

---

568 R. Arthur 'The Place of Norms in Tax Compliance' (1997) 56 *Tax Review* 216, at 218.

569 P Robinson and J Darley 'The Utility of Desert' (1997) 91 North Western University Law Review, 457.

570 Ibid, at 468.

571 The Police Foundation 'Drugs and the Law: Report of the Independent Inquiry into the Misuse of Drugs Act 1971' (2000) at 115 internet source, http://www.policefoundation. org.uk., accessed 17/10/2007.

572 L Friedman *The Legal System: A Social Science Perspective*, Russell Sage Foundation, 1975, at 118-19.

The experimental evidence presented by Nadler did suggest that a perceived injustice can result in less respect for the law.[573] Compliance with the law decreases when many members of the society perceive that a particular law is unjust in accordance with their perception of what is just and fair. In the experiments conducted, *Experiment One* tested the influence of perceived unjust legal rules regarding civil forfeiture, distribution of the income tax burden and the right to privacy. In this experiment, Nadler demonstrated that perceived unjust legal rules cause people to be more likely to engage in law breaking in their daily lives.

From Nadler's research, it is shown that perceptions of the justice of taxation (policy, laws and administration) can either increase or decrease compliance with taxation. It can increase compliance when taxpayers perceive the system to be fair, but will decrease compliance if the system is perceived unfair. Fairness of taxation flies through the window when, as is the case in Tanzania, a night nurse and the hard working school teacher are taxed fully on their small pay, but the same does not apply to Ministers and Parliamentarians who, in addition to higher pay, tax free allowances and tax exempt gratuities, are taxed lightly on earnings. This disparity can have a serious impact on taxpayer attitudes.

Conclusion

This chapter has attempted to show that voluntary taxpayer compliance is affected, not only by tax administrators in the application of tax laws, but also by the soundness of the policies forming the basis for the laws administered by the tax authority. Therefore there is a need for the government to demonstrate to its people that the taxes they pay are fair and the revenue is used for worthy causes. The government must show visibly that the taxes it receives from taxpayers are well conceived and are also applied to the best interests of the taxpayers themselves.

The point has been made that an important attribute of good governance is the ability of government to formulate sound policies for the people it governs. It can also be said that at the centre of sound taxation policy is the fair treatment of taxpayers, including a fair distribution of the tax burden and a fair manner of collecting taxes. The fairer the tax burden is allocated and realised, the easier it is to win the hearts of taxpayers to voluntarily support the government in its tax objectives.

Taxation policies and administrative procedures can be geared towards creating a conducive environment for a friendlier interaction

---

573 J. Nadler Flouting the Law"(2005) 83 *Texas Law Review*, 1399, p.1426.

between the tax administration and the taxpayers. The slogans adopted by the TRA on the occasion of the TRA's tenth anniversary are indeed instructive, "From Tax Collector to Partner in Development" and "Together we Build the Nation". Similar sentiments are echoed in Uganda where the URA uses the slogan "Building Uganda Together". This reflects the change of mindset spoken about previously and has the potential to foster cooperation between the tax administration and the taxpayers.

The service standards and the commitment to serve the taxpayers as are contained in the TRA and the URA Taxpayer's Charters are a good starting point. However, for these service standards and expectations to achieve the intended results, they must be enforceable by law. It is the force of law which can make service commitments an effective instrument, as that gives the taxpayers the ability to realize them in court, instead of being mere pronouncements in taxpayer charters which exist by the grace of the tax administration.

Good tax administration adheres to a high performance standard and public expectation. The fundamental performance expectations which define a just system in a democratic society are well known in the perceptions of taxpayers. Any action by a government agency which is contrary to those performance expectations will undermine confidence in that agency. These expectations come in addition to legal rights such as the presumption of innocence, the right of appeal without any let or hindrance, and the right to property.

Arguing for the government and its agencies to adhere to the due process of law, Mr. Justice Brandeis wrote that,

> If the Government becomes a law breaker, it breeds contempt for law; it invites every man to become a law unto himself; it invites anarchy.[574]

The overriding need to collect as much tax as is possible should not detract the policy framer, the legislator and the administrator, from the needs of those governed. Ultimately, the government exists for the people and taxes must be paid only for the peoples' good. The justice of taxation must be maintained.

---

574 *Olmstead v United States*, 277 U.S.438, 485 (1928).

7

Enforcement of Tax Compliance

Introduction

Throughout this study, the point has been made that non-compliance with taxation is a significant cost to the government.[575] In Tanzania, the TRA estimates that taxpayers who have been reached are less than half of the potential taxpayers.[576] Reports abound that the government is losing much revenue through non-payment of tax and that this non-payment is difficult to combat because the vice is widespread. For this reason, combating non-compliance must be a key function in the administration of taxes. Types of deviant taxpayer behaviour which the tax administration has to combat include:

- failure to report taxable activities;
- omission of taxable items from tax returns (whether deliberate or accidental);

---

575 The TRA, *From Tax Collector to Partner in Development – A Decade of TRA Transformation 1996-2006* at 3.
576 *The Citizen* Newspaper of 11th March, 2005 at 5, as no sufficient data was given by the report, this statement, while bearing some truth, may be exaggerated.

- tax evasion or fraud (illegal activities which if discovered would result in criminal prosecution); and

- tax avoidance (involving schemes which enable a person to escape tax).[577]

These forms of non-compliance are multi-faceted and the causes for their prevalence are also varied. Financial reward is just one of the many reasons for dodging tax. Other factors exist, including for instance, the thrill of winning against the system. For such people, self enrichment is not the objective; rather, it is the satisfaction which comes with beating the tax system. When faced with such a multifaceted problem, there can be no single response for dealing with it.

This study has argued that tax compliance requires a combination of strategies. A tax administration must adopt both voluntary tax payment measures, as well as effective measures to compel non-compliant persons to pay their taxes. The challenge for governments and tax administrations alike is how to determine the right mix between these two compliance strategies. For many tax administrations, there appears to be an irresistible attraction to enforcement as the most efficient way to combat tax non-compliance.[578] The justification could well be that a slight relaxation in enforcement can lead many compliant taxpayers to join the non-compliant. In this regard, the effectiveness of enforcement need not always be measured by the ability to increase the number of taxpayers, but rather, the ability to sustain the number of compliant taxpayers. Therefore, funding enforcement may in reality be funding to sustain compliance. This view should not detract from the need for expanding the tax base and the need for inclusive taxation.

The preference for enforcement measures is visible in Tanzania, where a big portion of tax compliance resources are put into enforcement measures. Voluntary compliance measures are not as well funded as those which seek to enforce tax compliance. In pursuing tax enforcement, there is great emphasis on improving tax investigation so that it leads to effective prosecution and punishment of tax offenders.

Why Enforcement is Preferred
Tax administrators' attraction to enforcement measures is understandable. The revenue effectiveness of enforcement is readily

---

577 G Cooper 'Analysing Corporate Tax Evasion' (1994) 50 Tax Law Review 33, at 35.
578 In reaching this conclusion, reliance is placed mostly on tax collections resulting from audits and investigations. No data is offered for results from voluntary compliance measures which would enable an objective comparison to be made.

measurable. Enforcement measures are also said to have a direct deterrent effect which increases tax compliance.[579] Relying on this thinking, some people have suggested that the most efficient way to combat non-compliance is to enact very significant penalties for tax evasion,[580] so that the 'would be' evaders are discouraged from contemplating such conduct. This view seems to have its foundation in the philosophical propositions of Jeremy Bentham, who wrote that since the profit of the crime is the force which urges man to delinquency, then the pain of the punishment is the force which must be employed to restrain him from it"; and "if the first of these forces be the greater, then crime will be committed; but if the second, then crime will not be committed.[581]

The other response to non-compliance is a legislative response. However, the limitation in fighting tax evasion and avoidance using legislation is now widely recognized. The House of Lords' successive decisions in *IRC v Burmah Oil*,[582] *Ramsay v IRC*[583] and *Furniss v Dawson*,[584] decided between 1980 and 1984, recognized that drafters of legislation cannot foresee the multiplicity of schemes by which taxes can be avoided so as to come up with water-tight legislation capable of preventing such non-compliance.[585] A Legislative response to tax evasion and avoidance also results in too much detail and complexity in tax legislation, which is undesirable. Modern day tax thinking is that tax laws ought to be simple and understandable to taxpayers. Complex tax legislation is difficult to comply with and detracts from making tax legislation understandable.

The effectiveness of tax investigations and audits in combating non-compliance is relative.[586] It is dependent on the resources available to the tax administration to enable it to undertake sufficient audits to uncover a significant number of non-compliant persons, as well as deter others because of the knowledge that they will be caught. No tax authority has resources at such levels as to be able to rely entirely on audits and investigations.

---

579 C O Rossotti 'Modernizing Americas' Tax Agency', (1999) 83 *Tax Notes* 1191 at 1195.
580 J Andreoni, B Erard and J Feinstein 'Tax Compliance' (1998) 36 *Journal of Economic Literature* 818 at 824.
581 J Bentham, *Principles of Penal Law*, Edinburgh, 1843.
582 IRC v Burmah Oil (1980) STC 731.
583 Ramsay v IRA (1982) AC 300.
584 Furniss v Dawson (1984) AC 474
585 G S Cooper 'Analysing Corporate Tax Evasion' in G S Cooper *Avoidance and the Rule of Law*, IBFD Amsterdam 1997, at 35.
586 *Ibid.*

Tax investigations tend to go hand in hand with prosecution and punishment. One compliments the other. It is one thing to uncover tax fraud, but if the discovered fraud is not effectively prosecuted and sufficiently punished, it leaves the offender feeling immune to sanction. The failure to prosecute and punish criminal behaviour also frustrates the enthusiasm of the investigators.

Investigation, prosecution and punishment of tax offences are, however, not an easy task. Prosecution of tax cases, especially, is a complex process. Canada, which has a common law legal system similar to that of Tanzania, provides instructive lessons on how prosecuting tax delinquency is problematic. In dealing with tax evasion cases, the courts in Canada insist that the criminality test applicable to other areas of crime must apply as well to tax evasion cases. Prosecutors must establish *mens rea* and prove the wilful intention to dodge tax on the part of the accused. In *Regina v Branch*,[587] the accused admitted the failure to file tax returns for four years. The question at the trial was whether this failure was coupled with an intention to evade tax so that it could be said he had "willfully evaded payment of taxes." In his defence, it was argued that the failure to file tax returns was not intentional or wilful because he was emotionally disturbed and could not attend efficiently to many of his affairs.

The court found that the necessary *mens rea* to convict for tax evasion was lacking and acquitted him. The judge said,

> ... In my opinion the word evasion implies something of an underhand or deceitful nature ... a deliberate attempt to escape the requirement of paying tax on income that had been earned. This intention can be inferred from acts of omission or commission. Mere failure to file tax returns and to pay tax for four successive years cannot suggest an attempt to evade the payment of taxes.[588]

Another example of the application of stringent criminal law tests to cases of tax evasion is the case of *Regina v Hummel*.[589] Here, the accused was charged with wilful evasion of payment of taxes and making false and deceptive statements in tax returns. The court acquitted the accused on a finding that there was no *mens rea*. These two cases demonstrate that successful prosecution of tax evasion or other tax offences, especially where proof of intent is required, is not always an easy affair.

---

587 *Regina v Branch* (1976) CTC 193.
588 *Ibid.* at 195.
589 *Regina v Hummel* (1971) CTC 803.

The Tax Enforcement Strategies of the TRA

In its tax compliance strategies, the TRA puts great emphasis on tax enforcement. It relies heavily on investigation and punishment of tax offenders. There is wide use of the audit and investigation powers as discussed earlier. Investigations are coupled with criminal prosecutions leading to various forms of punishment.

Much effort by the TRA was put into strengthening the Tax Investigation Department (TID). The TID, which had about 25 investigation officers (19 male and 6 female) in 2005,[590] had grown to 80 investigators by 2010 with an additional 27 supporting staff. According to a TRA report,[591]

> the role of the Tax Investigation Department is to minimize the occurrence of tax fraud through identification and investigation of fraudulent cases, collecting evaded taxes and recommending prosecution of offenders with a view to improve compliance with tax laws.[592]

The organizational changes, which occurred within the TRA, have affected the Tax Investigation Department as well. On the recommendation of DANIDA, USAID, the Swedish International Development Agency (SIDA) and the German International Cooperation Agency (GTZ), together with the World Bank,[593] who are the major development partners for the TRA, the TRA has adopted an integrated approach to tax administration. It has moved away from a tax-type to a tax-function approach. As a result, the singular departments for income tax, VAT and stamp duty. which existed previously as separate administrative units, were merged in 2005 in what is now called the Department of Domestic Revenue. Even before this merger occurred, all large taxpayers were transferred in October 2001 to the Large Taxpayers Department (LTD), in an effort to provide them a one-stop service centre for all their tax affairs (except for customs matters).[594]

In like manner, the TID also adopted an integrated approach to tax investigations and audits, such that audit visits are now carried out for all taxes at the same time, by the same officer(s), in respect of each investigation.[595]

---

590 The TRA, *Annual Report 2004/05*, at 22. The staff position has tended to fluctuate over the years, affected by departmental transfers, dismissals and deaths.

591 Tax Investigation Department, *Annual Performance Report for 2002/2003*.

592 *Ibid.* 1.

593 Annual Review Reports on the Tax Administration Project (TAP) funded under the basket funding administered by the World Bank,

594 The TRA, *A Decade of TRA Transformation 1996-2006*, Tanzania Revenue Authority, Dar es Salaam, 2006, 54.

595 The TRA, Tax Investigation Department Report to the TRA Management, December 2002, at 2.

In order to enable the TID to carry out its functions, the TRA transferred officers from other departments to the TID. As these were drawn from tax collecting departments, they are able to use their experience in tax affairs to carry out investigation work. In addition, these officers were given professional training in investigation techniques relating to documentary evidence and in computer forensic audit.[596]

The TID put together a Business Intelligence Unit, which is responsible for developing a data bank containing business intelligence, which the TID is able to share with other departments at the TRA Head Office and its Zone Offices to improve the quality of investigations and audits. The Business Intelligence Unit became operational in July 2005. The TID also installed three hotline phones in the Northern Zone (Arusha, Moshi, Manyara areas), Southern Highland Zone (Iringa, Mbeya and Ruvuma areas), and Lake Zones (Mwanza, Bukoba, Shinyaga and Kigoma areas), as well as one hotline for the Dar es Salaam Zone; These hotlines are used by members of the public to report tax irregularities.[597]

In line with these initiatives, the TID computers were linked to the Customs ASYCUDA++ system, and in August 2006 a radio communication system was installed in all the TID Zone Offices.[598] An Internet facility that enables the distribution of orders and instructions was established to link the TID at Head Office in Dar es Salaam to the TID Dar es Salaam Zones I and II. Further radio connections were installed for Mbeya, Dar es Salaam, Zanzibar, Arusha and Mwanza.[599]

The TID set up an investigation office for Zanzibar in December 2003, which is headed by a Principal Tax Investigation Officer. The total workforce for this office is four investigation officers equipped with one motor vehicle, several computers and a communication system Surveillance equipment was also procured and deployed to the Zanzibar office. All of these investigation initiatives implemented by the TRA are captured in the National Investigation Policy which the TRA started implementing in July 2007.[600]

Effectiveness of Investigations and Tax Audits
Having been set up in 2001, the TID carried out operations for the first time as a full fledged investigation department during the year 2002/03. It investigated a total of 466 taxpayers for suspected tax fraud and other

---

596 *Ibid.* 3.
597 *Ibid.* 4-5.
598 *Ibid.* 4.
599 *Ibid.* 6.
600 *Ibid.* 6.

tax irregularities.[601] The cases investigated had a total revenue potential of Tzs 8,807,000,000. An amount of Tzs 4,525,100,000 was recovered, representing a 51% recovery rate.[602]

It is notable that in the first year of performance following the restructure, the TID performed below the mark it had set before reorganization.[603] The recovery rate for 2001/02 was 58%.[604] However, the recovery rate achieved for both years was well above the benchmark recovery rate set for the TID by the TRA which was 26% for 2002/03 and 25% for 2001/2002. A tabulation of tax investigation results for 2002/03 is shown in Table 10 below:

TABLE 10: TID INVESTIGATION CASES FOR 2002/03
(VALUES ARE IN BILLION TANZANIAN SHILLINGS)

TID	Investigations	Potential Revenue	Arrears and doubtful claims	Recoverable Arrears	Tax Recovered	Tax Outstanding	Recovery Rate
VAT	79	4,928.0	12.1	4,915.9	1,942.2	2,973.7	39.4%
Income Tax	103	2,265.6	-	2,265.6	1,328.5	937.1	58.6%
Customs	284	1,613.4	-	1,613.4	1,254.4	359.0	77.7%
Total	466	8,807.0	12.1	8,794.9	4,529.1	4,269.8	51.4%

* Source: The TRA Investigation Department Annual Report for 2002/03

** Values are in Billion Tanzania Shillings

Among the taxpayers investigated for 2002/03, the TID recommended 72 cases for prosecution. However, only 29 were taken up for prosecution. The TID relies on the Legal Services Department (LSD) of the TRA for advice on which cases can be successfully prosecuted, and also for undertaking the prosecutions in the courts. The LSD returned the rest of the cases to the TID, either for additional investigation, or rejected as unfit for prosecution.[605] Table 11 below shows the investigations breakdown for 2002/03.

---

601 The TRA, *Tax Investigation Department Annual Report for 2002/03.*
602 *Ibid.* 1- 2.
603 *Ibid.* 2.
604 *Audit and Investigation Department Report 2001/02,* 1.
605 The TRA, *Tax Investigation Department Annual Report for 2002/03,* 2.

TABLE 11: CASES INVESTIGATED AND ACTION TAKEN

	Action Taken	Total
1	Cases investigated	466
2	Cases recommended to the LSD for prosecution	72
3	Cases settled under compounding offence procedure	288
4	Cases referred back to the TID for further investigation	22
5	Criminal cases prosecuted	29
6	Criminal cases completed	11
7	Criminal cases decided in favour of the TRA	8
8	Criminal cases decided in favour of the taxpayer	3

* Source: The TRA Tax Investigation Department Annual Report for 2002/03

In its first year following reorganization, the TID continued to develop the investigation skills of its staff. Officers attended a two-month course on basic criminal investigation techniques conducted between February and April 2002.

The tax investigation work undertaken by the TID involves surveillances, travel and communication. The TID annual report for 2002/03 says that the TID was handicapped by a lack of working tools and enumerated the following factors which constrained performance:[606]

- inadequate working tools such as computers, radios, desk phones, cellular phones and motor vehicles;
- failure by taxpayers or their authorized accountants and auditors to comply with various TID notices to supply information or attend inquiries as permitted under the tax laws;
- inadequate professional skills for the TID staff when dealing with complex investigations;
- shortage of staff at Headquarters which is more serious at Zone, Regional and District level; and
- poor record keeping by taxpayers which makes it difficult to track taxable activities.

Annual Reports for the years 2003/04 and 2004/05 show no improvement in the performance of the TID. The reports also show that the constraints on performance noted by the TID in the first year of

606 *Ibid.* at 13.

operations still persisted. Table 12 below shows a summary of the cases investigated by the TID for the year 2003/04.

TABLE 12: TID INVESTIGATION CASES FOR 2003/04
(VALUES ARE IN BILLION TANZANIA SHILLINGS)

TID	Investiga-tions	Potential Revenue	Arrears and doubtful claims	Reco-verable Arrears	Tax Reco-vered	Tax Out-standing	Reco-very Rate
VAT	51	3,136.6	-	3,136.6	1,716.0	1,420.6	55%
Income Tax	85	6,489.6	-	6,489.6	3,223.8	3,265.8	50%
Customs	111	6,286.8	100.7	6,186.1	4,816.8	1,369.0	77%
Total	247	15,913.0	100.7	15,812.3	4,659.6	16,912.3	62%

* Source: The TRA Investigation Department Annual Report for 2003/04

** Values are in Billion Tanzania Shillings

One of the highlights of investigation work undertaken in 2003/2004[607] was the interception of two mining company expatriates by officers of the TID at Mwanza Airport; one was a South African and the other, an Australian, both suspected of attempting to leave the country without paying their taxes. A search carried out on their personal effects, including information on the taxpayer's laptop computer, revealed that the required level of employment taxes for the year ending December 2004, had not been paid. Some of the employment tax deducted by the taxpayers' employers had not been remitted to the TRA under the PAYE scheme. A total of Tzs 463 million as principal tax and penalties was recovered.

For the year 2003/2004, the TID identified the following areas as causing tax revenue leakage:[608]

- failure to register taxpayers;
- the keeping of false books of accounts for purposes of evading taxes;
- the use of the Zanzibar port and airport to land goods for trans-shipment to mainland Tanzania without payment of proper duties (because of poor customs control in Zanzibar);

---

607 The TRA, *Tax Investigation Department Annual Report for 2003/04*, at 2-3.
608 *Ibid.* 5.

- the use of false documents to clear goods through customs (e.g., false invoices, mis-declaration of goods and mis-classification of goods);
- smuggling through Tanzania's long and porous borders;
- overstatement of expenses to reduce income tax;
- failure to declare dividends and persistent reporting of losses by private companies;
- misuse of tax exemptions given by Tanzania Investment Centre to approved enterprises;
- splitting of remuneration paid to expatriate employees by private companies so that only a small portion of what they were paid was declared to the TRA for PAYE purposes, but the bigger part was paid off-shore into the employee's bank account;
- the laundering of money through real estate transactions;
- failure to withhold tax on payments to non-residents (e.g. fees for technical or management services); and
- failure to record and report payments to foreign or local directors of companies.

The above areas of concern are cited repeatedly in subsequent TID reports,[609] indicating that these problems have not been resolved. It is noted that for 2003/04, the TID did not meet the target of having at least 30% of its completed investigations cases sent for criminal prosecution. According to the 2003/04 annual report, the failure to achieve the targeted level of prosecutable cases resulted from inability to obtain the level of evidence required to ensure successful prosecutions.[610]

For the year 2004/05, the TID directed its efforts to identifying new areas of tax delinquency and following-up outstanding taxes. These efforts resulted in the recovery of Tzs 7,702,800,000 for both current taxes and tax arrears. During that year, the TID concluded 259 investigation cases with a revenue potential of Tzs 22,083,100,000. The average revenue contribution per case was Tzs 85,300,000. The tax recovery rate for 2004/05 was only 22%, much lower than the recovery rate achieved in 2003/2004, which was 62%. Table 13 below shows the TID investigation performance for 2004/05.

---

609 The TRA, *Tax Investigation Department Annual Reports for 2003/04 to 2006-07.*
610 The TRA, *Tax Investigation Department Annual Report for 2003/04.*

TABLE 13: TID INVESTIGATION CASES FOR 2004/05
(VALUES ARE IN BILLION TANZANIA SHILLINGS)

TID	Investiga-tions	Potential Revenue	Arrears and Doubtful Claims	Reco-verable Tax	Tax Reco-vered	Tax Out-standing	Reco-very Rate
VAT	63	9,145.8	402.5	8,743.3	1,522.3	7,221.0	17%
Income Tax	84	9,936.9	108.7	9,828.2	1,692.4	8,135.8	17%
Customs	112	3,000.4	-	3,000.4	1,444.9	1,555.5	48%
Total	259	22,083.1	511.2	21,571.9	4,659.6	16,912.3	22%

* Source: The TRA Investigation Department Annual Report for 2004/05

** Values are in Billion Tanzania Shillings

There has been no noticeable improvement in investigation performance for succeeding years. The constraints on good performance noted in the initial years have only been partially resolved.

The shortage of tax investigation officers, which is noted in all previous annual reports of the TID, persisted in the year 2005/06.[611] The annual plan for the TID, which was drawn up in March 2005 in time for the start of the TRA financial year on 1st July 2005, envisaged a staffing increase by July 2006 upon completing the merger of the VAT Department and Income Tax Department. Excess staff from merged departments would be deployed to the TID. However, the expanded operations of the new Domestic Revenue Department absorbed nearly all the staff. Only a few officers were transferred to the TID, well below its staffing requirement. All the transferred officers were assigned to the Business Intelligence Unit, so that this Unit could start operations.

The integration of the VAT and Income Tax Departments also disrupted the operations of the TID, because the office space requirements of the new Domestic Revenue Department necessitated the re-location of the Dar es Salaam Tax Investigation Zone offices twice during July and August 2006. The physical movement of files, electronic equipment and furniture, impaired the TID operations substantially.[612]

The year 2005 was also an election year for Tanzania. The TRA was required to join other officers from the Police Force and State Security

---

611 The TRA, *Tax Investigation Department Annual Report for 2005/06*, 3.
612 *Ibid.* 5.

to undertake patrols during the 2005 general elections. Twenty-four hour patrols were conducted daily along the coastal stretch from Kisiju in Mkuranga District of Dar es Salaam to Saadan in Bagamoyo District. This operation lasted for 28 days. Various smuggled goods were intercepted and several other illegal activities affecting the security of the country and/or its economic interests were prevented.[613]

As many of the officers for this operation were drawn from the Customs Department and the TID, the use of the TID for this operation further deprived the TID of capacity to undertake normal tax investigations.

In 2005/06, the TID also attempted to focus on tax irregularities in the transit trade. Tanzania is surrounded by a number of countries which are land-locked and the port of Dar es Salaam is used as a shipping route for goods destined for the land-locked countries of Uganda, Burundi, Rwanda, Zambia, Malawi and the Democratic Republic of Congo. The TRA must ensure that transit goods which are allowed passage through Tanzania duty free must not be diverted into Tanzania for domestic consumption. Apart from the revenue loss which results from diverting transit goods, the sale of untaxed transit goods in Tanzania causes serious price distortions. However, monitoring and reconciling shipping and clearance documents for transit goods is a time consuming task, as most records are stored manually. Some TID staff were assigned to this task, reducing further the number of investigation officers available for normal tax investigations which are revenue yielding.[614]

The gathering of information through the Business Intelligence Unit proceeded in earnest during 2005/06. The intention was to gather data which would show the patterns of trading activities in terms of quantities, pricing, packaging and shipping. The typical patterns emerging would be used to test the veracity of the records of the taxpayer being investigated. During 2005/06, the TID gathered business information from eighty taxpayers relating to five business sectors, namely, hardware, textile, mining, construction and petroleum.[615]

In 2005/06, the TID also tackled the problem of undervaluation of imported motor vehicles, which results in payment of lower customs duties. The TID found that, out of 114 motor vehicles cleared through the Holili border station, 95 vehicles were undervalued. The declared purchase prices were much lower than the comparable market prices stored in the TID database. A total of 310 motor vehicles in Dar es

---

613 *Ibid*. 6.
614 *Ibid*. at 6-7.
615 *Ibid*. 2.

Salaam were also examined during this period. It was established that appropriate taxes had not been fully paid in respect of 117 motor vehicles. Tax amounting to Tzs 123,000,000 millions was recovered.[616]

A major constraint noted by the TID in 2005/06 is that courts take too long to complete the tax cases filed, and in most events convicted offenders get fines only, not jail terms. During 2005/06, 36 taxpayers were recommended for criminal prosecution and only 22 cases were completed. Convictions were obtained against 15 (worth Tzs 32,100,000 in tax revenue). Two taxpayers were acquitted (the tax claim against them was Tzs 42,200,000). Charges against five taxpayers were withdrawn. Although the success rate in criminal prosecutions arising from TID work is poor, the TID still believes that "the prosecution of tax evaders of itself has a deterrent psychological effect and to a large extent contributes in enhancing tax administration integrity."[617] However, the TID believes that, in a society where tax evasion is not viewed by the public as a serious criminal breach, jail terms would serve as a more effective deterrent. Fines alone, however substantial, are not seen as an effective deterrent against tax evasion.

The desire to use criminal prosecutions as a psychological tool for enhancing compliance persisted.[618] In 2006/07, the TID had 47 criminal cases in the courts. Of these, 27 were brought forward from 2005/06 and 20 were newly instituted cases. Of the 17 cases decided during 2006/07, there were 15 convictions with tax revenue amounting to Tzs 348,600,000; two taxpayers were acquitted (the tax claim against them was Tzs 99,500,000); and six cases were withdrawn. Moreover, for the first time, two tax offenders were sentenced to three-month jail terms for smuggling offences.[619]

During 2006/07, the TID made further efforts to improve the competence of staff.[620] It provided various training courses aimed at improving the investigator's skills in such areas as,

- evidence gathering,
- computer access and reconstruction of deleted data,
- transfer pricing,
- income splitting,

---

616 *Ibid*. 3.
617 The TRA, Tax Investigation Department Annual Report for 2005/06, at 1, Paragraph 2.1.
618 The TRA, Tax Investigation Department Annual Report for 2006/07.
619 *Ibid*. 1.
620 *Ibid*. 3.

- tax fraud investigation, detection, prevention and prosecution, and
- general intelligence.

Training in reconstruction of computer data has become necessary, because taxpayers who store data in computers often delete information in the wake of a tax investigation. In a bid to equip tax investigators with skills to reconstruct deleted data, fifteen officers were sent for a three-month computer forensic networking course in Germany.

In its annual report for 2006/07, the TID still decried the long delays attending criminal prosecution of tax offenders due to lengthy court procedures.[621] The TID also decried the fact that most of the criminal cases end up in payment of a fine. In part, the TID report recommended that,

> [i]n order to improve compliance a fine alone is not enough. Where laws permit, offenders should be sentenced to jail sentences, this would be a lesson to the general public which views tax evasion as a minor offence. There is a need for tax evasion to be included in serious criminal offences. However, getting a conviction is in itself a positive step.[622]

A comparison of taxpayer investigations undertaken in 2005/06 and 2006/07 is shown in Table 14.

---

621 The TRA, Tax Investigation Department Annual Report for 2006/07, 3.
622 *Ibid.* 3, Paragraph 3.2.

TABLE 14: TID INVESTIGATION CASES FOR 2005/06 AND 2006/07
(VALUES ARE IN BILLION TANZANIA SHILLINGS)

TID	Cases Investigated	Potential Revenue	Tax Recovered	Tax Recovery Rate
YEAR 2005				
Domestic Revenue	133 (49%)	9,208.0	1,718.7	18.7%
Customs Duties	139 (51%)	3,181.5	2,981.8	93.7%
TOTAL	272 (100%)	12,389.5	4,700.5	37.9%
YEAR 2006				
Domestic Revenue	135 (43%)	14,589.1	8,073.8	55.3%
Customs Duties	176 (57%)	3,401.4	1,100.2	32.3%
TOTAL	**311 (100%)**	**17,990.5**	**9,174.0**	**51%**

* Source: The TRA Investigation Department Annual Report for 2006/07

** Values are in Billion Tanzania Shillings

For the first quarter of the year 2007/08,[623] a total of 64 investigation cases were completed, with a revenue potential of Tzs 5,928,100,000, compared to 57 cases during a similar period for 2006/07. Out of the 64 cases, 60 were settled using compounding offence provisions, making a recovery of Tzs 4,918,600,000.[624]

During this quarter, the TID had 22 cases in the courts brought forward from 2006/07, while four new cases were freshly instituted. Of the 26 cases in court, only two were completed and decided in favour of the TRA. There was no case dismissed or withdrawn during the period. The other 24 cases were still at various stages of prosecution.[625] A summary of tax cases investigated in the First Quarter of 2007/2008 is shown in Table 15 below.

---

623 The TRA, *Tax Investigation Department Annual Report for 2007/08*, 1.
624 *Ibid*. 2.
625 *Ibid*. 2.

TABLE 15: TID INVESTIGATION CASES FOR THE FIRST QUARTER 2007/08
(VALUES ARE IN BILLION TANZANIA SHILLINGS)

Violations	Cases Completed	Potential Revenue	Tax Recovered	Tax Outstanding
Direct Taxes	29	4,391.6	3,316.5	1,075.1
Indirect Taxes	11	305.7	26.6	279.1
Domestic	40	4697.3	3343.1	1354.2
Customs	24	1230.8	189.0	1041.8
Total	64	5,928.1	3,532.1	2,396

* Source: The TRA Investigation Department Annual Report for 2007/08
** Values are in Billion Tanzania Shillings

The report for the first quarter of 2007/08 also notes that the gathering of business intelligence from various sectors of trade continued.[626] The sectors covered include hardware, petroleum, hotels, textiles, manufacturing and general merchandise. The business intelligence gathered was tested in tax investigations carried out on traders based in the Dar es Salaam, Mbeya, Iringa, Morogoro and Dodoma regions. The tax findings were still being analysed for trends and discrepancies at the time of this inquiry.

The TID expected to surpass the mark of 311 cases investigated in 2006/07, as well as the tax yield of Tzs 17,990,500,000 achieved in 2006/2007.[627]

In addition, the TID wants to encourage taxpayers with substantial disputed taxes to negotiate acceptable amounts which will resolve long running disputes and realize some tax for the government. Taxpayers with substantial long standing disputed liabilities are in the mining, major constructions, manufacturing, petroleum and telecommunications sectors.[628] By June 2010, eight substantial disputes had been settled with the TRA signing a memorandum of understanding with each of the taxpayers involved.

The TID has also unveiled plans for closer cooperation with the tax investigation wings of neighbouring countries such as Uganda, Kenya, Zambia, Burundi, Democratic Republic of Congo, Rwanda, Malawi and Mozambique, which share common borders with Tanzania, so that cross border transactions can be effectively monitored. The monitoring will cover imports, exports and transit goods.[629]

---

626 *Ibid.* 3.
627 *Ibid.* 3.
628 *Ibid.* 3-4.
629 *Ibid.* 5.

The TID has targeted the examination of fuel import data from Kisumu, Kenya, consignments of transit sugar through Tanzania to neighbouring countries, as well as transit fuel, in order to curtail the known revenue leaks. The TID is cooperating with the highway control authority, TANROADS, so that information extracted at road weighbridges can be matched with that given to customs, to prevent cheating.[630]

While the TRA has removed all of its tax investigation work from the Income Tax and VAT Departments and brought it under the TID, there are still some aspects of tax investigation being carried out by the Customs Department in its traditional role of securing the country's borders. One such function is the patrol of land borders and the territorial sea strip. Three patrol boats were acquired in 2001 by the Customs Department and deployed to monitor the Indian Ocean coast, Lake Victoria and Lake Tanganyika, which are known to be prone to customs irregularities.[631] An additional boat was acquired in 2005. The TRA also created the Flexible Anti-Smuggling Teams (FAST) responsible for surveillance and seizure of smuggled goods.[632] Although the public visibility of FAST has remained low key when measured against the rampant smuggling believed to exist, it nonetheless serves as a useful deterrent. The performance of FAST for the five years up to 2004/05 is shown in Table 16 below.[633]

---

630 *Ibid.* 5.
631 The TRA Annual Report for 2004/05, 21.
632 *Ibid.* 21, Paragraphs 3.3.3 and 3.3.4.
633 *Ibid.* at 21.

**TABLE 16: FAST PERFORMANCE FOR THE YEARS 2000/01 TO 2004/05
(VALUES ARE MILLION TANZANIA SHILLINGS)**

Description	2000/01	2001/02	2002/03	2003/04	**2004/05**
Cases detected	128	286	281	131	134
Cases Completed	105	198	150	95	62
Pending cases	23	88	131	36	72
Revenue Collected	156.9	444.2	201.7	119.3	203.6

* Source: The TRA Annual Report for 2004/05

** Values are in Million Tanzania Shillings

Limitations of the TRA's Enforcement Strategies

An important constraint on the TRA enforcement strategy, which the above research shows, is the inability of the TRA (and therefore government) to provide adequate resources for tax enforcement activities. The TID, which has 25 officers only, believes that it needs an additional 24 officers to attain an effective staffing level.[634] The fact that this need for additional staff has not been satisfied despite being repeated in every TID annual report since 2002 is indicative of an institutional inability to achieve optimum success with the tax enforcement strategy.

Other resource constraints, which compromise the effectiveness of the enforcement strategy of the TRA, include inadequate working tools for the TID, such as vehicles, computers, two-way radios and cellular phones. There is also the problem with the overall inefficiency of the court system, which causes delays in the completion of cases taken to court for prosecution.

Court delays in the disposal of tax cases result in significant tied-up tax revenue. The extent of the problem is better appreciated when one also considers that the many tax appeals pending with the Tax Revenue Appeals Board and the Tax Revenue Appeals Tribunal add to the tied-up revenue. The TID has no control over these disputes, because all tax cases involving litigation are handled by the Legal Services Department (LSD). The LSD is a department of the TRA headed by the Chief Legal Counsel, who is also the Secretary to the TRA Board of Directors. The LSD has 32 lawyers, 21 of whom are based at the TRA Headquarters, while 11 work with the TRA Zone offices in the regions.

---

634 The TRA, *Tax Investigation Department Annual Report for 2006/07*, at 5.

The LSD undertakes all criminal prosecutions arising from tax investigations (customs, income tax and value added tax). It also has responsibility for all tax appeals arising from objections to tax assessments and from other disputes arising from tax decisions made by the TRA officers. This is a significant responsibility on a department which has only skeleton staff.

As explained previously, there are three levels at which tax appeals are adjudicated. The Tax Revenue Appeals Board has original jurisdiction over all tax disputes.[635] Appeals go to the Tax Revenue Appeals Tribunal,[636] from which a final appeal lies to the Court of Appeal of Tanzania.[637]

The point made by the TID regarding the delay in disposing of tax criminal cases can also be made against the Tax Revenue Appeals Board and the Tax Revenue Appeals Tribunal, but in a different context. Tax appeals before these two bodies are determined with relative speed (within three to six months of being filed).[638] Appeals from the Tax Revenue Appeals Tribunal to the Court of Appeal continue to be a serious concern because it can take up to three or four years for an appeal to be heard by that court. Altogether, however, the large number of appeals filed by taxpayers tie-up significant amounts of tax revenue.

Tables 17, 18 and 19, below, show the number of tax assessments/ decisions which are taken on appeal to the Tax Revenue Appeals Board relating to income tax, value added tax and customs duties.

---

635 Section 16 of the *Tax Revenue Appeals Act No. 15 of 2000*.
636 *Ibid.* Section 16.
637 *Ibid.* Sections 25.
638 Criminal prosecutions in Tanzania take up to three or four years to conclude.

TABLE 17: INCOME TAX APPEALS FOR 2001 - 2010

	2001	2002	2003	2004	2005	2006	2007	2008	2009	2010
Dismissed	1	8	2	2	8	7	10	4	7	0
Upheld	0	6	3	8	7	3	6	3	10	3
Part Upheld	0	6	9	10	3	0	0	1	4	0
Settled	0	6	5	4	3	1	0	3	11	1
Withdrawn	0	9	3	4	4	1	0	1	2	0
Pending	0	0	0	0	0	2	8	0	20	25
Total	1	40	23	28	25	14	24	12	54	29

* Source: The TRA Tax Revenue Appeal Board - Appeals Register

TABLE 18: VALUE ADDED TAX APPEALS FOR 2001 - 2010

	2001	2002	2003	2004	2005	2006	2007	2008	2009	2010
Dismissed	2	4	6	6	10	2	5	4	2	0
Upheld	0	0	3	2	7	1	7	4	4	1
Part Upheld	0	1	3	0	2	0	2	1	4	0
Settled	0	1	3	1	1	0	1	2	1	0
Withdrawn	0	2	1	5	0	0	1	2	3	0
Pending	0	1	0	0	4	4	0	0	14	5
Total	2	9	16	14	25	7	16	13	28	6

* Source: The TRA Tax Revenue Appeal Board - Appeals Register

TABLE 19: CUSTOMS APPEALS FOR 2002 – 2010

	2002	2003	2004	2005	2006	2007	2008	2009	2010
Dismissed	5	7	3	6	2	3	6	2	1
Upheld	2	1	3	2	0	3	4	3	0
Part Upheld	5	1	2	0	0	0	1	2	0
Settled	0	0	0	1	0	0	0	0	0
Withdrawn	1	0	5	1	1	1	0	0	0
Pending	0	0	0	0	0	3	6	5	8
Total	13	9	13	10	3	10	17	12	9

* Source: The TRA Tax Revenue Appeal Board - Appeals Register

The above tables show that the number of tax appeals which go to the Tax Revenue Appeals Board is significant. A total of 480 tax appeals were brought by taxpayers against income tax, VAT assessments and customs between November 2001 and December 2010. Only cases which arose after the establishment of the unified tax appeal bodies under the Tax Revenue Appeals Act of 2000 are captured in the above Tables. Cases filed and determined under the previous non-unified tax tribunals are not included.

The 480 tax appeals involved disputed taxes amounting to Tzs 447,739,392,861, which (at an exchange rate of about Tzs 1200 to the American dollar) was well over 373 million US dollars. Table 20 below shows how this amount is distributed among income tax, customs and value added tax.

TABLE 20 VALUES FOR INCOME TAX, CUSTOMS AND VAT APPEALS BROUGHT
TO THE TAX REVENUE APPEALS BOARD 2002 TO 2010

Year	Total Income Tax	Total Customs	Total VAT
2002	24,680,855,759	1,426,633,937	791,805,762
2003	6,732,527,231	528,217,828	3,071,152,755
2004	145,604,704,695	5,586,694,913	13,871,877,773
2005	1,067,900,350	1,372,077,460	6,399,933,418
2006	4,872,583,757	1,114,252,822	12,507,831,315
2007	14,619,836,161	17,401,082,625	22,112,041,246
2008	23,210,222,870	6,805,701,978	24,759,037,274
2009	51,690,964,357	13,155,440,888	37,085,293,148
2010	24,455,689,964	3,248,223,679	1,214,416,539
TOTAL	276,637,950,208	48,706,456,763	122,394,985,890

* Source: The Tax Revenue Appeals Board – Appeals Register

It is notable that less than one third of the appeals filed with the Tax Revenue Appeals Board are taken on a second appeal to the Tax Revenue Appeals Tribunal. Only 132 appeals were taken to the Tax Revenue Appeals Tribunal for the period 2002 to 2010. A lot less make the final stage of appeal to the Court of Appeal of Tanzania. Only 33 appeals were taken to the Court of Appeal between 2002 and 2010.

An additional concern, however, is that the Court of Appeal is so congested that many of the appeals filed with that court remain pending for hearing. Table 21 below tabulates these numbers.

TABLE 21: APPEALS TO THE TRIBUNAL AND TO THE COURT OF APPEAL
2002 – 2007

Year	Tribunal	Court of Appeal
2002	10	0
2003	10	2
2004	7	3
2005	13	5
2006	38	12
2007	17	1
2008	23	4
2009	31	3
2010	27	3

* Source: The TRA Tax Revenue Appeal Board - Appeals Register

Conclusion

Given the many concerns discussed above regarding tax enforcement by the TRA, the overall success of this strategy is called into question, especially when pursued in isolation. Some emphasis needs to be re-directed to voluntary compliance efforts spearheaded by a more aggressive taxpayer education program. In addition, the service culture, which for the TRA is more word than deed, needs to be visible in TRA actions and in the way TRA officers interact with taxpayers. Equally, the partnership the TRA has announced should not be a partnership with government alone, but also with the taxpayers as the major stakeholders and the backbone of the tax system.

8

Summary of Findings and Recommendations

8.1   Summary of Findings

The findings of this research show that voluntary taxpayer compliance in Tanzania has not been achieved at a sufficiently high level. The modernization of the tax administration undertaken in the mid 1990s, of itself, has done little to change the negative taxpayer perception of the TRA and the tax system at large. It appears that tax administration reform has focused too much on the structure of the TRA and the performance of its functions, without sufficient attention being given to the interaction of tax officers with taxpayers and the impact of taxpayer attitude to the performance of the TRA. The TRA reform is being undertaken without sufficiently taking into account the other factors which influence taxpayer acceptance of the tax system.

The study has pointed to the following factors as undermining voluntary compliance with, and preventing public acceptance of, taxation:

- the process of tax legislation and tax policy formulation is not inclusive, as many who have a stake in taxation are not given the opportunity to participate;
- there are too many taxes administered by the TRA which makes it difficult for taxpayers to understand and comply with taxation;
- the tax rates used for the various taxes are high and are not aligned to ability to pay;
- the tax burden is not fairly distributed, because the tax base is too narrow as it does not include the significant informal sector or rural sector;
- taxes are administered in a high-handed manner; and
- there is a negative perception of the government and the tax system, which impacts on taxpayer compliance attitudes.

Tanzania's tax base is also very narrow. While a large part of this is attributed to avoidance and evasion activities, there is also a reluctance to seriously harness the informal and rural sectors. This is partly because of an unfounded belief that those operating in the informal and rural sectors live on the poverty line and no good would result from taxing them, and partly because of the political risk of antagonizing this important voting population. Figures making up the GDP in Tanzania show significant losses from failure to harness the informal sector. The DANIDA report referred to earlier,[639] showed that, in Tanzania, a significant 28% of GDP is generated from non-market production, and a further 15% from the informal sector. Combined, these two untaxed sectors make up 43% of the GDP. Maliyamkono's[640] research leads to the same conclusion. He shows that the untaxed informal sector has been growing steadily. It was 28.1% of GDP in 1986, 36.1% in 1996, and 48.1% in 2006.

In their examination of tax reforms in Tanzania, Uganda and Zambia, Rakner and Gloppen[641] observed that in all three countries the tax reforms have focused on increasing collection through improving the compliance of existing and known taxpayers. They agree with a recent evaluation by the British Department for International Development

---

639 DANIDA Project Document, Danish Support to Tanzania Revenue Authority Phase II 2003/04 – 2007/08, at 7.
640 Op cit. p 25.
641 L Rakner and S Gloppen. "Tax Reform and Democratic Accountability in Sub-Saharan Africa" at 10 of their joint paper, internet source http://www.ids.ac.uk/gdr/cfs/activities/Rakner-Gloppen.pdf.

(DFID) that the failure to tax the informal sector and agriculture and the continued tendency of granting tax exemptions to powerful businesses/ individuals with close political connections, provide the main reason why collections appear to have stagnated at a relatively low level. As for the reforms in Tanzania, Uganda and Zambia, Rakner and Gloppen say,

> A common trend in all three countries is an apparent lack of ability and/or political willingness to apply the tax law with full force to informal operators perceived to be electorally important. The way VAT has been introduced helps explain the failure to widen the population base of the tax system. A uniform VAT (with major exemptions) has replaced business turnover taxes and sales tax in the three countries. However, as food commodities are zero-rated and most agricultural inputs are exempted, VAT has not included many new groups into the tax net.[642]

On the unrealized revenue potential of the VAT, Maliyamkono[643] notes that, since inception, the VAT has been the most successful and robust tax producing revenue, equivalent to 6% of GDP (the combined total tax/GDP ratio is around 13%). Nonetheless, there is a wide range of remissions through special relief and zero rating, which means there is a potential to reduce the number of tax remissions where they are no longer justified and so further increase the contribution of VAT to total revenues.

The undue reliance on tax enforcement has only enhanced the public perception that the tax administration is high-handed. This research, however, has shown that the 'fear factor' alone can not effectively influence tax compliance patterns, because of the limited enforcement capacity of the TRA. The capability constraints which afflict the Tax Investigation Department of the TRA make it impossible for enforcement to have either the deterrent effect it has on tax delinquency in countries where detection and punishment is better resourced, or the positive compliance effect on would be evaders by closing the opportunity to cheat. In addition, the TRA is unable to rely on the severity of sanctions to send the right message because of its lack of capacity to undertake wide-scale investigations and obtain convictions, and because of the public perception (which has been shown to be the perception of the courts as well) that failure to pay tax is not a serious offence.[644] The TRA

---

642 *Ibid.* p11.
643 *Op cit* p21.
644 This is evident from the fact.

has undertaken over 200 criminal prosecutions since 2002; however, only two tax offenders have been sentenced to jail. Even in these two cases, the jail terms were two and three months only, not severe enough to send a message against tax delinquency.

This study also shows that the tax laws in Tanzania do not encourage taxpayers to comply voluntarily with taxes. Provisions relating to assessment and payment of tax are mostly premised on punishing non-compliance, rather than encouraging compliance. This approach alienates taxpayers from the tax system and does not inspire them to take ownership of the tax system.

The lack of adequate accountability for the government also impacts negatively on taxpayer compliance attitudes. The government is perceived to be corrupt. In 2008, a major corruption scandal unravelled, forcing the Prime Minister to resign and the President to dismiss the entire cabinet on 7th February 2008.[645]

Allegations of corruption have also been continually levelled against the TRA, as shown in the taxpayer perception surveys undertaken by the National Bureau of Statistics in 2003 and by PricewaterhouseCoopers in 2006.[646] As a result, taxpayer confidence in the tax system, necessary to promote voluntary taxpayer compliance, is lacking. It is encouraging to note that the Third Corporate Plan (2008/09 to 2012/13), currently being implemented, has four strategic goals which underscore a recognition by the TRA of the dissatisfaction taxpayers have with the present state of taxation. The four strategic goals are: (i) to broaden the tax base; (ii) to improve voluntary tax compliance; (iii) to improve customer service; and (iv) to enhance integrity. It remains to be seen if the lofty objectives of the TRA Third Corporate Plan will bring fundamental changes to the institutional culture of the TRA.

Relevance of Findings

In demonstrating the limited capacity of the enforcement strategy to drive taxpayer compliance, and in documenting the resource constraints of the TRA in mounting an effective detection and punishment scheme against tax delinquency, this study has made a case for refocusing tax

645 This event was front page news on the 8th February 2008 for all major daily papers in Tanzania, including the *Daily News*, *The African* and *The Guardian*, as well as other papers published in the Kiswahili language.

646 National Bureau of Statistics "Assessment of the Effectiveness of Taxpayer Awareness Programs and Attitude of Taxpayers Towards the TRA" National Bureau of Statistics Report, September 2003, Dar es Salaa; PricewaterhouseCoopers, "Stakeholders Perception Survey Report 2006," Large Taxpayer Department, the TRA, Dar es Salaam.

compliance efforts such that enforcement strategies are not pursued in isolation, but alongside voluntary compliance strategies.

mWith the appreciation that voluntary compliance can be the key to better performance of the tax system, the government should more seriously address factors such as fairness, accountability, trust in government and soundness of tax policies, which impact not only on compliance with tax laws, but on general compliance with all laws.

A taxpayer-centric thinking is now required for tax administrators. Fortunately, this approach is already emerging in the service oriented culture being adopted by the TRA, making the taxpayer an important partner in taxation.

Recommendations

i. There is a need to change the mind-set of tax administrators so that they accept the partnership which must exist between tax administrators and taxpayers.[647] For this partnership to succeed, there needs to be a real commitment to respect taxpayer rights that goes beyond rhetoric (in the form of non-enforceable taxpayer charters) to substantive recognition. As suggested by Professor Bentley,[648] taxpayer rights need to be recognized, not only because they reinforce tax compliance, but also because they are a matter of substantive law. Therefore, taxpayer rights must be sufficiently entrenched in the tax laws so that taxpayers may readily enforce them, which is not the case at present.

ii. Adequate resources need to be provided for those measures which promote voluntary taxpayer compliance such as the taxpayer education program of the TRA, which, currently, is not sufficiently resourced.

iii. Finally, there is a need to improve good governance so that the legitimacy of government is enhanced. With enhanced legitimacy of government and sufficient integrity within the tax administration, the foundation for better voluntary compliance will exist. As stated at the outset, taxpayers can voluntarily pay their taxes if they perceive the tax laws to be just, the tax administration to be fair and the government to be responsible.

647L P Feld and B. S. Frey "Trust Breeds Trust: How Taxpayers Are Treated" (2002) 3 Economics of Governance p.87.

648D Bentley *Taxpayers' Rights: Theory, origin and Implementation,* Series on International Taxation, Kluwer Law International, 2007, p.5.

Bibliography

Books

Adams, C., 1998, *Those Dirty Taxes: The Tax Revolts That Built America*. New York: Free Press.

Ayoki, M., Obwona, M. and M. Ogwapus, 2008, *Tax Reforms and Domestic Revenue Mobilisation in Uganda,* Kampala, Uganda: Fountain Publishers.

Barzel, Y. A., 2002, *Theory of the State: Economic Rights, Legal Rights, and the Scope of the State*, Cambridge: Cambridge University Press.

Bentley, D. (ed), 1998, *Taxpayers' Rights – An International Perspective*, The Revenue Law Journal, Queensland: School of Law, Bond University.

Bentley, D., 1998, "Classifying Taxpayers' Rights", in D. Bentley (ed), *Taxpayers' Rights – An International Perspective*, The Revenue Law Journal, Queensland: School of Law, Bond University.

Bentley, D., 2007, *Taxpayers' Rights: Theory, Origin and Implementation*, Series on International Taxation, Netherlands: Kluwer Law International.

Bird, R. M. and C. D. Jantscher (eds), 1992, *Improving Tax Administration in Developing Countries*, Washington DC: International Monetary Fund.

Blumstein, A., 1983, "Models for Structuring. Taxpayer Compliance" in Sawicki, P. (ed), *Income Tax Compliance: A Report of the ABA Section of Taxation International Conference on Income Tax Compliance*, Chicago, IL: American Bar Association.

Braithwaite, V., 2003, "A New Approach to Tax Compliance", in Braithwaite, V. (ed), *Taxing Democracy: Understanding Tax Avoidance and Evasion*, United Kingdom: Ashgate Publishing.Braithwaite, V., 1998, "Communal and Exchange Trust Norms: Their Value Base and Relevance to Institutional Trust", in Braithwaite, V. and M. Levi (eds), *Trust and Governance*, New York: Russell Sage Foundation.

Braithwaite, V., 2003, "Dancing with Tax Authorities", in Braithwaite, V., *Taxing Democracy: Understanding Tax Avoidance and Evasion*, United Kingdom: Ashgate Publishing.

Braithwaite, V., 2003, *Taxing Democracy*, United Kingdom: Ashgate, Publishing Ltd.

Brennan, G. and J. Buchanan, 1980, *The Power to Tax: Analytical Foundations of a Fiscal Constitution*, Cambridge, UK: Cambridge University Press.

Broomberg, E. B. and D. Kruger, 1998, *Tax Strategy (3rd Edition)*, London: Butterworths Publishers.

Budge, I., 1996, *The New Challenge of Democracy*, Cambridge: Blackwell Publishers.

Carmody, M., 1998, "Future Directions in Tax Administration of Community Confidence: The Essential Building Block" (Chapter 16), in Evans, C. and A. Greenbaum (eds), *Tax Administration: Facing the Challenge of the Future*, Sydney: Prospect Media.

Carroll, J. S., 1989, "A Cognitive-Process Analysis of Taxpayer Compliance", in Roth, J. A. and J. T. Scholz (eds), *Taxpayer Compliance*, Philadelphia: University of Pennsylvania Press.

Carroll, J. S., 1992, "How Taxpayers Think About Their Taxes: Frames and Values", in Slemrod, J. (ed), *Why People Pay Taxes*, Ann Arbour, Michigan: University of Michigan Press.

Clarke, J. and D. Wood, 2001, "New public management and development: the case of public service reform in Tanzania and Uganda", in McCourt, W. and M. Minogue (eds), *The Internationalisation of Public Management: Reinventing the Third World State,* Cheltenham: Edward Elgar.

Cooper, G. S., 1997, *Tax Avoidance and the Rule of Law,* Amsterdam: IBDF Publications.

Cowell, F. A., 1990, *Cheating the Government: The Economics of Tax Evasion,* Cambridge, MA: MIT Press.

Croome, B., 2010, *Taxpayers' Rights in South Africa,* Clairemont, South Africa: Junta & Co.

Cross, R. and C. Tapper, 1985, *Cross on Evidence* (6th edition), London: Butterworths.

De Soto, Hernando, 2000, *Why Capitalism Triumphs in the West and Fails Everywhere Else*, New York: Basic Books.

Dicey, A. V., 1885, *Introduction to the Study of the Law of the Constitution,* Rpt as 10th Edition, 1960, Macmillan.

Erard, B., 1992, "The influence of tax audits on reporting behaviour", in Slemrod, J. (ed), *Why people pay taxes: Taxpayer compliance and enforcement,* Ann Arbour, Michigan: University of Michigan Press.

Faundez, J., Footer, M. E. and J. J. Norton (eds), 2000 *Governance, Development and Globalization*, Oxford: Blackstone Press.

Finnis, J., 1980, *Natural Law and Natural Rights*, Oxford: Oxford University Press.

Fjeldstad, O. H., 2000, "Why People Pay Tax: A Study of Tax Compliance in Tanzania", *Den Ny Verden*, Vol. 33 No. 4.

Frampton, D., 1993, *Practical Tax Administration,* Bath: Fiscal Publications.

Frey, R. L. and B. Torgler (eds), 2002, *Changing the Social Norm of Tax Compliance by Voting,* Kyklos International Review for Social Sciences, Blackwell, Synergy.

Alm, J, McClelland, G. H. and W. D. Schulze, 1999, "Changing the Social Norm of Tax Compliance by Voting", *Kyklos International Review for Social Sciences*, 52.2:141-172.Friedman, L., 1975, *The Legal System: A Social Science Perspective*, New York: Russell Sage Foundation.

Ghai, Y., 1993, "Constitutions and Governance in Africa: A Prolegomenon", in Adelman, S. and A. Paliwala (eds), *Law and Crisis in the Third World*, Warwick: Centre for Modern African Studies, University of Warwick.

Glenday, G., 1997, "Capacity Building in the Context of the Kenya Tax Modernisation Program", in Grindle, M. S. (ed), *Getting good government: capacity building in the public sectors of developing countries*, Harvard, MA: Harvard University Press.

Gordon, R. K., 1996, "Law of Tax Administration and Procedure", in Thuronyi, V. (ed.), *Tax Law Design and Drafting*, Vol 1, Washington, DC: IMF.

Hart, H. L. A., 1968, *Punishment and Responsibility*, Oxford: Oxford University Press.

Hayden, G. and M. Bratton (eds), 1993, *Governance and Politics in Africa*, Boulder, CO: Lynne Rienner Publishers.

Hirst, P., 2000, "Democracy and Governance", in Pierre, J. (ed), *Debating Governance: Authority, Steering and Democracy*, Oxford, UK: Oxford University Press.

Howarth, P. and R. Maas, 2004, *Taxpayer Rights and Revenue Powers*, London, UK: Lexis Nexis.

Institute for Fiscal Studies, (ed), 1993, *Striking the Balance: Tax Administration, Enforcement and Compliance in the 1990s*, London: Institute for Fiscal Studies.

Casanegra de Jantscher, M., 1997, "Providing Resources to the Tax Administration", in Bolanos, D. (ed), *Necessary Attributes for a Sound and Effective Tax Administration*, Buenos Aires: Centro Interamericano de Administraciones Tributarias (CIAT) James, S. and C. Nobes, 1998, *The Economics of Taxation: Principles, Policy and Practice*, New York: Prentice Hall.

Kofele-Kale, N., 2000, "Good Governance as a Political Conditionality: An African Perspective", in Faundez, J., Footer, M. E. and J. J. Norton, (eds), *Governance, Development and Globalization*, Oxford: Blackstone Press Ltd.

Levi, M., 1998, "A State of Trust", in Braithwaite, V. and M. Levi, *Trust and Governance*, New York: Russell Sage.

Levi, M., 1997, *Consent, Dissent and Patriotism*, Cambridge, MA: Cambridge University Press.

Levi, M., 1988, *Of Rule and Revenue*, Berkeley, CA: University of California Press.

Lewis, A., 1982, *The Psychology of Taxation*, New York: Blackwell, Oxford/ St Martin's Press.

Luoga, F. D. A. M., 1995, "Formulation of Tax Policy in a Developing Country: Some Suggestions for Tanzania", in Mtaki, C. K. and L. X. Mbunda (eds), *Taxation Policy in Tanzania: Problems and Prospects*, Tanzania: Dar es Salaam University Press.

The Mahabharata, a sacred Hindu writing, Rpt., Thuronyi, V. (ed), 1996 *Tax Law Design and Drafting* (Vol 1), (Chapter 4, "Law of Tax Administration and Procedure"), .

Maliyamkono, T. L., Mason, H., Ndunguru, A., Osoro, N. E. and A. Ryder, 2009, *Why Pay Tax*, Tanzania: TEMA Publishing and Siyaya Publishing.

Maliyamkono, T. L. and M. S. D. Bagachwa, 1990, *The Second Economy in Tanzania*, London: James Curry.

Mbunda, L. X. and C. K. Mtaki (eds), 1995, *Taxation Policy in Tanzania: Constraints and Perspectives*, Tanzania: University of Dar es Salaam.

McGee, R. W. (ed), 2008, *Taxation and Public Finance in Transition and Developing Economies*, Miami, FL: Springer Science and Business Media.

McGee, R. W. and G G and B M'Zali, 2008, "Attitudes Towards Tax Evasion in Mali" (Chapter 27), in McGee, R. W. (ed), *Taxation and Public Finance in Transition and Developing Economies,* Miami, FL: Springer Science and Business Media.

McGee, R. W., 2004, *The Philosophy of Taxation and Public Finance*, Boston, MA: Kluwer Academic Publishers.

McGee, R. W. (ed), 1998, *The Ethics of Tax Evasion*, New Jersey: Dumont.

Mercuro, N. and S. G. Medema, 1997, *Economics and the Law: From Posner to Post-Modernism*, Princeton, NJ: Princeton University Press.

Messere, K. C., 1993, *Tax Policy in OECD Countries: Choices and Conflicts*, Amsterdam: IBDF Publications BV.

Michael, A. and B. Thompson (eds), 2002, *Cases and Material on Constitutional and Administrative Law*, Oxford: Oxford University Press.

Mpunguliana, R. G., 2000, *The Theory and Practice of Taxation in Tanzania*, Dar es Salaam: Tanzania Printing Services.

Neumann, M., 2000, *The Rule of Law: Politicizing Ethics,* United Kingdom: Ashgate Publishing.

OECD, 1990, *Taxpayers Rights and Obligations: A Survey of the Legal Situation in OECD Countries,* OECD.

Pearsall, J. (ed), 2002, *The Concise Oxford English Dictionary* (10th Rev Edition), Oxford: Oxford University Press.

Peters, B. G., 1991, *The Politics of Taxation: A Comparative Study,* Cambridge: Blackwell.

Pierre, J. (ed), 2000, *Debating Governance: Authority, Steering and Democracy,* Oxford, UK: Oxford University Press.

Pierre, J. and B. G. Peters, 2000, *Governance, Politics and the State,* New York: St Martins Press.

Rakner, L. and S. Gloppen, 2003, "Tax Reform and Democratic Accountability in Sub-Saharan Africa", in **Van de Walle, N., Ball, N. and V. Ramachandran,** *Beyond Structural Adjustment: The Institutional Context of African Development,* London: Palgrave – McMillan.

Raz, J., 1979, *The Authority of Law: Essays on Law and Morality,* Oxford, UK: Clarendon Press.

Riahi-Belkaoui, A., 2008, "Bureaucracy, Corruption and Tax Compliance", in McGee, R. W. (ed), *Taxation and Public Finance in Transition and Developing Economies,* Miami, FL: Springer Science and Business Media.

Roth, J. A. et al (eds), 1989, *Taxpayer Compliance,* Philadelphia: University of Pennsylvania Press.

Scholz, J. T., 1998, "Trust, Taxes and Compliance", in Braithwaite, V. and M. Levi (eds), *Trust and Governance,* New York: Russell Sage.

Shefrin, S. M. and R. K. Triest, 1992, "Can Brute Deterrence Backfire? Perception and Attitude in Taxpayer Compliance", in Slemrod, J. (ed.), *Why People Pay Taxes: Tax Compliance and Enforcement,* Ann Arbour, MI: University of Michigan Press.

Silvani, C. and K. Baer, 1993, S*triking the Balance: Tax Administration, Enforcement and Compliance in the 1990s,* London: Institute for Fiscal Studies.

Slemrod, J. (ed), 1992, *Why People Pay Taxes,* Ann Arbour, MI: University of Michigan Press.

Slemrod, J., 1989, "Complexity, Compliance Costs and Tax Evasion", in Roth, J. A. et al, (eds), *Taxpayer Compliance,* Philadelphia: University of Pennsylvania Press.

Smith, K., 1992, "Reciprocity and Fairness: Positive Incentives for Tax Compliance", in Slemrod, J. (ed), *Why People Pay Taxes: Tax Compliance and Enforcement,* Ann Arbour, MI: University of Michigan Press.

Tamanaha, B. Z., 2004, *On the Rule of Law; History, Politics and Theory,* Cambridge, MA: Cambridge University Press.

Tanzani Revenue Authority, 2006, *A Decade of TRA Transformation 1996-2006,* Dar es Salaam: Tanzania Revenue Authority.

Taylor, N., 2003, "Understanding Taxpayer Attitudes through Understanding Taxpayer Identities", in Braithwaite, V., *Taxing Democracy,* United Kingdom: Ashgate Publishing.

Thuronyi, V. (ed)., 2000, *Tax Law Design and Drafting Vol I,* Netherlands: Kluwer Law International.

Tiley, J., 2008, *Revenue Law (6th Edition),* Portland, OR: Hart Publishing.

Torgler, B., 2007, *Tax Compliance and Tax Morale: A Theoretical and Empirical Analysis,* Cheltenham: Edward Elgar.

Trebilcock, M. J. and R. J. Daniels, 2008, *Rule of Law Reform and Development,* Cheltenham: Edward Elgar.

Tyler, T. R., 1998, "Trust and Democratic Governance", in Braithwaite, V. and M. Levi (eds), *Trust and Governance,* New York: Russell Sage Foundation.

Tyler, T. R., 1990, *Why People Obey the Law,* New Haven, CT: Yale University Press.

Wenzel, M., 2003, "Tax Compliance and the Psychology of Justice: Mapping the Field", in Braithwaite, V. (ed), *Taxing Democracy: Understanding Tax Avoidance and Evasion,* Burlington, VT: Ashgate.

Whitehouse, C. and P. Vaines, 2002, *Revenue Law – Principles and Practice (20th Edition),* London: Butterworths Lexis Nexis.

Journal Articles

Andreon, J., Erard, B. and J. Feistein, 1998, "Tax Compliance", *Journal of Economic Literature*, 36: 818.

Arthur, R., 1997, "The Place of Norms in Tax Compliance", *Tax Review*, 56: 216.

Avery, J. J., 1996, "Tax Law: Rules or Principles?", *Fiscal Studies*, 17: 63.

Baldry, J. C., "Income Tax Evasion and the Tax Schedule: Some Experimental Results", *Public Finance*, 42: 357.

Bankman, J. and T. Griffith, 1987, "Social Welfare and the Rate Structure: A New Look at Progressive Taxation", *California Law Review*, 75: 1905.

Bardach, E., 1989, "Moral Suasion and Taxpayer Compliance", *Law and Policy*, 11: 10.

Barzel, Y., 2003, "A Theory of the State: Economic Rights, Legal Rights, and the Scope of the State", *Journal of Economic Literature*, 41, 3: 943.

Becker, G. S., 1968, "Crime and Punishment: An Economic Approach", *Journal of Political Economy*, 76: 169.

Bentley, D., 1996, "Formulating a Taxpayer's Charter of Rights: Setting the Ground Rules", *Australian Tax Review*, 25: 97.

Bentley, D., 1994, "The Commissioner's Powers: Democracy Fraying at the Edges?", *Revenue Law Journal*, 4: 85.

Bird, R. M., 2004, "Administrative Dimensions of Tax Reform", *Asia Pacific Tax Bulletin*, 10, 3: 134.

Bird, R. M., 1999, "Tax Policy and Tax Administration in Transitional Countries", *International Studies in Taxation: Law and Economics*, Lindecrona, G., Lodin, S. and B. Wiman (eds), : p. 71.

Block, M., 1991, "Optimal Penalties, Criminal Law and the Control of Corporate Behaviour", *Boston Law Review*, 71, 2: 395.

Blumenthal, M., Christian, C. and J. Slemrod, 2001, "Do Normative Appeals Affect Tax Compliance? Evidence from a Controlled Experiment in Minnesota", *National Tax Journal*, 54: 125.

Boyd, C. W., 1986, "The enforcement of tax compliance: Some theoretical issues", *Canadian Tax Journal*, 34, 3: 588.

Cheibub, J. A., 1998, "Political Regimes and the Extractive Capacity of Governments: Taxation in Democracies and Dictatorships", *World Politics*, 50: 349.

Cheng, E. K., 2006, "Structural Laws and the Puzzle of Regulating Behaviour", *Northwestern University Law Review,* 100: 655.

Citrin, J., 1998, "Do People want Something for Nothing: Public Opinion on Taxes and Government Spending", *National Tax Journal,* 32: 113.

Cullis, J. G. and A. Lewis, 1997, "Why People Pay Taxes: From a Conventional Economic Model to a Model of Social Convention", *Journal of Economic Psychology,* 18: 305.

De Juan, A., Lasheras, M. A. and R. Mayo, 1994, "Voluntary Tax Compliant Behaviour of Spanish Income Tax Payers", *Public Finance,* 49: 90.

Dean, P. K. T., Keenan, T. and F. Kenney, 1980, "Taxpayers' Attitudes to Income Tax Evasion: An Empirical Study", *British Tax Review,* 25: 28.

Devas, N., Delay, S. and M. Hubbard, 2001, "Revenue authorities: are they the right vehicle for improved tax administration?", *Public Administration and Development,* 21: 211.

Feld, L. and B. S. Frey, 2002, "Trust Breeds Trust: How Taxpayers Are Treated", *Economics of Governance,* 3: 87.

Fjeldstad, O. H., 2003, "Fighting fiscal corruption, Lessons from the Tanzania Revenue Authority", *Public Administration and Development,* 23, 2: 165.

Fjeldstad, O. H., 2001, "Taxation, Coercion and Donors: Local Government Tax Enforcement in Tanzania", in *The Journal of Modern African Studies,* 39, 2: 289.

Fjeldstad, O. H. and J. J. Semboja, 2001, "Dilemmas of Fiscal Decentralisation: A Study of Local Government Taxation in Tanzania", *Forum for Development Studies,* 27, 1: 7.

Fjeldstad, O. H. and J. J. Semboja, 2001, "Why People Pay Taxes: The Case of the Development Levy in Tanzania", *World Development,* 29: 2059 (also in *IDS Bulletin* 33, 3: 21).

Goldberg, D. Q., 1996, "Between the Taxpayers and the Executive: Laws Inadequacy; Democracy's Failure?", *British Tax Review,* 9: 42.

Goldsmith, A. A., 1999, "Africa's Overgrown State Reconsidered: Bureaucracy and Economic Growth", *World Politics,* 51: 23.

Graetz, M., Reinganum, J. and L. Wilde, 1986, "The tax compliance game: Toward an interactive theory of law enforcement", *Journal of Law, Economics and Organisation,* 2, 1: 1.

Grasmick, H. and W. Scott, 1982, "Tax Evasion and Mechanisms of Social Control: A Comparison with Grand and Petty Theft", *Journal of Economic Psychology*, 2: 213.

Grasmick, H. G. and D. E. Green, 1980, "Legal Punishment, Social Disapproval and Internalisation as Inhibitors of Illegal Behaviour", *Journal of Criminal Law & Criminology*, 71: 325.

Holmes, J., 1986, "The Taxing Power", *Arizona Law Review*, 134: 32.

Howe, G., 1977, "Reform of Tax Machinery", *British Tax Review*, 97: 90.

James, S. and C. Alley, 1999 "Tax Compliance, Self Assessment and Administration in New Zealand - Is the Carrot or the Stick More Appropriate to Encourage Compliance?", *New Zealand Journal of Taxation Law and Policy*, 5, 1: 3.

Joulfaian, D. and M. Rider, 1998, "Differential Taxation and Tax Evasion by Small Business", *National Tax Journal*, 51: 675.

Kahan, D. M., 2002, "Signalling or Reciprocating? A Response to Eric Posner's Law and Social Norms", *University Richmond Law Review*, 36: 367.

Kahan, D. M., 2003, "The Logic of Reciprocity: Trust, Collective Action and Law", *Michigan Law Review*, 102: 71.

Kahan, D. M., 2001, "Trust, Collective Action and Law", *Boston University Law Review*, 81: 333.

Kaplan, S. E. and P. M. Reckers, 1985, "A Study of Tax Evasion Judgements", *National Tax Journal*, 38: 97.

Kasipillai, J., 2001, "Voluntary Tax Compliance in Malaysia", *The Electronic Journal of Insurance and Risk Management* 14

Kidder, R. and C. McEwen, 1989, "Taxpaying Behaviour in Social Context: A Tentative Typology of Tax Compliance and Non-compliance", *Taxpayer Compliance*, 2: 47.

Kinsey, K., 1984, "Survey data on tax compliance: A compendium and review", *American Bar Association*, 1.

Kirchler, E., 1998, "Differential Representations of Taxes: Analysis of Free Associations and Judgments of Five Employment Groups", *Journal of Social Economics*, 27: 117

Klepper, S. and D. Nagin, 1989, "The Anatomy of Tax Evasion", *Journal of Law, Economics and Organisation*, 5: 1.

Kornhauser, M. E., 2005, "Doing the full Monty: Will Publicizing Tax Information Increase Compliance?", *Canadian Journal of Law and Jurisprudence*, 18, 1: 2.

Kornhauser, M. E., 1987, "The Rhetoric of the Anti-progressive Income Tax Movement: A Typical Male Reaction", *Michigan Law Review*, 86: 465.

Kramer, S., 1990, "An Economic Analysis of Criminal Attempt: Marginal Deterrence and the Optimal Structure of Sanctions", *Journal of Criminal Law and Criminology*, 81: 398.

Lederman, L., 2003, "Tax Compliance and the Reformed IRS", *Kansas Law Review*, 51: 971.

Lederman, L., 2003, "The Interplay between Norms and Enforcement in Tax Compliance", *Ohio State Law Journal*, 64: 1453.

Lehmann, G., 1995, "The Reform That Does Not Reform and the Simplification That Does Not Simplify: The Tax Law Improvement Project Fiasco", *Butterworth's Weekly Tax Bulletin*, 301.

Levi, M. and L. Stoker, 2002, "Political Trust and Trustworthiness", *Annual Review of Political Science*, 3: 475.

Mathews, P., 1983, "Ignorance of the Law is No Excuse?", *Legal Studies*, 3: 174.

McAdams, H. R., 1997, "The Origin, Development, and Regulation of Norms", *Michigan Law Review*, 96: 338.

McGee, R. W., 1994, "Is Tax Evasion Unethical?", *Kansas Law Review*, 42: 411.

McGee, R. W., 1996, "Tax Advice for Latvia and Other Similarly Situated Emerging Economies", *International Tax & Business Lawyer*, 13: 223.

McGee, R. W., 1993, "Principles of Taxation for Emerging Economies: Some Lessons from the U.S. Experience", *Journal of International Law*, 12: 29.

McGraw, K. M. and J. T. Scholz, 1991, "Appeals to Civic Virtue Versus Attention to self Interest: Effects on Tax Compliance", *Law and Society Review*, 25: 471.

Milliron, V. and D. Toy, 1988 "Tax compliance: An investigation of key features", *Journal of the American Tax Association*, 9, 2: 84.

Mitchell, C. N., 1988, "Willingness to pay: Taxation and tax compliance", *The Memphis State University Law Review*, 15: 127.

Nadler, J., 2005, "Flouting the Law", *Texas Law Review*, 83: 1399.

Odd-Helge, F. and T. Bertil, 2003, "Fiscal Corruption: A Vice or a Virtue?", *World Development*, 31: 1459.

Pocarno, T. and C. Price, 1993, "The Effects of Social Stigmatization on Tax Evasion", *Advances in Taxation*, 5: 197.

Prebble, M., 1990, "Tax compliance and the use of tax information", *Australian Tax Forum*, 7, 2: 207.

Rakner, L., 2001, "The Politics of Revenue Mobilisation: Explaining Continuity in Namibian Tax Policies", *Forum for Development Studies*, 28, 1: 19.

Raskolnikov, A., 2006, "Crime and Punishment in Taxation: Deceit, Deterrence and Self-Adjustment Penalty", *Columbia Law Review*, 106: 569.

Roberts, M. L. and P. A. Hite, 1994, "Progressive Taxation, Fairness and Compliance", *Law and Policy*, 16: 27.

Robinson, R. and J. Darley, 1997, "The Utility of Desert", *North Western University Law Review*, 91: 457.

Rosen, H. S., 2001, "Tax Consensus: Waiting for a New Consensus of the Experts", *Tax Notes*, 95: 1267.

Rosenberg, J. D., 1996, "The Psychology of Taxes, Why They Drive Us Crazy, and How We Can Make Them Sane", *Virginia Tax Review*, 16: 155.

Rossoti, C., 1999, "Modernizing America's Tax Agency", *Tax Notes*, 83: 1191.

Santiso, C., 2001, "Good Governance and Aid Effectiveness: The World Bank and Conditionality", *Georgetown Public Policy Review*, 7: 1.

Scholz, J. T., 2003, "Contractual Compliance and the Federal Income Tax System", *Journal of Law and Policy*, 13: 139.

Scholz, J. T. and M. Lubell, 1998, "Trust and Taxpayers: Testing the Heuristic Approach to Collective Action", *American Journal of Political Science*, 42: 398-417.

Schwartz, R. and S. Orleans, 1967, "On Legal Sanctions", *University of Chicago Law Review*, 25: 274.

Shavell, S., 1985, "Criminal Law and the Optimal Use of No-monetary Sanctions as a Deterrent", *Columbia Law Review*, 85: 1232.

Silberman, M., 1976, "Towards a Theory of Criminal Deterrence", *American Sociological Review*, 41: 442.

Smith, A. T. H., 1985, "Error and Mistake of Law in Anglo-American Criminal Law", *Anglo-American Law Review*, 14: 3.

Spicer, M. W. and L. A. Becker, 1980, "Fiscal Inequality and Tax Evasion: An Experimental Approach", *National Tax Law Journal*, 33: 171-175.

Spicer, M. W. and S. B. Lundstedt, 1976, "Understanding Tax Evasion", *Public Finance*, 31: 295-305.

Therkildsen, O., 2000, "Understanding Taxation in Poor African Countries: A Critical Review of Selected Perspectives", *Forum for Development Studies*, 28, 1: 99.

Thurman, Q. C., 1991, "Taxpayer noncompliance and general prevention: An expansion of the deterrence model", *Public Finance*, 46, 2: 289.

Wallschutzsky, I., May 1989, "Achieving Compliance in Developing Countries", *Bulletin De La Société Géologique De France*, 234-244.

Webly, P., 1987, "Audit Probabilities and Tax Evasion in a Business Simulation", *Economic Letters*, 25: 267.

Witte, A. D. and D. F. Woodbury, 1985, "The Effect of Tax Laws and Tax Administration on Tax Compliance: The Case of the U.S. Individual Income Tax", *National Tax Journal*, 38, 1: 1.

World Bank, 2000, *Reforming Public Institutions and Strengthening Governance* Washington, DC: World Bank.

World Bank, 1994, *Governance: The World Bank Experience,* Washington, DC: World Bank.

World Bank, 1993, *Governance,* Washington, DC: World Bank.

World Bank, 1992, *Governance and Development,* Washington, DC: World Bank.

World Bank, 1991, *Managing Development: The Governance Dimension,* Washington DC: World Bank.

World Bank, 1989, *Sub-Saharan Africa: From Crisis to Sustainable Development,* Washington DC: World Bank.

Papers and Reports

Tanzania Revenue Authority, 2001, "Amendments made to Tax Laws from 1996 to 2001", Dar es Salaam.

Tanzania Revenue Authority, 2001/02 to 2007/08, *Annual Report*, Dar es Salaam.

International Monetary Fund, 1999, "Manual of Fiscal Transparency", Washington DC.

Tanzania Revenue Authority, 2001, "Proposals for the Review of the Tax Structure in 2001/2002", Dar es Salaam..

Ministry of Finance, and FAD-IMF, 1997, "Tanzania: Strengthening the Tax System", Dar es Salaam.

Tanzania Revenue Authority Taxpayer Education Department, 1999, "Tax Administration and Structure in Tanzania", Dar es Salaam.

Ministry of Finance and FAD-IMF, 1997, "Tanzania: Proposals for Tax Reform in 1995/96 and Beyond", Dar es Salaam.

Annan, K., 1999, "Preventing War and Disaster", in *1999 Annual Report on the Work of the Organisation*, New York: United Nations.

Bank of Tanzania, 2005, "Creating Optimal Conditions for Foreign Investment", Occasional Publication, December.

Bank of Tanzania, 2006, *Annual Report 2005/06*.

Barbone, L., Das-Gupta, A., De Wulf, L. and A. Hansson (World Bank Tax Policy and Administration Thematic Group), 1999, "Reforming the Tax Systems: The World Bank Record in the 1990s", Washington, DC: World Bank.

Blumstein, A., "Models for Structuring Taxpayer Compliance - Income Tax Compliance", 1983, in P. Sanicki, "A Report of the ABA Section of Taxation, International Conference on Income Tax Compliance", Chicago, IL: American Bar Association.

Maghji, Zakhia (Minister for Finance), 14 June 2007, "Budget Speech to Parliament", Dar es Salaam.

DANIDA, October 2003 "Danish Support to the Tanzania Revenue Authority, Phase II 2003/04 – 2007/08", Danida File 104, Tanzania 213.

Frey, B. S. and L. P. Feld, 2005, "Tax Compliance as the Result of Psychological Contract: The Role of Incentives and Responsible Regulation", Centre for Tax System Integrity.

Institute of Fiscal Studies (ed), 1993, "Striking the Balance: Tax Administration, Enforcement and Compliance in the 1990s", London: IFS Sixth Residential Conference.

Tanzania Investment Centre, 2006, "Investment Opportunities in Tanzania", Dar es Salaam: TIC Publication.

James, S., 2000, "The Taxpayer as a Cooperative Citizen", Paper presented at the XXV Annual Colloquium on Research in Economic Psychology & SABE Conference on "Fairness and Cooperation", Vienna, Austria.

Luoga, F. D. A. M., 2004, "Divergent Tax Administration Practices and the Collapse of Accountability in Taxation: the Emerging Realities in Tanzania", (unpublished paper).

Luoga, F. D. A. M., 2002, "Tax Reform, Constitutionality and the Human Rights Dimension: An Analysis of the Pitfalls in the Tanzanian Tax Reform Approaches" (Booklet), Warwick, UK: University of Warwick, School of Law.

Mansfield, H. K., 1983, "The role of sanctions in taxpayer compliance", in *The Report of the ABA section of tax invitational conference on income taxpayer compliance,* Sawicki, P. (ed), Washington, D.C.: the American Bar Association.

Mbunda, J. J., November 2004, "Customs and Excise Department: Practical Experience on Processing of Customs Data in Tanzania", Paper presented by the Tanzania Revenue Authority at Workshop on the Compilation of International Merchandise Trade Statistics, Addis Ababa, Ethiopia:, UN Department of Economic and Social Affairs, Statistics Division.

Messere, K. C., 1993, "Tax Policy in OECD Countries: Choices and Conflicts", Amsterdam, Netherlands: IBDF Publications BV.

Morgan, S. and K. Murphy, December 2001, "The 'Other Nation': Understanding Rural Taxpayers' Attitudes Toward the Australian Tax System", Canberra, Australia: Centre for Tax System Integrity Working Paper No 26, The Australian National University.

National Bureau of Statistics, September 2003, "Assessment of the Effectiveness of Taxpayer Awareness Programs and Attitude of Taxpayers Towards TRA", Dar es Salaam: National Bureau of Statistics.

Osoro, N. E. et al, 1999, "Enhancing Transparency in Tax Administration in Tanzania", Dar es Salaam: EAGER/PSG Research Report, Department of Economics, University of Dar es Salaam.

PricewaterhouseCoopers, 2006, "Stakeholders Perception Survey Report", Dar es Salaam: TRA Large Taxpayer Department.

Tanzania Presidential Commission of Enquiry, 1991, "Report of the Presidential Commission of Enquiry into Public Revenues, Taxation and Expenditure", Dar es Salaam: Government Printers.

Sawicki, P., 1983, "Income Tax Compliance: A Report of the ABA Section of Taxation", in Blumstein, A., *Models for Structuring Taxpayer Compliance*, Washington, D.C.: the American Bar Association.

Silvani, C. and K. Baer, 1977, "Designing a Tax Administration Reform Strategy: Experiences and Guidelines", an I.M.F Working Paper (WP/97/30/1977), Washington, D.C.: International Monetary Fund.

Smith, K. W., December 1990, "Reciprocity and fairness: Positive incentives for tax compliance", Paper presented at the Conference on Tax Compliance and Tax Enforcement, Ann Arbour, MI: Office of Tax Policy Research, School of Business Administration, The University of Michigan.

Smith, K. W., 1988, "Will the real noncompliance please stand up? Complexity and the measurement of noncompliance", Paper prepared for the American Bar Foundation, Washington, D.C..

Steward, C. and D. Harstein (Working group of the ABA), 2004, "Internal Revenue Service Tax Exempt and Government Entities, Voluntary Fiduciary Correction of PTs", Washington, D.C.: American Bar Association.

Tanzi, V. and A. Pellechio, 1995, "IMF Working Paper 95/22", Washington, D.C.: the International Monetary Fund.

Centre for International Development, 2001, "The Africa Competitiveness Report 2000/2001", Harvard, MA: Harvard University.

Tanzania Ministry of Planning, Economy, and Empowerment, June 2007, "The Economic Survey 2006", Dar es Salaam: Government of Tanzania.

Therkildsen, O., October 2003, "Revenue Authority Autonomy in Sub-Saharan Africa: The Case for Uganda", Paper prepared for the workshop on "Taxation, Accountability and Poverty" 23-24 October, Danish Institute for International Studies

Torgler, B., 2003, "Tax Morale: Theory and Empirical Analysis of Tax Compliance", PhD Dissertation, Basel: University of Basel.

Tanzania Revenue Authority, 2000, "TRA Annual Report for 1998/1999", Dar es Salaam: Government of Tanzania.

Tanzania Revenue Authority, 2001, "TRA Tax Revenue Report for August 2001", Dar es Salaam: Government of Tanzania.

United Nations Human Development Report Office, 2001, *Human Development Report 2000*, New York: United Nations.

United Nations Human Rights Commission, 2001, "Millennium Report 2000", Geneva, Switzerland: the Office of the United Nations High Commissioner for Human Rights.

Wenzel, M., 2001, "Misconceptions of Social Norms about Tax Compliance: A Pre-Study", Canberra, Australia: Centre for Tax System Integrity Working Paper No. 7, The Australian National University.

World Bank, 1991, "Managing Development: The Governance Dimension - 1991 Report", Washington, D.C.: World Bank.

Internet Sources

CIDA, "Human Rights, Democratisation & Good Governance", Programme Paper of the Canadian International Development Assistance (CIDA), at http://www.acdi.gc.ca/cida, accessed on 3/8/2005.

Baine, Mary, 2006, "Address by the Rwanda Revenue Authority Commissioner General", Kigali, at http://www.rra.gov.rw/en, accessed 13/11/2007.

Dhillon, A. and J. G. Bouwer, 6/7/2005, "Reform of Tax Administration in Developing Nations", Occasional Paper, Montgomery Research Institute, Tax Volume 1, at http://www.revenueproject.com, accessed 26/1/2007.

Gatheru, W. and R. Shaw (eds), 1998, *Our Problems Our Solutions: An Economic and Public Policy Agenda for Kenya*, Nairobi: AGENDA Publication Series, Institute of Economic Affairs, at http://www.iea.or.ke/ourpoblems.asp, accessed 1/5/2001.

Maina, E., 1998, "Reduction and Payment of Domestic Debt", in Gatheru, W. and R. Shaw (eds), *Our Problems, Our Solutions*, at http://www.iea.or.ke/ourpoblems.asp, accessed 1/5/2001.

United Nations High Commission for Human Rights, at http://www.unhcr.ch/huridocda.nsf, accessed 3/8/2005.

Rakner, K. and S. Gloppen, 2000, "Tax Reform and Democratic Accountability in Sub-Saharan Africa", at http://www.ids.ac.uk/gdr/cfs/activities/rakner-gloppen.pdf, accessed.

Slemrod, J., 2005, "Testimony given before the President's Tax Reform Panel on 14th March 2005 in Washington", athttp://www.bus.umich.ed, accessed 28/5/2006.

Stanford Encyclopaedia of Philosophy, at http://setis.library.usyd.edu.au/stanford, accessed 3/8/2005.

Police Foundation, 2000, "Drugs and the Law: Report of the Independent Inquiry into the Misuse of Drugs Act 1971", at http://www.policefoundation.org.uk, accessed 17/10/2007.

Government of Tanzania, "The Tanzania Census 2002 Report", at http://www.tanzania.go.tz/census, accessed.

United Nations Development Program, 1997, "Policy paper on governance and how it relates to human development", at http://magnet.undp.org, accessed 3/8/2005.

United Nations Development Program, 1997, "Governance for sustainable human development", at http://magnet.undp.org, accessed 3/8/2005.

Waruhiu, H., 1998, "An Economic and Public Policy Agenda for Kenya", in Gatheru, W. and R. Shaw (eds), *Our Problems Our Solutions: An Economic and Public Policy Agenda for Kenya*, at http//www.iea.or.ke/ourpoblems.asp, accessed 1/5/2001.

Waruhiu, H., 1998, "Taxing the People", in Gatheru, W. and R. Shaw (eds), *Our Problems Our Solutions: An Economic and Public Policy Agenda for Kenya*, at http://www.iea.or.ke/ourproblems.asp, accessed 1/5/2001.

World Bank, 1991, "Managing Development: The Governance Dimension - 1991 Report", athttp://www.worldbank.org/, accessed 3/8/2005.

Zambia Revenue Authority, "Taxpayer's Charter", Lusaka: Zambia Revenue Authority, athttp://www.zra.org.zm/charter.php, accessed 13/11/2007.

Newspapers

The African, 8th February 2008, front page report of the corruption scandal and the sacking of the cabinet in Tanzania.

The Citizen, 22nd March 2007, page 8 Editorial.

Daily News, 8th February 2008, front page report of the corruption scandal and the sacking of the cabinet in Tanzania.

Daily News, 6th January 2008.

Daily News, 20th November 2006, report on the speech of the Minister for Finance at the Taxpayers' Day celebrations.

The Guardian, 8th February 2008, front page report of the corruption scandal and the sacking of the cabinet in Tanzania.

The Guardian, 20th November 2006, report of the Minister for Finance speech at the Taxpayers' Day celebrations.

Policy Documents

Bank of Tanzania, June 2007, "Monetary Policy Statement".

Tanzania Revenue Authority, "Draft TRA Third Five Year Corporate Plan 2008/2009 to 2012/2013 to be adopted in 2008", Dar es Salaam: Tanzania Revenue Authority.

President's Office, Planning Commission, October 1996, "National Investment Promotion Policy," Dar es Salaam, Tanzania.

East African Community Secretariat, 2004, "Protocol on the Establishment of the East African Customs Union adopted on 2nd March 2004", Arusha, Tanzania: EACS.

Tanzania Revenue Authority, "Second Five Year Corporate Plan 2003/2004 to 2007/2008", Dar es Salaam, Tanzania.

Tanzania Revenue Authority, Education Department, "Taxpayer's Charter", Dar es Salaam.

Tanzania Revenue Authority, "First Five Year Corporate Plan 1998/99 to 2002/2003", Dar es Salaam, Tanzania.

United Nations Economic and Social Council, 5 January 2006, "Report of the Committee of Experts on Public Administration", E/C.16/2006/4.

United Nations Human Rights Commission, "Resolution 2000/64", New York: UNHRC.

Tanzania Revenue Authority, Education Department, April 2007, "VAT General Guide, TRA Booklet PN No 1", Dar es Salaam.

Statutes and Statutory Instruments

Tanzania.

"Companies Act", 2002 (Chapter 212).

"Constitution of the United Republic of Tanzania of 1977", 2005 Edition, Dar es Salaam: Office of the Attorney General (Chapter 2).

"Drugs and Prevention of Illicit Traffic in Drugs Act No 9", 2002.

"Immigration Act No 7", 1995 (Chapter 54).

"Income Tax Act No 11", 2004 (Chapter 262).

"Land Act", 1997 (Chapter 113).

"Local Government (District Authorities) Act No. 7", 1982 (Chapter 287).

"Local Government (Urban Authorities) Act No. 8", 1982 (Chapter 288).

"Local Government Finances Act No. 9", 1982 (Chapter 290).

"Pools and Lotteries Act No 23", 1967 (Chapter 42).

"Stamp Duty Act", 1972 (Chapter 189).

"Sugar Industry Act No 26", 2001 (Chapter 251).

"Tanzania Revenue Authority Act No. 11", 1995 (Chapter 399).

"Tax Revenue Appeals Act No 15", 2000 (Chapter 408).

"The Urban Authorities (Rating) Act No. 2", 1983 (Chapter 289).

"Value Added Tax Act No 24", 1997 (Chapter 148).

"Written Laws Miscellaneous Amendment Act", 2007.

Uganda

"Customs Tariff Act No. 17", 1970.

"Excise Tariff Act", (Chapter 174).

"Income Tax Act", 1997, (Chapter 340).

"Stamp Duty Act", (Chapter 172).

"Traffic and Road Safety Act No. 15", 1998.

"Value Added Tax Act", 1995 (Chapter 349).

Kenya

"Air Passenger Service Charge Act" (Chapter 475).

"Betting, Lotteries and Gaming Act" (Chapter 131).

"Customs and Excise Tariff Act" (Chapter 472).

"Directorate of Civil Aviation Act" (Chapter 394).

"Entertainment Tax Act" (Chapter 479).

"Income Tax Act" (Chapter 470).

"Kenya Revenue Authority Act", 1995 (Chapter 469).

"Parliamentary Pensions Act" (Chapter 196).

"Road Maintenance Levy Fund Act No. 9", 1993.

"Second Hand Motor Vehicle Purchase Tax Act" (Chapter 484).

"Stamp Duty Act" (Chapter 480).

"Traffic Act" (Chapter 403).

"Transport Licensing Act" (Chapter 404).

"Value Added Tax Act" (Chapter 476).

"Widows and Children's Pensions Act (Chapter 195).

East Africa Community Laws

"East African Customs and Excise Management Act No 1", 2005 (Chapter 26).

Rwanda

"Law No. 15", 1997.

"Law on Direct Taxes on Income, Law No. 16", 2005.

"Law on Tax Procedure, Law No. 25", 2005.

"Customs Law, Law No. 21", 2006.

"Import Duty Law, Law No. 27", 2004.

"Code of Value Added Tax, Law No. 06", 2001.

"Ministerial Order No. 006/03/10/Min", May 2003.

Zambia

"Zambia Revenue Authority Act No. 23", 1993.

Cases

Associated Newspapers Group v Fleming, 1973, AC 628.

Baron v Canada, 1993, 1 CTC.

Bilbie v Lumley, 1802, 2 East 469.

Briggenshaw v Crabb, 1948, 30 TC 331.

Bull v United States, 1935, 259 U.S. 247, 259.

Calico Industries v Pyaraliesmail Premji, 1983, TLR 28.

CIR v Newman, 1947, 159 F 2d 848.

Commissioner General TRA v Samuel John Ezekiel Tax Appeal No. 13, 2005.

D A Park-Ross v The Director, Office for the Investigation Serious Economic Offences, 1995, (2) SA 198 (C).

DTP v Commissioner General TRA, Appeal No. 5, 2006.

Flood v Kuhn, 1972, 407 U.S. 258, 293 n.4.

Funke v France, European Court of Human Rights, 25 February 1993, Series A No 256-A.

Furniss v Dawson, 1984, 1 All ER 530 (HL).

IRC v Burmah Oil, 1980, STC 731.

IRC v Duke of Westminster, 1936, AC 1.

Karibu Textile Mills Ltd v The Minister for Finance and the Honourable Attorney General, 2005, Misc. Commercial Case No. 43 (unreported).

McCulloch v Maryland, 1819, 17 U.S. 316, 431.

MNR v Kruger Inc, 1984, CTC 506.

Olmstead v United States, 1928, 277 U.S.438.

R v Butterwasser, 1948, 1 KB 4, (1947) 2 All ER 415.

Ramsay v IRC, 1982, AC 300 (HL).

Regina v Branch, 1976, CTC 193.

Regina v Hummel, 1971, CTC 803.

Samuel John Ezekiel v Commissioner General, 2004, TRA Tax Appeal No. 11.

St Aubyn v Attorney General, 1952, AC 15.

Thibaudeau v Canada, 1995, 1 CTC 212.

Yero Transport Services Ltd v Attorney General & 2 Others, 2001, Civil Application No. 58/2001, Court of Appeal of Tanzania (unreported).

www.ingramcontent.com/pod-product-compliance
Lightning Source LLC
Chambersburg PA
CBHW021036210326
41598CB00016B/1035